Visual Basic 6.0 Win32 API Tutorial

Jason Bock

Wrox Press Ltd. ®

Visual Basic 6.0
Win32 API Tutorial

© 1998 Wrox Press

wrox

Published by Wrox Press Ltd. 30 Lincoln Road, Olton, Birmingham, B27 6PA
Printed in USA
ISBN 1-861002-4-32

Trademark Acknowledgements

Wrox has endeavored to provide trademark information about all the companies and products mentioned in this book by the appropriate use of capitals. However, Wrox cannot guarantee the accuracy of this information.

Credits

Author
Jason Bock

Development Editor
Dominic Shakeshaft

Editors
Craig A. Berry
Kate Hall
Dominic Lowe

Technical Reviewers
Edward Ferron
Guy Fouche
John Harris
David Jewell
David Liske

Technical Reviewers
Duncan Mackenzie
Marc H. Simkin
Rob Vieira
Terri Watkins
Donald Xie

Design/Layout
Noel Donnelly

Cover
Andrew Guillaume
Concept by Third Wave
Photo by Carroll Studios, Inc.

Index
Diane Brenner

Acknowlegements

First and foremost, I'd like to thank my wife Elizabeth for supporting me during this project. I feel very fortunate to have met her, and even more amazed that she's my wife (especially with all the nights that I came home from work, turned on the computer, and wrote until 3:00 A.M). Sometimes, I wonder why I got so lucky. I love her dearly.

I have to thank everyone who was involved with this book from Wrox Press. This includes (but is not limited to) Dominic Shakeshaft, Dominic Lowe, Kate Hall, Craig Berry and all those who reviewed the book before it came to press. They were dealing with a rookie this time around, and I bet it showed, especially during the editing process. My thanks for their patience and commitment to helping me make this a better book.

I also would like thank the following people for their technical knowledge and ideas: Steve Clementi, Bill Daley, Dexter Jones, and Rob Swenson. Whether they like or dislike VB, or Microsoft, or any other issue in the computing realm, they have their act together, and they've all helped me see a bigger IT picture. (Plus, Rob makes some of the finest homebrewed beer around, and I have no problem sampling his newest creations.)

Thanks also to all of my friends who had nothing to do with the book, but kept me sane by getting me away from this collection of words to go golfing, play tennis, or see Pat McCurdy sing his heart out at a local bar. I've recently heard the phrase, "You work to live, and not the other way around." I'm grateful that I have friends who have different interests and talents than mine - they help make my life more than just programming in VB.

Finally, special thanks must go to my parents, Ronald and Mary. Whenever I work on some kind of project that takes a lot of effort - be it a musical recording, a master's thesis, or this book - I remember one phrase that they said to me when I was graduating from high school. Our yearbooks had a section in the back where the parents of the seniors could send in a picture of their son or daughter along with a phrase to send them off into the "real world". This is what they said to me:

> You have been blessed with so many gifts, and we have been blessed with you. The whole world is yours. Go for it.

I don't give this quote as an ego-booster; rather, I think that it summarizes the kind of encouragement, love, and support that my parents gave me when I was growing up (and still do to this day). Of this, I am grateful beyond words.

Table of Contents

Introduction

To start off this book, I thought I'd give a brief summary as to why I decided to write it in the first place. I started to program in Visual Basic over 3 years ago using version 3.0. It was my first language out of college that I developed in, and it was also my first "real-world" project. I really didn't know what I was doing, other than putting buttons and labels and other interesting controls all over my forms ... along with writing some code. Needless to say, my first project was a nightmare. I felt that I was flying blind most of the time, scrambling to try and figure out how to get my code to work. Upgrading to VB 4.0, 16-bit version made it much, much worse. It took me a month to get my project stable again after control upgrades and bugs completely fouled up the program.

After spending more time in the tool, I started to notice what VB couldn't do. I had problems reading file sizes consistently. I couldn't get the title bar to flash if a major problem occurred. I couldn't get a program to shell synchronously. VB's buttons didn't let you add pictures. And this really started to annoy me! I knew other programs were doing this; why couldn't VB? That's when I started to find out more about API calls and what they could do.

Initially, I was told by other developers to avoid them at all costs. "You'll always get a GPF", "That's low-level stuff for C programmers", etc., etc. To be honest, I was almost scared to even touch the little beasts for fear of causing major havoc on my end-users' PCs. However, the more time I spent learning about them, I realized just how much more you could accomplish by using them.

Right now (especially with versions 5.0 and 6.0), I'm convinced that VB is finally a serious Windows development tool. It may not be the most pain-free environment to pull some of the more advanced OS features off, but virtually everything is there for a developer to use. It's not just a tool for front-ends anymore.

With all that said, you do have to invest some time learning more about the Windows OS, and that's not a trivial task. I'm still finding out new things every day. I think it's safe to say that a fair amount of non-Windows developers come to VB and have a blast going control nuts on forms (just like I did) without having a good understanding of the fundamentals of the OS. VB has to be approached with a Windows perspective, not the other way around.

Who Should Read This Book

Therefore, I've written the book for the VB developer who is familiar with the fundamentals of VB: They can create projects, slap together some usable forms and write good VB code.

I should point out that this is not a book that defines every Win32 API call that can be made. Other authors in the field have already done that (rather well, I might add), and I have no desire to repeat their work. This book is written to introduce you to the fundamentals of Win32 development and how they can be applied to real-world application development. Hopefully, after reading this book, you'll be able to see other calls and have a firm understanding of how they operate and any potential problems to avoid.

Tools Needed

The only tool you'll really need is VB. Make sure that you've installed the API Declaration Viewer with it - we'll use it extensively in this book. Also, this book is dedicated to Win32 development ONLY; no 16-bit development will be addressed.

What's Covered in This Book

In Chapter 1, we'll take a look at what a dynamic link library (DLL) is and the benefits of using dynamic linking over static linking. We'll go over how an API call is made in VB and use a couple of calls in a simple example. I'll also show you the API Declaration Loader program that comes with VB and how you can use it to make the declarations easier.

Chapter 2 will look at some of the potential traps and pitfalls that usually occur to the newcomer - I'll also show you some tips that you can use when using calls that are unfamiliar. Then, we'll take a high-level look at the main program that will be used throughout the book: The Encryption Program. I'll describe why I chose this project as the basis for API development.

Chapter 3 will use calls from `kernel32.dll`. This DLL is responsible for most of the low-level OS work, like multithreading and memory management. We'll use most of the file management calls to encrypt and decrypt files. We'll also use this chapter to compare VB's file calls with the API calls.

Chapter 4 will address the calls that can be made from `user32.dll`. This DLL is responsible for the visual components that exist within the Windows OS, like application windows and command buttons. We'll use calls to make message boxes without using VB's `MsgBox` function along with doing some form and menu manipulation.

Chapter 5 will take a look at the calls in `gdi32.dll`. This DLL is responsible for any graphical drawing and/or manipulation of icons, bitmaps, etc. We'll create non-rectangular windows, rotate text in labels, and other control twists and manipulations.

Chapter 6 will be a digression of sorts. We'll move away from the Win32 calls and demonstrate how you can make other calls from other DLLs. To do this, we'll use calls from `winmm.dll` and `shell.dll`. We'll use the first DLL to play sounds at key points in the program, while the second DLL will be used to display the Copy dialog box you see in the Windows Explorer program.

Chapter 7 moves into a concept that cannot be done within VB 4.0: API calls that require a callback. We'll use a real-world example to explain what a callback is, and write some pseudo-code to bring the example to more familiar territory. Then I'll introduce the `AddressOf` operator in VB and what it can and cannot do.

Chapter 8 is devoted to a callback example written within a COM component. We'll use the appropriate API calls to create our own timer component. Once we've successfully created the component, we'll use it within the Encryption project.

I don't assume in this chapter that you're an expert in developing components in VB. Although I do talk about COM to a degree, I've tried to focus on the callback APIs and the problems that occur when hiding the calls within a class.

Code Examples

Any of the projects that are given in the book can be downloaded form Wrox's web page at `www.wrox.com`.

Conventions Used

We use a number of different styles of text and layout in the book to help differentiate between the various types of information. Here are examples of the styles we use along with explanations of what they mean:

Bulleted information is shown like this:

- **Important Words** are in a bold font.
- Words that appear on the screen, such as menu options, are a similar font to the one used on screen, e.g. the File menu.
- Keys that you press on the keyboard, like *Ctrl* and *Enter*, are in italics.
- All file, function names and other code snippets are in this style: `Video.mdb`.

Code shown for the first time, or other relevant code, is in the following format,

```
Dim intVariable1 As Integer

intVariable1 = intVariable1 + 1
Debug.Print intVariable1
```

while less important code, or code that has been seen before, looks like this:

```
intvariable1 = intvariable1 + 1
```

Code you need to type into an Immediate window, or for a browser's URL appears like this:

```
http://www.wrox.co.uk
```

Finally, background information will look like this,

And vital, not-to-be-missed information looks like this.

Tell Us What you Think

This was my first writing project, and I've found it to be a rewarding experience (just as long as I had enough caffeine around). However, you may have suggestions for improvement, or you might have some questions on some of the sections. You can contact me at:

> **feedback@wrox.com**
> **http://www.wrox.com**
>
> or
>
> **http://www.wrox.co.uk**

I'm always looking for constructive criticism on anything that I do, so don't hesitate to let me know what you think of this book.

1

API Fundamentals

An API call is a complex beast. Even relatively simple calls can have complex and confusing parameters with such descriptive names as **dwRop**. And the complex ones - where on Earth do you start with them? Well, I'm not going to be revolutionary. I'm going to start at the best place of all - the beginning. Therefore, in this chapter we'll start from square one and cover all the groundwork that we'll need to use API calls. In fact by the end of chapter API calls will seem like second nature, allowing us to get ahead with the real job of cracking open the real functionality of Windows. In this chapter we'll cover:

- ❑ The basics of an API call
- ❑ Dynamic and Static linking
- ❑ The syntax of API calls
- ❑ The API Viewer
- ❑ Undocumented APIs

We'll also get our hands dirty by demonstrating a couple of API calls in action. So let's get cracking, we've a lot of ground to cover in this chapter.

What Does API Stand For?

If you've been wondering what the acronym stands for, it's **A**pplication **P**rogramming **I**nterface. For all of the perceptions that exist about the Win32 APIs (such as "they're hard", "they crash my program", or "they're unbelievable"), all that they really are is a set of functions that any programmer can use to access all of the services that Windows has. To be more specific, Windows groups the core APIs into three files: `kernel32.dll`, `user32.dll`, and `gdi32.dll`. I'll define what a DLL is in a moment, and we'll cover functions from each of these files in this book. However, to clarify what APIs are, let's use a very simple example in VB.

Suppose, after months and months of research and development, you came up with a set of functions that demonstrated computer consciousness. You open VB, add a new module to your project, and type the following functions:

```
Public Function Speak() as String

    Speak = "Hello, World!"

End Function
```

```
Public Function Question() as String

    Question = "What is the meaning of life?"

End Function
```

```
Public Function Answer() as String

    Answer = "42"

End Function
```

```
Public Function Work() as String

    Work = "ZZZZZZZZ"

End Function
```

You compile your code, and you see that everything works as planned. Excited to show your fellow programmers your creative insights, you copy your VB module (appropriately titled AI.BAS, of course) to a network drive that everyone in the IT department can see. Guess what, you've just published your own set of APIs! You've put together a set of procedures that share similar functionality – which is computer consciousness – and published the functions for others to see.

So if it's this easy to create APIs (and to get a computer to think), why is there such a fuss about them at times in the VB community? Well, as you will see, we've only begun to scratch the surface…

Static and Dynamic Linking

OK, everyone in your company now knows how innovative you are. You've received the appropriate raise and promotion, and the technical questions flood your voice and e-mail every day. Your APIs are being used in all of the newest projects, and the company's stock is riding high. Plus, you're on the cover of all the computer magazines in the world. In short, life is good.

But problems soon begin to arise. Other programmers are starting to catch your visionary ideas and want to make some changes. You quickly compile a list of these innovations:

```
Public Function Shout() as String

    Shout = "HEY!!!!!!!!!!!!"

End Function
```

```
Public Function DemandNewSalary(CurrentSalary as Double) as Double
```

```
        DemandNewSalary = DemandNewSalary(CurrentSalary + 10000.0)

End Function


Public Function ScaryQuestion(EmployeeName as String) as String

    ScaryQuestion = "What are you doing, " & EmployeeName & "?"

End Function

Public Function Speak(EmployeeName as String) as String

    Speak = EmployeeName & ", prepare to be assimila...er, " & _
            "I mean, assisted."

End Function
```

After your review, you realize that you've got some big problems to worry about. Let's take a look at some of the issues:

❑ The `DemandNewSalary` has a couple of dangerous pitfalls that won't be caught by VB's compiler. It is a recursive function that doesn't stop. Eventually, the function will cause an error once the stack space in the computer is exhausted. Another error may be raised before this one, though - you might overflow the value of `CurrentSalary` (although some may argue that this is a nice feature and not a bug).

❑ Suppose that somebody wants to change the behavior of the `Speak` function. How would this effect the programs that currently use the old implementation of Speak? They'd have to reopen their project, recompile their apps, and try to get the new executable out to the thousands of users. Plus, now there's an argument to the function, and some programs may not have an employee name to pass in – another problem. But who would really want this statement to come out of their computer, anyway?

❑ Three new functions have been added: `DemandNewSalary`, `ScaryQuestion`, and `Shout`. It's the same situation as the previous point: Current compiled programs would have to do a recompile to use these functions.

❑ You may have noticed that every time an application wants to use your APIs, they have to compile the same code over and over again. If five different programs are using the same code within their programs, this becomes a great source of inefficiency.

❑ Even worse, since you've copied your code out to a public server, who knows what other changes programmers have made to your APIs? You now have another problem where `Speak` in one program may return a completely different result from the response you originally intended.

These are the problems of **static linking**. Basically, whenever you compile an application in VB, all of the code is linked into an executable (EXE) that Windows can use. However, if you change the code after the compilation, these changes won't be seen by the executable. You have to recompile the app to apply the changes.

This may not seem like a big deal if you're writing an application at home to keep track of your finances. You can easily get away with recompiles, because the only executable resides on your computer and nowhere else. Plus, you have complete control over the source code. So, static linking would be fine in this situation.

However, in the world of business application development, your user base may range anywhere in size from 10 to 10,000 and beyond. Even worse, these users may be anywhere on the globe. This could lead to a big distribution problem! Here's a picture to demonstrate the chaos that can ensue if there isn't a short leash kept on that source file:

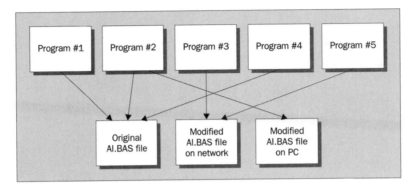

As you can see, the situation is pretty ugly. Five programs are using three different versions of the source code. In fact, one program is using different calls from different versions! This is a scenario that I would not want to be a part of (but, unfortunately, I've seen programmers who are, and it seems to make you age a bit). Once the code is compiled into the EXE, there's no way to change it other than doing a full recompile.

However, with **dynamic linking**, most of these problems are minimized. Without delving into the details of how you create a **dynamic link library** (DLL), the nice aspect of DLLs is that the APIs are centralized in a binary file that has a specialized executable format that Windows can read. This means that no one can go into the file and start changing the code around. Also, once this file is on a user's PC and five programs need to use the APIs, they all use one file, and they don't have the code compiled into their own executables. We see a much calmer picture when dynamic linking is used:

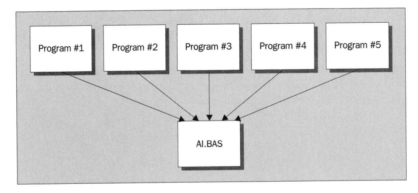

This is a much nicer situation to be in. All of the programs are using the same code base. If the DLL changes, the code still makes the same call and automatically gets the new implementation. (We'll discuss how VB loads and calls functions in DLLs later on in the chapter.)

Even with all of the advantages listed above, there are some disadvantages to dynamic linking. You still have to distribute a new copy of the DLL every time changes or additions are made to the API set. However, this would only require a file copy to the PC and not a full recompile of the applications.

Also, a dynamic function call is a bit slower than a static call, since the calling application has to somehow find out where the function resides within another file (the DLL). If you statically link the function into your program, the function is already within the EXE, so the invocation is quicker. Furthermore, you can't break the interface, meaning that you can't change, delete or add new parameters to a call. This occurs both on the DLL side as well as a client of the DLL.

For example, if you create a DLL, you can't change the **signature** of the call once programs start to use it. Older programs would not be able to successfully invoke this function anymore and your support calls would keep you awake at night.

Conversely, if you call a function from a DLL in VB, you have to make sure that the calls are correct, since VB will not "enforce" the contract for you. If you don't declare the function right, you'll eventually get a run-time error when you try to call it (we'll deal with data type issues more in Chapter 2).

With all of that said, there are times when you should statically link and other times when creating DLLs is the right choice. This is more of a design issue that would be weighed in during the analysis phase of a project. However, we're more concerned with the APIs that Windows has to offer, so let's start to investigate how you can use those in VB.

Description of API Call Keywords

To begin with, let's go over how you would make a Win32 API call in VB, and then we'll take a look at each part in more detail.

> Before we look at an API call declaration, I should make one point clear. All of the DLLs we'll deal with in this chapter are the "standard" flavor of DLLs; they're not ActiveX/COM DLLs that you can make within VB.

Therefore, when you make components in VB (and you'll make a couple in this book), don't try to invoke the functions using this syntax. Now, have a look at this general declaration of an API call in VB:

```
[Public | Private] Declare Sub|Function name Lib _
"libname" [Alias "aliasname"] [([arglist])] [As type]
```

There are a lot of parts to this call, so let's break it down and see what it all means.

- ❑ **Public or Private**: This defines the scope of the declaration. If it's declared `Public`, then any procedure within your project can call the procedure; otherwise, only the module where the declaration was made can use the procedure. Note that you can't make an API `Public` if it's declared in a form or class module; this can only be done in code modules. If you omit this keyword, VB will default the declaration to be `Public`.
- ❑ **Declare**: This keyword is used for API calls only. Standard procedures that you create in VB don't use this keyword.
- ❑ **Sub or Function**: This lets VB know if the procedure will return a value (`Function`) or not (`Sub`).

- ❏ **name:** This is the name that you will use in your VB code to call the procedure. This may or may not be the same name that the DLL uses for the procedure.

- ❏ **Lib:** A keyword required when making an API declaration.

- ❏ **libname:** This is the file name of the DLL. You can either give a full file path (like `C:\Windows\System\kernel32.dll`) or just the file name (like `kernel32`). Be forewarned, though. If you hard-code a full file path in your project, make sure that the DLL file stays there. Depending on a multitude of issues (such as installing the application, the OS the user has, etc.), the file may not be where it was when you were developing the system, which would cause an error to occur when the API call was made.

- ❏ **Alias:** This isn't required for the declaration, but it can be useful when procedure-naming conflicts arise. For example, if the API call is named `RaiseRent` and you have a call within your application with the same name, you can name the API call `APIRaiseRent` and use the `Alias` keyword to define the actual name of the call. A classic example of this is the `SetFocus` API call. This definitely conflicts with VB's `SetFocus` method.

- ❏ **Aliasname:** If the `Alias` keyword was used, you have to give either the procedure name or its ordinal number (I'll explain what this number is later).

- ❏ **arglist:** This is where all of the arguments that the procedure needs go, if any exist. Note that the names of the arguments don't matter, but the way the variable is passed into the API (by value or by reference) along with the data type definitely matters. We'll investigate this further in Chapter 2.

- ❏ **As type:** If the API call is a function, then this will define the return type.

As you can see, the declaration syntax is very similar to any other procedure declaration you would make in VB. The only differences are a few keywords: `Declare`, `Lib`, and `Alias`. However, before we get into some examples, I'd like to define what an ordinal number is and how Windows finds your DLL.

The Ordinal Number

An ordinal number is simply a number that is associated with the function call within a DLL. This isn't a requirement for API calls - some functions do not have ordinal numbers. If you know the ordinal number of an API call, you can use it in the `Aliasname` section. For example, say a DLL called `StringCalls.DLL` had a function in it called `TwistString`, with an ordinal number of 255. You could make the call using the number like this:

```
Declare Sub TwistString Lib "StringCalls" Alias "#255" _
    (ByVal lpStr as String, ByVal lpLen as Long)
```

Note that you have to put the pound sign (#) before the number for VB to realize that you want to find the function through its ordinal number. Technically, if you use an ordinal number it does make the call a bit faster. However, under Win32 the use of ordinal numbers is not recommended as they vary between NT, Win95, and so on. For simplicity's sake, we won't be declaring APIs using ordinal numbers in this book.

Finding the DLL

Most, if not all, of the examples you will see in this book simply declare the name of the DLL in the name section of the declaration. However, within your corporation, other DLLs that were developed in-house may reside on the PC as well. If you use these DLLs and you are not responsible with their installation, how can you be sure if Windows will be able to find the DLL? Fortunately, there's a simple rules list that Windows adheres to in finding the specified DLL, and here it is:

1. First, Windows looks in the directory where the application resides (specifically, the location of the application executable). If it's here, that's the one that's used.

2. Next, Windows looks within the current directory. If it's here, it's used.

3. Next, Windows looks in the Windows system directory, whatever it may be (it differs between 95, 98 and NT). If it's here, it's used.

4. For NT Only: The next step is to look in the 16-bit Windows system directory. If it's here...(you know the rest).

5. Next stop (and hopefully our last) is the Windows directory.

6. If it's reached this stage we're getting desperate. Windows tries to search all of the directories listed in the PATH environment variable.

7. Finally, Windows is going to try a last ditch effort and scan the list of directories mapped in a network.

If everything fails, Windows passes an error back to Visual Basic, notifying you that it's sick and tired of trying to find your DLL. Well, it doesn't actually say that, but it does raise an error when it can't find the file. As the list shows, Windows will try to be as thorough as possible, but now that you know the search tree, try to keep your files somewhere near the top. It will make the first API call to this DLL much quicker.

Of course, you could avoid all of this hassle by declaring an explicit path for your DLL. If you specify a full file path (e.g. C:\WOMBAT\WIZARD.DLL) then Windows will only look in that particular directory.

Now that we've gone through the declaration syntax, let's go through a simple example using a couple of time counters from the Win32 API.

> I should note here that, since the Win32 APIs were written in a low-level language like C, most of the variable names use a naming convention called Hungarian notation. Turn to Appendix B to read more about the Hungarian notation. I would suggest looking at how this notation works for educational purposes, but it is not a requirement to understand it in this book.

A VB Example: GetTickCount and QueryPerformanceCounter

There are times when you'd like to analyze your code from a performance standpoint. You may think that your new idea for a procedure will speed things up, but you had better make sure that you have some hard core data to back up your speculation. There are a lot of tools in the marketplace that can do this for you, but if you just want to test one section of code in a procedure, you may want to set up the analysis yourself - setting up a full performance test is probably overkill. You'll need a clock that has high precision to see the differences in your test runs; a clock that only has a resolution of a second won't cut it in the world of computers. Win32 has a couple of API calls that you can use for this kind of scenario: GetTickCount and QueryPerformanceCounter. These calls are a good starting point to introduce APIs, since they vary in complexity, yet they do virtually the same thing. Let's take a look at each of the calls in more detail before we start coding the test example that uses these calls.

GetTickCount

This is one of the easiest calls to make out of all the API calls, so we'll start with this one first:

```
Declare Function GetTickCount Lib "kernel32" _
    Alias "GetTickCount" () As Long
```

As you can see, it's a function that returns a value of a Long type. The Alias is shown here for completeness; it's not needed for the function to work.

> *In fact if you try typing this declaration into VB6 then you'll see a funny thing happen. If you set the* Alias *to be the same as the funtion's name itself then VB will simply remove the* Alias *arguement from your code.*

The return value is the number of milliseconds that have elapsed since the OS was booted. For example, if you called this function and got the value 23033123, you know that 23033.123 seconds have elapsed since you powered up the computer (or 6 hours, 23 minutes, and 53.123 seconds – take your pick).

QueryPerformanceCounter

This one isn't as straightforward:

```
Declare Function QueryPerformanceCounter Lib "kernel32" _
    (lpPerformanceCount As LARGE_INTEGER) As Long
```

Again, this is a function that returns a Long value. However, in this case, the value means something different. If you get a nonzero value, that means that the installed hardware on the PC supports a high-resolution timer. If you get a zero, you can't use this function – the hardware doesn't support this kind of timer.

So what **is** a high-resolution timer, anyway? It's a timer that may be provided by the computer's processor. Its resolution varies from processor to processor, but it's usually at a much finer scale than what you'd get using `GetTickCount`. For example, the resolution of `GetTickCount` is 1 millisecond. The high-resolution timers you will find usually have resolutions of 1 microsecond.

Anyway, we still have to address the argument list. As you probably know, there isn't a data type in VB called `LARGE_INTEGER`, so if you guessed that this is a user-defined type (UDT), you're right. Here's how `LARGE_INTEGER` is defined:

```
Public Type LARGE_INTEGER
    LowPart As Long
    HighPart As Long
End Type
```

It's a simple UDT, but its meaning is a little esoteric. What the OS is trying to do is return a 64-bit value back to you to let you know what counter value the high-resolution timer is at, but some languages don't have a native 64-bit integer type. Therefore, a UDT was defined to get around this problem. The `HighPart` contains the high 32 bits, while the `LowPart` contains the low 32 bits. Here's a diagram that shows how this is laid out in memory:

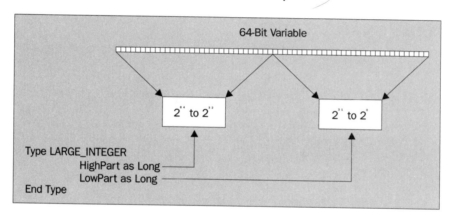

Let's take a look at a simple example. Say you called `QueryPerformanceCounter` with a UDT variable called `udtCounterValue`. After the call was made, you have the following values in the UDT:

```
udtCounterValue.LowPart = 20394
udtCounterValue.HighPart = 23
```

To figure out what the actual tick value is, you have to multiply 23 by 2^{32}, and then add that to 20394. This gives you 98784268202 (we'll have to use a `Double` data type to handle a value of this magnitude as you'll see later on). But why did I use the 2^{32}? The reason is that we have to "bit-shift" the bits stored in `HighPart` 32 bits to the left. What does this mean? Well, multiplying a number by 2 accomplishes a single bit-shift for us. For example, the number 4 in binary format looks like this: 0100. If we multiply 4 by 2, we get 8, which is 1000 in binary format. Notice that each bit is shifted one over to the left. In our case, we need to do this 32 times; hence, the 2^{32} factor.

There's a catch, however, to using `QueryPerformanceCounter`. The value given in the UDT is dimensionless. It isn't the number of milliseconds that have passed since the computer was turned on like the value that `GetTickCount` returns. That value has a dimension of time. In `QueryPerformanceCounter`'s case, the data point is taken at some place in time, but we don't know if the measurement was made in seconds, or milliseconds, or microseconds. To determine how the value can be converted into a time unit that we're comfortable with, you have to make a call to `QueryPerformanceFrequency`. It's almost identical to `QueryPerformanceCounter`:

```
Declare Function QueryPerformanceFrequency Lib "kernel32" _
    (lpFrequency As LARGE_INTEGER) As Long
```

The only difference is that the UDT contains the number of ticks that the high-resolution timer will produce in a second. For example, let's say you called `QueryPerformanceFrequency` and found out through the UDT that the high-resolution timer produced 100,000 ticks per second. Therefore, each tick is worth one microsecond with this timer. You then called `QueryPerformanceCounter` twice – once at the start of your procedure, and again at the end. You get two tick values: 50,000 and 75,000, respectively. To find out how long your procedure took, you subtract the ending value from the starting value - which is 25,000 - and divide that by 100,000, giving you 0.25 seconds.

Analyzing the For...Next Loop

Now that we've gone through the definitions of `GetTickCount` and `QueryPerformanceTimer`, let's look at how they work in a coding example and the differences between them. First, create a new Standard EXE project in VB. As always, you get a standard form to start out with. You'll need to add a label, a text box, and two command buttons to this form. Rename the form as `frmCounter` and change its `Caption` property to **Simple Timer Test**. Change the `Caption` properties of the command buttons to **Test GetTickCount** and **Test QueryPerformanceCounter**. Finally, name the **Test GetTickCount** button `cmdTestGetTickCount` and the **Test QueryPerformanceCounter** button `cmdTestQueryPerformance`. Also, name the text box `txtCount`.

By now, your form should look something like this:

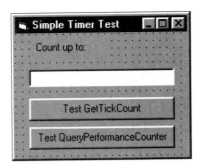

Now you need to add a module to this project. Do this by selecting <u>P</u>roject then Add <u>M</u>odule from the main menu, then select <u>O</u>pen from the window that appears.

You should now have a module which we'll simply call `Lib` for now. The three API calls that were shown in the previous section for `GetTickCount`, `QueryPerformanceCounter`, and `QueryPerformanceFrequency` need to be included in this library along with a declaration for the `LARGE_INTEGER` UDT.

Type in the API declarations:

```
Declare Function GetTickCount Lib "kernel32" _
    Alias "GetTickCount" () As Long
```

```
Declare Function QueryPerformanceCounter Lib "kernel32" _
    (lpPerformanceCount As LARGE_INTEGER) As Long
```

```
Declare Function QueryPerformanceFrequency Lib "kernel32" _
    (lpFrequency As LARGE_INTEGER) As Long
```

Then the User Defined Type:

```
Public Type LARGE_INTEGER
    LowPart As Long
    HighPart As Long
End Type
```

Now let's code the method that will use the GetTickCount function. Add this code to the form's Declarations section:

```
Private Sub TestGetTickCount()

On Error GoTo error_TestGetTickCount

'   This method uses GetTickCount
'   to test the for...next loop.

Dim lngC As Long
Dim lngEnd As Long
Dim lngLoop As Long
Dim lngStart As Long

'   Get the loop's ending value.
lngLoop = CLng(txtCount.Text)

'   Get a starting tick value.
lngStart = GetTickCount

'   Now run the loop.
For lngC = 1 To lngLoop
Next lngC

'   Get an ending tick value.
lngEnd = GetTickCount
'   Show the results.
MsgBox "Total Time = " & CStr((lngEnd - lngStart) / 1000#)

Exit Sub

error_TestGetTickCount:

MsgBox CStr(Err.Number) & "   " & Err.Description

End Sub
```

Let's take a look at this method in more detail. First, we convert the value in the text box to a long type and store that in `lngLoop` (if the data in the box isn't numeric, we'll catch the error and display the error message to the screen). Then, we get a starting tick count using `GetTickCount`, and store that in `lngStart`. Next, we run the `For…Next` loop as long as `lngLoop` dictates. Once the loop is done, we get the ending tick value and store that in `lngEnd`. Finally, we display the value of the loop to the user through a message box. Note that we divide the difference between the ending and starting values by 1000 to convert the milliseconds to seconds.

To test the high-resolution timer, the code is similar with a few minor twists:

```
Private Sub TestQueryPeformanceCounter()

On Error GoTo error_TestQueryPeformanceCounter

' This method tests the high performance timer.

Dim dblEndResult As Double
Dim dblFrequency As Double
Dim dblResult As Double
Dim dblStartResult As Double
Dim lngC As Long
Dim lngLoop As Long
Dim udtStart As LARGE_INTEGER
Dim udtEnd As LARGE_INTEGER
Dim udtFreq As LARGE_INTEGER

If QueryPerformanceFrequency(udtFreq) = 0 Then
    MsgBox "No counter available."
Else
    ' We already have the frequency of the counter.
    ' Get the loop's ending value.
    lngLoop = CLng(txtCount.Text)
    ' Get a starting tick value.
    Call QueryPerformanceCounter(udtStart)
    ' Now run the loop.
    For lngC = 1 To CLng(lngLoop)
    Next lngC
    ' Get an ending tick value.
    Call QueryPerformanceCounter(udtEnd)
    ' Calculate the difference.
    dblEndResult = (CDbl(udtEnd.HighPart) * 2 ^ 32) + _
                CDbl(udtEnd.LowPart)
    dblStartResult = (CDbl(udtStart.HighPart) * 2 ^ 32) + _
                CDbl(udtStart.LowPart)
    dblFrequency = (CDbl(udtFreq.HighPart) * 2 ^ 32) + _
                CDbl(udtFreq.LowPart)
    dblResult = dblEndResult - dblStartResult
    ' Show the results.
    MsgBox "Total Time = " & CStr(dblResult / dblFrequency)
End If

Exit Sub

error_TestQueryPeformanceCounter:

MsgBox CStr(Err.Number) & "  " & Err.Description

End Sub
```

The process is virtually the same, except that we first have to make a QueryPeformanceFrequency call to see if a high-resolution timer exists (note that by doing this, we already have the frequency of the timer in udtFreq). If it does, then we can begin the analysis. We get a starting counter value and store it in udtStart. We then run the loop as before, and get an ending counter value, which is stored in udtEnd. This is where we differ from GetTickCount's implementation. We have to convert the 64-bit values stored in the LARGE_INTEGER UDTs to a data type we can manage. Therefore, we convert the values to Double types using the conversion routine stated before. I'll admit that you may lose some precision by doing this depending upon the value of HighPart, but for our purposes this will suffice. Finally, we compute the tick difference between dblEndResult and dblStartResult, and divide that value by the timer's frequency value stored in dblFrequency. This is the value that is displayed to the user.

To make the project complete, add the following calls to each button's Click events:

```
Private Sub cmdTestGetTickCount_Click()

TestGetTickCount

End Sub
```

```
Private Sub cmdTestQueryPerformance_Click()

TestQueryPeformanceCounter

End Sub
```

Program Results

So what's the difference between the two API calls? Here's a table that lists the times taken for the loop to terminate, and what GetTickCount and QueryPerformanceCounter return (of course, your results will probably differ from mine):

Loop Value	TestGetTickCount	TestQueryPerformanceCounter
100000000	21.211	21.1916961397275
10000000	2.117	2.15382004391626
1000000	0.204	0.214193164484822
100000	0.015	2.11175178933606E-02
10000	0.002	2.11703179738179E-03
1000	0	2.21257480011398E-04
100	0	3.26857640925929E-05
10	0	1.3409544243115E-05
1	0	1.17333512127257E-05

As you can see, for large loop values, we get virtually the same results. However, below 1000, `GetTickCount`'s resolution is not fine enough to determine how long the loop took; the high-resolution timer still gives a reading.

Of course, these values will differ from PC to PC. I've also blatantly ignored any numerical issues when I convert the 64-bit values into `Double` variables. However, the purpose of this example is to illustrate how API calls are made and the varying level of difficulty between them.

The API Viewer

Since there are hundreds of calls that you could make within VB, it's nearly impossible to remember every aspect of each call. Microsoft has added a tool that is installed with the VB environment, and it's called the **API Viewer**.

Loading the API Viewer

To load the API viewer into VB you must select Add-In Manager from the Add-Ins menu option. You should see the following window:

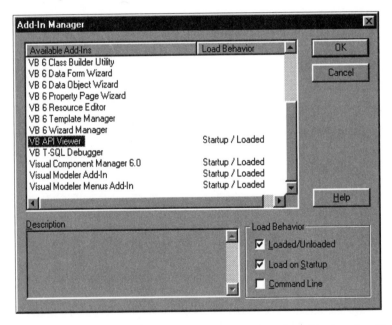

You need to check the Loaded/Unloaded checkbox and the Load on Startup checkbox. Now, whenever you load up VB, you can go to the Add-Ins menu and the API Viewer option will be there. Do this now, and you should see the following:

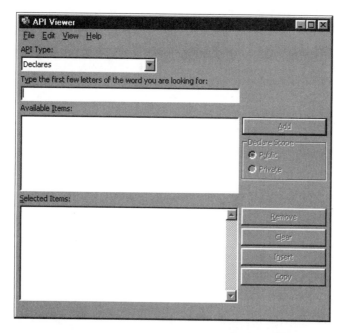

Admittedly, it's not one of the prettiest user interfaces you'll ever see, but it's very effective at helping you out with your declarations. First, you load up a text file that the program can read by selecting the `Win32api.txt` file. (Note: If this is the first time you're running the program, you have to select the file using the File | Load Text File... menu option. After that, the text file will show up as a menu option.) After the load is complete, you can opt to search for declarations, types, or constants by changing the value in the API Type combo box, as this screen shot shows:

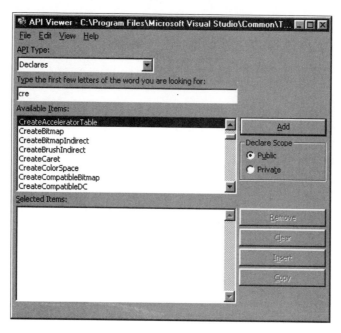

Once the values are loaded in the list box, you can type in the first letters of the item you're looking for, and the list will select the "best fit". Once you find what you're looking for, click the Add button, which will add this to the Selected Items: list. When you add items to the list, you should note that you can select the scope of the item before you add it to the list by selecting the correct Declare Scope option button. You can also change how the items are displayed in the list by changing the viewing option. There are two options listed under the View menu: Line Item and Full Text. If Line Item is checked, the program will only show the name of the item. Otherwise, the full implementation will be shown.

You can add as many items as you want, and once you're finished, you can press the Copy button. All of the contents in the Selected Items: box are copied to the clipboard, and you can directly paste them into your VB module. Here's a screen shot of what the program looks like after you've added a couple of items.

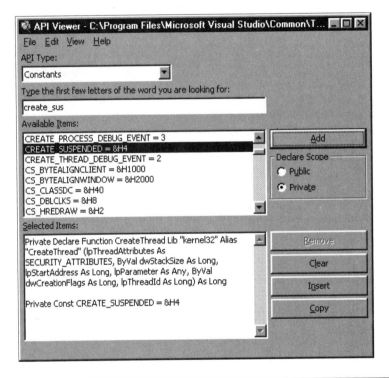

A word of warning to users of this application: Some of the declarations may not be correct! One of the more famous foul-ups is `GetPrivateProfileString`, a call that allows you to read information in an INI file. Developers who pasted this declaration into their code in earlier versions of VB suddenly ran into memory exceptions, and didn't have a clue as to why (in Chapter 2, we'll discuss why this happens). If you run into problems, look at what you pasted in to your project - this may be where the error lies. Microsoft usually posts fixes to the API text file, so if you find problems with the loader, check out their MSDN site to see if any updates have been made.

You may have noticed that the program asked you if you wanted to convert the text file to an Access database when you loaded the file. Even if you don't want to now, you can do this at any time - it's a menu option underneath <u>F</u>ile. It claims that there's a speed difference in doing this. While I haven't really noticed a big difference between the two, the nice thing about converting it to a database is that now you have a repository of all the API calls you can make in VB! With a little bit of work, you could expand this for other developers to use, along with adding some other information (like being able to document possible problems with the declarations). It's just a thought, but there may be some value in documenting what you've done for other developers to read.

I should also note that if you've used the API Viewer from previous versions of VB, you will have noticed that even though the application did change with the advent of VB 6.0, the differences are minor. But, there's one nice addition to the Viewer that I've found very appealing. If you look under the <u>V</u>iew menu option, you'll see an option called <u>L</u>oad Last File. As you may have seen when you opened up the `Win32api.txt` file, there were other text files that you could have loaded as well (like the `mapi32.txt` file). If you're using a particular API text file a lot and you simply want the program to load that file every time it runs, make sure that this menu option is activated. It saves a couple of keystrokes or mouse clicks!

Other API Sources

We've gone over an example that showed you what some of the Win32 API calls can do for you. However, that's only two! You may be wondering how you can find out what some of the other calls are and how they operate. Even though we'll go over a lot more in the rest of the book, it's a good idea to give you some sources of information to help you out in discovering new territories:

- ❑ **Microsoft's Web Site** is probably one of the best sites I've found on the APIs. This isn't a surprise - since they wrote them, they should be! They have a web site devoted entirely to the Win32 APIs – it's located at `http://www.microsoft.com/win32dev/`. You can also look at their VB site as well as their Search site.
- ❑ **Wrox's Web Site** located at `http://www.wrox.com/`, not only contains a wealth of information on forthcoming books, but features articles on topics of interest to all VB programmers, including API.
- ❑ **Dan Appleman's Visual Basic 5.0 Programmer's Guide to the Win32 API** is another source of information for VB developers. It's not a book to read through from start to end; I use it for reference purposes. It documents the fundamentals of each call very well though, so keep it close by when you need some help.
- ❑ **Win32 Programming** by Brent Rector and Joseph Newcomer is another solid reference book. It's not written for VB programmers, so don't look for any support in this area. However, it contains a wealth of information on the Win32 APIs – it's probably the book you'll need to use when you're really stuck and all other roads have hit dead ends.
- ❑ **The Visual Basic Programmer's Journal** is a great magazine to subscribe to. It has articles for any VB programmer at any level. I've always found some neat tricks that you can pull off in VB by delving into the APIs in each article. Check out `http://www.devx.com` for subscription information.

No doubt that there's more books and web sites that I could possibly list in the space provided. The best thing to do is to search for VB web sites. There is a lot of information out there if you have access to it - it's made my programming life much easier.

Quick View and Undocumented APIs

Along with the technical documentation listed above, there's also a utility in Windows that lists the routines supported by a DLL, Quick View. If you're the type of person that wants to understand more of what's going on, this is another place to look.

Quick View is an accessory that is not initially selected during the Windows 95 and 98 setup programs. If you need to add it to your PC, put your Windows CD-ROM into your disk drive and follow these steps:

From your Start menu select Settings | Control Panel. Double-click on Add/Remove Programs and the Add/Remove Programs Properties dialog appears:

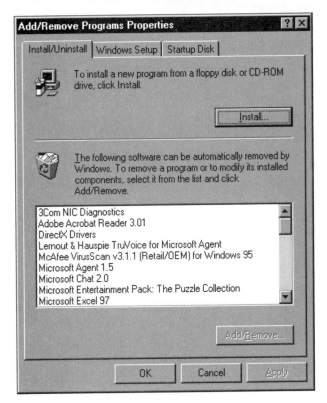

Select the Windows Setup tag and highlight Accessories as in this screenshot:

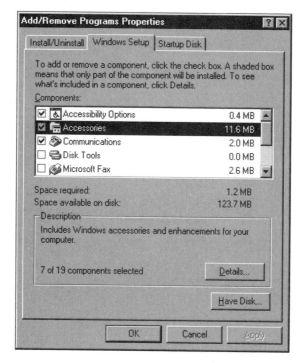

Now click on the <u>D</u>etails... button. Now check the Quick View box:

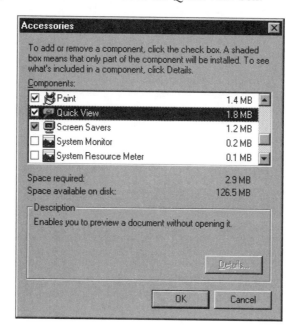

Now you can click **OK** twice and Quick View will be added to your PC.

To get this utility to work, open Windows Explorer, and find `kernel32.dll` (it should be located in the Windows system directory). Make sure the file is selected, and choose <u>F</u>ile | <u>Q</u>uick View. This option works with virtually any file, but when you use it on a DLL, you get a bunch of information that most of us won't ever spend more than 1 second looking at! Here's a sample of some of the information in `kernel32.dll`:

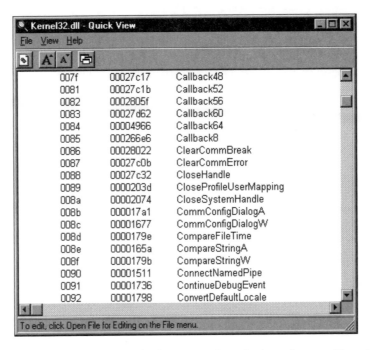

We won't go into the gory details here. Suffice to say that it's more than you'll probably ever want to see about DLLs. I'll leave the interpretation of this data as an exercise for the interested reader.

Well, there **is** one thing that I want to mention about using Quick View on DLLs. If you look at the screen shot I did, you'll see some functions, like `Callback64`, that you'll never find any documentation on. These functions are appropriately named **undocumented APIs**, and they're not that uncommon. One of the main reasons they're there is to allow the developers of the DLL to provide some special functionality that only they want to use. Since it's undocumented, you're on your own to figure out what it does. Microsoft will not help you if you try to use one of these APIs and run into major problems.

> Every so often, I hear somebody mention that Microsoft has an unfair advantage in their Win32 APIs because they actually have "secret" APIs. I won't get into the discussion of where Microsoft has advantages over other companies, but at least one employee from Microsoft has stated that there are no "secret" APIs. There may be undocumented calls, but they are open for the public to try. You can find this article at: `http://msdn.microsoft.com/developer/news/Nielsen_QA.htm`. In my opinion, this is probably an issue over semantics, but I'm more concerned about what Microsoft gives you over what they may hide - it's less stressful that way.

VB has its own undocumented calls as well. The ones that you hear about the most are called `VarPtr`, `StrPtr`, and `ObjPtr`. They return pointers to variables. The first one works for any data type, the second is used for string data types, and the third is used for objects only. They're very useful functions, and you'll see them pop up on occasions in this book, but make sure you use them only when necessary.

The Limits of Visual Basic

One of the main points of this book is to not only introduce you to the concept of APIs but also demonstrate some of their capabilities in projects. However, although you can use most of the calls in VB, there are times when aspects of the call simply prevent you from using it. I'll go through a simple example that will demonstrate this kind of limitation.

Dynamically Loading DLLs

As we saw before, VB uses a specific syntax to let the compiler know that you're making a function call to a DLL. But how does VB do this internally? I haven't had the luxury of working with the VB development team at Microsoft to see how they get the VB tool to work, but I've found three calls that actually come from the `kernel32.dll` that allow you to do this. Here are their declarations:

```
Declare Function LoadLibrary Lib "kernel32" _
    Alias "LoadLibraryA" (ByVal lpLibFileName As String) As Long
```

```
Declare Function GetProcAddress Lib "kernel32" _
    (ByVal hModule As Long, ByVal lpProcName As String) As Long
```

```
Declare Function FreeLibrary Lib "kernel32" _
    (ByVal hLibModule As Long) As Long
```

The first one, `LoadLibrary`, takes as its only parameter the name of the DLL file to load into your application's process space (note that this string has to be null-terminated in order for the call to work - I'll explain why in Chapter 2). This function follows the same rules stated before in this chapter to search for the given file. If it finds it, it returns a non-zero value, which is a handle to the module (we won't worry about what this means for now). Once the DLL is in memory, you can try to get the address to a function within the DLL (warning bells should be ringing in your head right about now) by using the `GetProcAddress` function. The first argument is the return value from `LoadLibrary` - the second argument is the name of the call that you want to eventually invoke (again, null-terminated, just like `lpLibFileName`). If you get a non-zero value back, `GetProcAddress` has determined that the function you were looking for does exist in the DLL loaded. After you're done calling the function, you should unload the DLL using the `FreeLibrary` function.

Suppose we created a small VB example to demonstrate this functionality. It might have an opening screen that looks like this:

DLL Function Addresses

DLL Name:

Procedure Name:

Find it!

It's very simple. It tries to find the function within the DLL given in the text boxes. If it can, it comes up with the following message box:

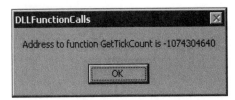

If it can't, it barks at you:

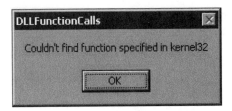

This is all well and good, and this is essentially what VB does for you underneath the scene whenever you call a DLL function. However, there's one big problem with all of this if you tried to perform this same task within VB code, and that's the return value from `GetProcAddress`. What do you do with it? There is no way that you can invoke a function in VB if you have the function's address. (OK, there is that wonderful keyword introduced in VB 5.0 called `AddressOf` that deals with address to functions, but we'll get to that later and it doesn't help us here anyway.) If you were a C or C++ programmer, this wouldn't be a stumbling block for you since they allow you to declare variables that point to functions. Remember that VB has inherent limitations in its design when it comes to pointers and addresses. VB simply doesn't expose them through any keyword or operators (save for the undocumented calls I mentioned before). In most cases, this isn't a limitation at all. A lot of studies have been done on programming projects, and one of the main sources of bugs is the use (or misuse) of pointers. VB isn't the only language not to expose pointers either - Java is another language that doesn't allow this.

However, when you want to write some extremely efficient code, this limitation starts to become very evident. For example, I once ran into the problem where a large number of spreadsheets had to be produced to show salary information. However, each spreadsheet had its own set of rules to calculate these numbers, and there were well over three hundred of them. Wouldn't it be nice to just simply figure out the rule tree for each spreadsheet, store that in an INI file, and let VB dynamically call whatever functions from whatever DLLs it needs to at run-time? But you just can't do this in VB.

> *Well, technically, you can do this with the* `CallByName` *function. However, this only works with COM objects and not the DLLs that we will come to know and love.*

All that said don't let this example be a deterrent from using the Win32 APIs in VB. This is the exception, and not the norm. I don't know of an exact percentage that tells you how many calls can be used in VB, but I would guess that it's over 95%. If you hit the brick wall, you have to resolve yourself to the fact that VB does have its limitations where other languages don't. If it comes to that, either find a good C++ book, or hope that you can find someone who knows how to program in it. (C++ programmers do exist, by the way, and we should be very thankful for their existence. I mean, did you **really** believe the rumors that VB was written in QuickBasic?)

Summary

That's it. All you need to go ahead and start using API calls in your applications. I hope you enjoyed my book and Good Luck!

Just kidding. But to be fair we have covered all the essentials of using API calls and you could probably quite easily start incorporating them into your programs. However, there is still so much more that we have yet to discuss.

In this chapter we:

- ❑ Covered the fundamentals of API calls
- ❑ Familiarized ourself with the API Declaration Loader
- ❑ Saw some undocumented calls
- ❑ Looked at two different calls that were similar in design but very different in implementation

Now that we've covered the basic we can go ahead and really start to learn about the API. In the next chapter, we'll look at some of the problematic areas of the API calls in VB and how you can avoid some nasty pitfalls. I'll also introduce the Encryption Program, an application that we will be using throughout the rest of the book to test other API calls.

2

API Pitfalls to Avoid and the Encryption Program

In the previous chapter, we looked at the basics of an API call and went over some examples of how to use them in VB. So you should now be ready to get down to some of the real nitty-gritty.

In this chapter we'll be investigating how API calls work at a much lower level. This will allow you to avoid some of the classic problems that have tripped up many other VB programmers in the past.

In this chapter we'll cover:

- ❑ Data Types and API calls
- ❑ Error handling with API calls
- ❑ Other troublesome calling issues

Finally, we'll be introduced to the Encryption Program. We will use this application throughout the rest of this book as a test ground for our Win32 development. In this chapter we'll build the UI for this project as well as covering how the encryption algorithm will function although we'll leave the coding for the next chapter.

The Differences in Data Types

If you've ever programmed in languages other than Basic, you've probably noticed that most of the data types are very similar overall, but not exactly the same. For example, if you added the following variable declaration in Visual Basic:

```
Dim intCount as Integer
```

You would have a variable that could hold integer values from -32,768 to 32,767. However, if you make the following declaration in Visual C++:

```
int intCount;
```

intCount would have a range of -2,147,483,648 to 2,147,483,647.

I'm already envisioning a response like, "Well, what does this have to do with us? We're VB programmers, not Pascal or C programmers." True, you don't have to worry about other languages when you're in VB. But when you make an API call, you're starting to walk out of the world of Visual Basic and into foreign territory. There are a lot of little surprises in store for the VB developer who doesn't take the time to figure out the exact data type that should be passed into an API call. For example, say a C programmer made a DLL for you on April 1st named HaHa.DLL, and said that the Gotcha function takes one integer parameter called WatchOut. It also returns a string. Ignoring the subtle hints, you add the following declaration to your code:

```
Declare Function Gotcha Lib "HaHa" (WatchOut as Integer) as String
```

This looks like it should work OK, but if you try and use this function like a VB function, you will soon run into a few problems. After this chapter is done, you'll be able to see the warning signs immediately. For now, let's go over the data types that can do cause trouble if you're not careful (I'll leave the method of revenge that should be incurred upon that C developer as an exercise to the reader).

> **By the way, even though I'm going to show you code in C, don't think that you've got another language to learn. I'm only doing this to demonstrate the differences in data types between languages, especially with a language that is used to create DLLs. Appendix A lists the data types you should use in VB for the C data types found in most DLL calls.**

Visual Basic Strings and API Calls

If you stay within the Visual Basic world, strings are pretty straightforward. Variable-length strings by definition grow and shrink with no special coding tricks. Here's a code snippet to demonstrate this:

```
Dim strTest as String

strTest = "First value."
strTest = ""
strTest = "Make it relatively bigger than before."
```

There's no magic going on here. VB is handling whatever memory allocation is needed to add and remove space as needed. C programmers don't have that luxury. They have to declare their strings using character arrays, like the following C code line:

```
char strTest[13] = "First value.";
```

C also requires that you end, or **terminate**, any string with the null character '\0'. Most VB programmers use the returned value from Chr$(0) to create this character. When you declare strTest in C this way, you don't have to explicitly add the null character to the end of the initialization value - it's done for you. Therefore, even though the string is only twelve characters long, we have to make sure there's room for that terminating character. You could allow the compiler to figure out how much space strTest needs by changing the code like this:

```
char strTest[] = "First value.";
```

but you could never have more than 13 characters in `strTest` after this declaration.

Of course, C has pointers and addresses that makes string manipulation much faster than VB, so if you have a lot of string processing going on in your application, you may want to have that friendly C programmer down the hall create a DLL for you to speed that up. (You may also want to tone down that revenge thing I mentioned before a little bit). But that's exactly where one of our problems lie. In C, strings are usually declared of the type `LPSTR`, or **l**ong **p**ointer to a **str**ing. Here's what that looks like in memory:

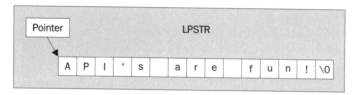

> **Technically, the acronym LPSTR is a bit deceiving. In C, LPSTR is typed as:**
>
> ```
> typedef CHAR* LPSTR
> ```
>
> **This means that LPSTR is actually a pointer to the first character of a string.**

As we have seen, this string is just an array of characters. In VB, however, strings are actually of a type called `BSTR`. Here's what this looks like:

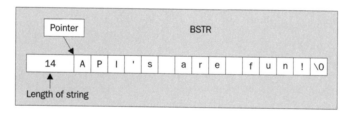

VB used to use the `HLSTR` *data type to define its strings. I won't go into the memory structure here, but if your fellow VB programmer who's stuck on maintaining a 16-bit application in version 3.0 is having problems with API calls and strings, you may want to start looking at this type. They used a pointer to a pointer to the first character in the string, which really made things confusing.*

You may wonder why you don't see the termination character whenever you use strings in VB. It's one of those magical features of the tool - it simply hides it from you whenever you read from or write to strings. Technically, it is there and as we'll find out, it can be quite useful.

Differences Between Fixed and Variable Length Strings

Fixed-length strings are similar to variable-length strings in that they both hold character information. Also, you pass a fixed-length string `ByVal` just like you would for a variable-length string. The only way they differ is that with fixed-length strings...well, they're fixed in size. As we saw with variable-length strings, we can grow and shrink the string with ease. However, as this following line of code shows:

```
Dim strFixed as String * 5
```

we can only have 5 characters in the string at one time. Personally, I use variable-length strings when I make API calls that require strings as parameters, but there are always exceptions.

As you can see, there's one big difference between BSTRs and LPSTRs, and it's the length parameter that's tacked onto the beginning of the BSTR. There's a nice feature to this - VB doesn't have to calculate the length of a string every time the Len is called. It simply looks up the value stored within the string, and passes that back to the caller. (Of course, VB must change this value when the string changes length.) However, one major drawback of this is that a DLL function expects a different type of string. The DLL doesn't want a BSTR - it wants a LPSTR.

So how do you get around this? Is there some convoluted method to convert a BSTR into a LPSTR? The answer is no - once again, VB handles all of this for you. Let's look at a simple API call to illustrate this - it's called FindWindow:

```
Declare Function FindWindow Lib "user32" Alias "FindWindowA" _
    (ByVal lpClassName As String, ByVal lpWindowName As String) _
    As Long
```

This function will return a window handle for a window that matches the information given. What we're more concerned about here is how we're going to get that information to FindWindow correctly.

> **You may wonder why the function is really called FindWindowA in the DLL. This is the ANSI declaration; a Unicode version called FindWindowW exists as well. We'll cover Unicode later on in the chapter.**

As it turns out, it's the ByVal keyword that saves us. When you pass a variable of a String type using this keyword, VB will actually pass a reference, or pointer to be exact, to your string. Furthermore, since your string is actually null-terminated internally, you don't have to append a termination character to the end of your string every time you call an API that requires a string.

There are a couple of catches here. The function will stop at the first null terminating character in the string. Remember that when VB passes the string to the API, it's actually passing the address of the first character to the call. Therefore, the call really has no idea how long the string is, or, more accurately, how much memory you've allocated to hold the string's contents. It's depending upon that end character to notify the DLL when the end of the string has been reached. So make sure that there are no null characters within the string when you pass it! Although you probably won't throw a memory exception if you do this, any of the data that exists past the first null character will not be read by the DLL.

Another catch is the keyword overloading. Although you have explicitly declared that the string should be passed ByVal, the string could get modified within the DLL. This is a head-twister when you first read it. You're passing it ByVal, but it's acting as though you passed it ByRef! Why is this the case? I really, really wish I knew! Personally, it would make sense to me that if the DLL function can change the contents of a variable, it should be passed ByRef. But that's not the case. This is one of those little quirks of the VB environment that, whether or not it makes logical sense, you must follow to ensure your strings are handled correctly by DLL functions.

Also, be sure that you read the documentation on the call you're making - since the DLL is actually referring to your string variable, they can alter the contents of the string itself. This is usually what you want to have happen in most calls, just don't be surprised if the data is different after an API call.

Usually when the DLL will change your string, it also will ask you to tell it how long the string is. For example, let's take a look at the following API call to illustrate this scenario:

```
Declare Function GetWindowsDirectory Lib "kernel32" _
    Alias "GetWindowsDirectoryA" (ByVal lpBuffer As String, _
    ByVal nSize As Long) As Long
```

This function returns the full path of the Windows directory. The `lpBuffer` is the variable that `GetWindowsDirectory` will fill with the path, and `nSize` is the length of the string. This function will return the length of the string copied into `lpBuffer` on success (minus the termination character), and zero on failure. Note that if the string you passed in wasn't big enough, this function will return the length of the buffer required. Here's how you'd get the path in VB:

```
Dim lngRet as Long
Dim lngSize as Long
Dim strWindowsPath as String

lngSize = 255
strWindowsPath = String$(lngSize, " ")

lngRet = GetWindowsDirectory(strWindowsPath, lngSize - 1)

If lngRet <> 0 then
    If lngRet > lngSize Then
        '  We have to make the call again
        '  with a bigger string!
    Else
        strWindowsPath = Left$(strWindowsPath, lngRet)
    End If
End If
```

What we're really doing here is creating a memory buffer. We use the `String$` function to fill the string with 255 spaces. After calling `GetWindowsDirectory`, we check the return value (note that we didn't have to use the `ByVal` keyword for the two arguments, since the function was declared with the arguments `ByVal`). If everything's OK, we get rid of the spaces in `strWindowsPath` using the `Left$` function. Note that we passed in the length of the string minus 1. This is kind of a "safety net". Since we know that we've allocated for 255 characters, and we also know that the string is null-terminated underneath the covers, we should expect that the DLL will only use those 255 characters. But to be safe, we'll tell the function that we've only allocated enough space for 254 characters.

The problem lies with initializing the string and passing in the right length value. If we're not careful in our code, we may pass in a value like 2555 for `nSize`. The DLL thinks that you've allocated 2555 bytes in your string, and it might try to use them all. If it actually tries to go past that 255th byte, you're in big trouble! Whatever memory exists past that 255th byte, we didn't allocate it. Therefore, you're almost guaranteed to cause a memory exception in this case. This is a classic problem that many VB programmers have run into, so make sure you pass in the size correctly!

Another problem with allocating the string is not doing it at all. In this case, the value of nSize always corresponds to the size of the string. However, some functions do not have arguments that allow you to tell the function how much space is available in a buffer, and require that you allocate enough space in a string. If you don't do this, it's possible that the DLL might try to write to a location in memory that your string hasn't allocated, and a memory exception will occur. Again, make sure the string is allocated correctly for the function used.

> One nice trick that you can use to make sure you always pass in a nice, "safety net" value for string lengths is by using the Len function on the string, and then subtracting one from the value. This will ensure that the DLL function has enough valid space to write data to.

There's one more issue we need to address with strings. We now know how to pass them in, but what happens if the call **returns** a string? You may think that it's not that big of a deal, but if you're guessing that it gets really ugly, you're right. Fortunately, these calls are the exception and not the rule, but we still need to understand what we need to do to make the call correctly. Let's look at another API call:

```
Declare Function GetEnvironmentStrings Lib "kernel32" _
    Alias "GetEnvironmentStringsA" () As String
```

All this API call does is return the current Windows environment settings. Note, though, that the **Declaration Loader** says the call returns a String data type. From what we just went through with string lengths, do you think this code will work?

```
Dim strEnv as String

strEnv = GetEnvironmentStrings
```

When I tried to do this, I got a bunch of garbage. DLL functions don't return a String data type the way you would in VB. They're actually returning a LPSTR - a pointer to the first character in a string. In fact, if you did some more research on this call, you'd see how the function was declared for a C point of view:

```
LPVOID GetEnvironmentStrings(VOID)
```

That LPVOID is telling us that we're getting a pointer back. As you know, VB doesn't have any kind of pointer operations to help us out, so it looks like we're stuck. Fortunately, there's an API call that can help us out here, and by using this call, we'll move into another area where memory exceptions can really nail you: typeless variable declaration.

> *To find out what the function declarations look like in C (like I did above for* GetEnvironmentStrings*), go to Microsoft's search site at* http://search.microsoft.com/default.asp. *All of the Win32 documentation is at their Premier level, but registering for this level of service is free.*

Using the Any Keyword

There's an API call that comes in really handy when you need to move blocks of memory around. It's called CopyMemory:

```
Declare Sub CopyMemory Lib "kernel32" _
    Alias "RtlMoveMemory" (lpvDest As Any, _
    lpvSource As Any, ByVal cbCopy As Long)
```

This procedure allows you to copy memory from one location to another. It does this by reading memory from a source (lpvSource) and copying it to another location in memory (lpvDest). The size of the copy is determined by cbCopy.

This procedure has been used by many VB programmers to solve a number of problems. I don't have the space to go over each application of the call, but if you use it, beware of the first two parameters. The first two characters of the argument names should point out (no pun intended) that these are pointers to blocks of memory. Furthermore, the declaration is made with the arguments As Any. The Any keyword is not a data type, like Variant; rather, it's used to let virtually any data type into the function call (it's analogous to the void keyword in C). This makes the call extremely flexible, since it will take virtually anything you pass into it. You can copy memory from longs to longs, from arrays to arrays, and so on. However, by doing this, you've left yourself wide open to a lot of errors. For example, what happens if you pass in a pointer to a string as the source, a pointer to a long as the destination, and set the length of the string as cbCopy? It may work, but I would never bet on it. You have to make sure what kind of information will go where, and if it will make any sense once it gets there.

It's even worse with strings. As we saw before, we have to pass in the string ByVal to force VB into passing a pointer to the first character in the string. The same holds true in this case. If we have a pointer to the string, it may seem like we could just pass in the value of this pointer ByRef. However, this would cause a memory exception, since we're not adhering to what VB is doing for us underneath the scenes.

Let's create an application called TestAPIStringReturn. This program simply makes a call to GetEnvironmentStrings and puts that information into a VB string. First off, before we jump into the code, we need to initialize the project. Add a module called StringLib, and add the CopyMemory declaration I gave before to this module. However, the GetEnvironmentSetting declaration, which should also be added to the StringLib module, has to change a bit:

```
Declare Function GetEnvironmentStrings Lib "kernel32" _
    Alias "GetEnvironmentStringsA" () As Long
```

Also, add a form to the project with one command button. Change the property values in this project according to the following table:

Object	Name	Caption
Form	frmStringReturn	Test API String Return
Command Button	cmdAPIGet	Call API

It's not a very complex project, as the following screen shot shows:

Here's the call that uses the `CopyMemory` procedure to get the information returned to use via a pointer from `GetEnvironmentStrings`. The following code should be typed into the code window of your form:

```
Private Sub TestStringRet()

    Dim lngRet As Long
    Dim strDest As String

    lngRet = GetEnvironmentStrings

    strDest = String$(1000, " ")

    CopyMemory ByVal strDest, ByVal lngRet, Len(strDest) - 1

    Debug.Print strDest

End Sub
```

We call this function from the `Click` event of `cmdAPIGet`:

```
Private Sub cmdAPIGet_Click()

    TestStringRet

End Sub
```

Let's take a look at what this method is doing in more detail. First, we get the pointer to the string via `GetEnvironmentStrings`:

```
lngRet = GetEnvironmentStrings
```

Then, we allocate space for our destination buffer `strDest` using the `String$` function.

```
strDest = String$(1000, " ")
```

Next, we use the handy `CopyMemory` procedure to copy 1000 bytes from the string pointed at by `lngRet` to `strDest`:

```
CopyMemory ByVal strDest, ByVal lngRet, Len(strDest) - 1
```

Finally, we print out the contents of `strDest` to the **Debug** window:

```
Debug.Print strDest
```

Depending upon the length of the environment string, you may end up with a bunch of null characters in `strDest`*. I won't demonstrate it here, but you could use string functions like* `Instr$`*,* `Left$`*, and* `Mid$` *to find the first occurrence of a null and take off that character and any others that follow it.*

You'll notice that both pointer parameters were passed in `ByVal`, even though the declaration says the parameters are going to be used by reference. This is good, since we're passing in pointers to strings as our values. If we made the call this way:

```
CopyMemory strDest, lngRet, Len(strDest)
```

we'd throw a memory exception (trust me, I've tried it - if you really must have a go yourself make sure that you save everything first). Also, you may have wondered why I arbitrarily buffered `strDest` with 1000 space characters. Since we don't know the length of the string that `lngRet` is pointing at, I just picked a number that I thought would be large enough to handle the result. Obviously, if you wanted to use this function in a production application, you'd have to be more creative to make sure you're getting all of the environment information into `strDest`.

The reason we could get this to work in the first place is because we handled the data types correctly on our end. By declaring the data type `As Any` in the API call, you're forced to make sure that the data you're copying from can be stored in the destination location you've given. If we take another look at the `FindWindow` procedure, you'll notice that VB wouldn't have allowed a `Long` to be passed into either of its arguments:

```
Declare Function FindWindow Lib "user32" Alias "FindWindowA" _
    (ByVal lpClassName As String, ByVal lpWindowName As String) _
    As Long
```

VB won't do a type check when you use `As Any`, you're on your own. However, by passing in two strings `ByVal`, the call is successful.

I'd suggest that you always type your arguments whenever possible. It makes your VB coding life a lot less painful. Sure, there are exceptions - like the one we just covered - but make sure you know what's going into your code, because VB is going to drop the ball on those data types.

The GetPrivateProfileString Fiasco

Remember in Chapter 1 when I said that I'd get back to this function? Well, now is the time to reveal what the big stink about this function was. The function itself isn't the problem; it's the declaration from the **API Viewer** that causes it. If you pasted the declaration from the version supplied in VB 4.0 because you wanted to read INI files, you got something like this:

```
Declare Function GetPrivateProfileString Lib "kernel32" _
    Alias "GetPrivateProfileStringA" (ByVal lpApplicationName _
    As String, lpKeyName As Any, ByVal lpDefault As String, _
    ByVal lpReturnedString As String, ByVal nSize As Long, _
    ByVal lpFileName As String) As Long
```

Many VB programmers started to have a lot of problems in using this call, and if you look at the declaration hard enough, you'll see why. It's that second parameter that is causing all the problems. If you look at Microsoft's documentation for this parameter, you'll see this definition of `lpKeyName`:

> **Pointer to the null-terminated string containing the key name whose associated string is to be retrieved. If this parameter is NULL, all key names in the section specified by the `lpAppName` parameter are copied to the buffer specified by the `lpReturnedString` parameter.**

If the parameter is a string value, why isn't it passed in `ByVal` like all the others? The hitch is when you have to pass in a null value. Declaring a string like this:

```
Dim strNull as String
strNull = ""
```

does not make the string null as far as a DLL function is concerned! VB has added a string constant called `vbNullString`, which you should use when you need to pass in a null value to a string parameter. Microsoft posted the fix on their web site, which said that the declaration should be (incidentally, this is the declaration you will get if you use the **API Viewer** with Visual Basic 6):

```
Declare Function GetPrivateProfileString Lib "kernel32" _
    Alias "GetPrivateProfileStringA" (ByVal lpApplicationName _
    As String, ByVal lpKeyName As Any, ByVal lpDefault As String, _
    ByVal lpReturnedString As String, ByVal nSize As Long, _
    ByVal lpFileName As String) As Long
```

However, I disagree with this declaration, since the data type declaration for the `lpKeyName` argument has been left as `As Any`. The function's declaration clearly states that the argument expects a pointer to a null-terminated string; so why would anyone want to pass in a UDT or `Long`, etc. to this function? I usually declare `GetPrivateProfileString` like this:

```
Declare Function GetPrivateProfileString Lib "kernel32" _
    Alias "GetPrivateProfileStringA" (ByVal lpApplicationName _
    As String, ByVal lpKeyName As String, ByVal lpDefault As String, _
    ByVal lpReturnedString As String, ByVal nSize As Long, _
    ByVal lpFileName As String) As Long
```

It makes my life a lot easier when I use it this way!

I think the reason why this mistake got more publicity than all of the other bugs that VB has had is that a lot of programmers needed to manipulate INI files. Therefore, this call probably got more use than, say, `GetProcAddress`. Whenever you make an API call, it's a good idea to find out exactly what the DLL is expecting. Check the SDK from Microsoft whenever possible - it might save you a lot of pain when you're trying to find a very subtle bug with parameter data types.

Arrays and API Calls

Arrays are pretty simple to use, but they tripped me up the first time I had to use them in a call. Granted, I didn't know what I was doing, so I'm trying to stop you from wasting time here.

Anyway, let's take a look at a call that we'll be using a lot throughout this book. It's called `ReadFile`:

```
Declare Function ReadFile Lib "kernel32" Alias "ReadFile" _
    (ByVal hFile As Long, lpBuffer As Any, ByVal _
    nNumberOfBytesToRead As Long, lpNumberOfBytesRead As _
    Long, lpOverlapped As OVERLAPPED) As Long
```

This comes straight from the **API Viewer**. Remember what I said about not taking that tool at its word? We need to make some changes here:

```
Declare Function ReadFile Lib "kernel32" Alias "ReadFile" _
    (ByVal hFile As Long, lpBuffer As Byte, ByVal _
    nNumberOfBytesToRead As Long, lpNumberOfBytesRead As _
    Long, ByVal lpOverlapped As Long) As Long
```

We'll deal with UDTs shortly. We've already dealt with the traps that can bite you by using the `Any` keyword for data types, which is why I've explicitly declared the type. I'm more concerned here with the `lpBuffer` variable. If you read the documentation on this call, it will tell you that this is a buffer that the DLL will put file information into. That's why we declare it as a `Byte` data type, since it seems very natural to handle file information in a `Byte` format. If we had decided to store the file information in a `Long` array that would be fine as well, but there are many data conversions that we would have to deal with. For example, say we needed to read in a file that was 16 bytes long. If we used a long array, we'd only have 4 elements, but we would have to do some bit manipulation to separate out each `Byte` from a `Long` array element. Since VB doesn't have a lot of intrinsic bit manipulation functions (especially the really cool ones like shift-left and shift-right), it's easier to use a type that maps to the file extremely well.

Now that we've got some of the data declaration issues out of the way, we can tackle the array issue. If an API is going to fill a buffer for us and we decide to use an array, we have to pass in the first element of the array to the call. Note that I didn't say "element 1". It doesn't matter what the first element is - in fact, we could pass in any element of our array into the call. For example, each of the `ReadFile` calls would work in this example:

```
Dim bytFile(1 to 10) as Byte
Dim bytFile2(1 to 10) as Byte
Dim lngHFile as Long
Dim lngRet as Long
Dim lngTotalBytes as Long

'  Code to open the file would go here.
'  lngHFile is the handle to the file.

lngRet = ReadFile(lngHFile, bytFile(1), 10&, lngTotalBytes, 0&)
lngRet = ReadFile(lngHFile, bytFile2(6), 5&, lngTotalBytes, 0&)
```

In the first call, we're trying to read 10 bytes from a file and passing that information into `bytFile`. In the second example, we're only reading 5 bytes and we're starting at element 6. The first five elements in `bytFile2` won't be changed after the second `ReadFile` call.

When I tried to pass in an array to a DLL the first time, I wrote this:

```
lngRet = ReadFile(lngHFile, bytFile(), 10&, lngTotalBytes, 0&)
```

This didn't work. When you pass in an array, VB is actually passing in a pointer to the element of the array that you specify (which is why the parameter is passed in by reference). If I had read up on the documentation, I would have saved myself hours of frustration. I had assumed that the call would be able to "know" what it should do with my buffer.

The only place you should be concerned with arrays and API calls is telling the DLL how much space you've allocated. For example, let's rewrite the first call to `ReadFile` to virtually guarantee that we crash our application:

```
Dim bytFile(1 to 10) as Byte
Dim bytFile2(1 to 10) as Byte
Dim lngHFile as Long
Dim lngRet as Long
Dim lngTotalBytes as Long

' Code to open the file would go here.

lngRet = ReadFile(lngHFile, bytFile(1), 15&, lngTotalBytes, 0&)
```

In this case, we've told the DLL that there are 5 more elements from the starting point than what we've allocated for in memory. As we saw with strings, there's no way that the DLL knows how long your array is - you have to specify that yourself. In this case, the DLL is going to try and write to elements 11, 12, 13, 14, and 15. However, the area of memory that exists after our array is off limits, so the chance of a memory exception occurring is quite high when the DLL goes beyond the array boundaries - if you want to experiment with this don't forget to save your work.

UDTs and API Calls

UDTs are usually not a problem when it comes to API calls. Whenever an API call requires a UDT to be passed in as a parameter, it needs to be passed in by reference. For example, the `GlobalMemoryStatus` allows you to find out the current status of some OS memory parameters. Here's what the call looks like:

```
Declare Sub GlobalMemoryStatus Lib "kernel32" _
    (lpBuffer As MEMORYSTATUS)
```

That last parameter is a UDT - here's its definition:

```
Type MEMORYSTATUS
    dwLength As Long
    dwMemoryLoad As Long
    dwTotalPhys As Long
    dwAvailPhys As Long
    dwTotalPageFile As Long
    dwAvailPageFile As Long
    dwTotalVirtual As Long
    dwAvailVirtual As Long
End Type
```

Don't forget that you can get this information from the API Viewer as well, but you have to go to Types instead of Declares.

As we stated before, the MEMORYSTATUS UDT is passed in by reference. Therefore, the DLL may modify the contents of the variable, but in most cases this is exactly what we're looking for.

Note that we saw this same situation with the calls we made in Chapter 1 for the high-resolution timer calls that used the LARGE_INTEGER UDT.

The following code would work just fine in VB:

```
Private Sub GetMemoryStatus()

    Dim udtMemory as MEMORYSTATUS

    GlobalMemoryStatus udtMemory

    '  Code can be added here to use the memory information
    '  stored in udtMemory.

End Sub
```

Once the call is made, each value in udtMemory will be changed to reflect some aspect of the current Window memory allocation. If for some reason you won't pass in a UDT to the call, simply add another call (or change the one you already have) that will accept a Long data type ByVal. This situation arises when you need to make a call that needs a SECURITY_ATTRIBUTES UDT as an argument (we'll see this in the next chapter for the CreateFile call). If you're programming in NT, you can use some security features that define how processes can share system objects. However, this has no meaning in the Win9x world. By redefining the argument as a Long data type, you can pass in a null pointer value, or zero in the VB world. This passes in a null pointer to the function call, which will know that you didn't pass in the UDT. You'd have to redefine the argument's data type in these cases. In fact, take a look at our array discussion we just went through. We redefined ReadFile such that we could ignore the OVERLAPPED UDT.

The only issue that should really concern you when you need to use a UDT is memory alignment. The rules that govern UDT memory alignment are as follows:

- ❑ A byte can exist anywhere within a structure
- ❑ An integer must exist at an address location that is evenly divisible by two
- ❑ A long must exist at an address location that is evenly divisible by four

Therefore, if your type has a `Byte` data type declared along with some other types, VB has to "pad" the structure with some extra memory so the UDT fits the rules. For example, let's take a look at this type:

```
Private Type WeirdType
    ByteType As Byte
    LongType As Long
End Type
```

If you declared `udtWeird` as a `WeirdType` UDT and called `Len(udtWeird)`, you would get a 5. However, calling `LenB(udtWeird)` would return an 8. Since the first type is a `Byte`, VB has to add three extra bytes to make sure that `LongType` exists at a proper memory location. `LenB` returns the actual memory size, including any byte padding that the UDT needs to follow the rules stated above. `Len` simply returns the length of the UDT "as-is," without the memory padding added in. Here's a diagram to demonstrate what the UDT looks like in code, and how it is actually lined up in memory:

Most APIs are aware of the memory alignment issue and follow the requirements stated above. But what about strings? For example, say we changed `WeirdType` so that it looks like this:

```
Private Type WeirdType
    ByteType As Byte
    LongType As Long
    StringType As String * 5
End Type
```

Now what happens if we call `Len` and `LenB`? We get 10 and 20, respectively. But why? We know that VB is adding offsetting memory to get `LongType` in the correct spot. But it looks like we're only adding 5 more bytes with `StringType`. Well, guess what - we've run into yet another topic: **Unicode**.

Unicode and VB String Types

Internally, VB handles its strings as Unicode strings. A Unicode string is just like any other string; the difference is that a character is defined as being 2 bytes long, rather than the standard 1 byte that we're used to. The reason for this is that many languages have more than 256 characters in their alphabets, so Unicode was created to support any language currently used by mankind (can you think of a language that has more than 65,535 characters?).

This usually doesn't impact any VB code, but as soon as you tackle the APIs, you may start to see where the Unicode standard effects you. For example, in our extended `WeirdType` UDT, we noticed that the byte count went up to 20 when we added the fixed string. If we look at the memory layout, we'll see why an extra 5 bytes have been added:

The string is actually taking up 10 bytes of memory. Although we usually don't see this, DLLs really care about memory allocation, especially when strings are involved. In fact, as we'll see in Chapter 3, a UDT that has a `String` data type has a size parameter as well. This is to inform the DLL how much memory the UDT is taking up.

Although VB handles strings internally as Unicode strings, it will automatically handle the ANSI/Unicode conversions for us. However, if an API call specifically needs a Unicode string, you have to run though some hoops to do this. For now, we can declare a `Byte` array to retrieve the information, and then use `StrConv` to convert the `Byte` array's information to a string that we're comfortable with.

An API call that ends with the letter `W` needs Unicode strings. In one of the previous sections, we looked at the `FindWindow` call. There's a counterpart to the declaration that we made, and it's called `FindWindowW` in the DLL. You'll notice that our `FindWindow` call is actually calling `FindWindowA`. Furthermore, if you ever use the OLE or COM APIs, they only take Unicode strings, so you'll have to use the proper calls to communicate with them. However, to keep things simple we'll stick with the ANSI calls whenever possible in this book.

*By the way, don't try looking for Unicode calls in the **API Viewer**. All of the calls are aliased to use the ANSI version of the call. So if you try to search for `FindWindowW`, you won't find it. Nor, for that matter, would you find `FindWindowA`. The only call that will show up is `FindWindow`, which is actually calling `FindWindowA`. If you want to find out if a call like `FindWindow` has a Unicode version of the call, check the Microsoft SDK, or do a **Quick View...** on the DLL that contains the call in question.*

So Why 20 Bytes?

Before we leave the issue of strings and Unicode, I wanted to address an issue that, as of the writing of this book, is still unresolved. Let's break down the WeirdType structure element by element. The first one is a byte. Since the second element is a long, we know that VB will add three bytes between the byte variable and the long variable. This gives us 8 bytes. Well, we know the string is 10 bytes in length, so shouldn't that lead to 18 bytes?

You might think that LenB is taking into consideration the null-termination character at the end of the string, or something like that. Two odd things counter this idea, though. If you increase the length of the string to 6, you still get 20 from LenB. Plus, if you define WeirdType in a VB 5.0 application, you'll get 18 from LenB!

I hate pleading ignorance on this subject, but unfortunately I don't have a choice. I wish that I could give you a clear-cut answer as to why this is so, but I can't. Plus, I bet somebody out there has a simple answer as to what's going on. But I've asked some real gurus of the language, and they can't answer this dilemma.

I'm not too thrilled that there is this discrepancy, though, between the two languages. Granted, I doubt anyone's figured out what the byte length of their UDTs are, and stores those values in constants. If somebody did that in 5.0, they have a potentially big surprise coming up when the application gets ported over to 6.0! This goes to show you that, from version to version, VB may change things beneath the scenes. It may be subtle or it may be dramatic, but it happens. Something changed with LenB, and I'd really like to know what that is.

I have a hunch that this might have something to do with the fact that you can now pass UDTs as typed arguments from class modules in 6.0. Maybe the VB designers had to do something below the VB level to pull this off. This gets into issues with COM and marshaling, something that's best left for other discussions, but I wouldn't be surprised if this new feature is a part of the problem.

Other API Calling Issues

We've covered the majority of issues, problems, and errors that most VB programmers run into when using the API calls. The rest of them are pretty minor, so I've lumped them together into this "Other" category.

Currency Variables

The Currency data type is only valid inside of VB; no API calls that I'm aware of can handle it. If you need to pass in information from a Currency variable to a DLL, convert it to a Double or a Long. You may lose some precision, but that's the best you can do now.

Single and Double Types

The Single data type maps to the float type in C, and the Double type maps to the double type in C. However, none of the Win32 calls use floats or doubles, so unless you're using a custom DLL written in-house, you won't have to worry about it in this book.

Pointers to Functions

Some API calls need a function to call back to inform the calling application of some event. We'll address this (no pun intended) in chapters 7 and 8.

Window Handles

Most of the graphical API calls need a window handle to change something about a particular window. Thankfully, all of the forms and most of the controls (remember, most controls are windows) have a hWnd property, so you can just pass in that value straight into the API (by the way, window handles are declared using the Long data type).

Boolean Return Values

Watch out if a function says it returns zero on error, and nonzero on success. This doesn't translate to VB's True/False Boolean values, where False does equal 0, but True is equal to -1. Use the CBool function on these return values, since CBool will return True for any nonzero value.

Variants

Variants are used with any OLE or COM API calls, but none of the Win32 calls use this type. Therefore, I would strongly suggest avoiding using variants with Win32 calls.

Revisiting the Gotcha Function

Remember that evil C programmer that tried to fool us on April 1st? Well, let's take a look at that call again:

```
Declare Function Gotcha Lib "HaHa" (WatchOut as Integer) as String
```

Two big problems should immediately jump out at you:

❑ We're passing in an Integer data type, but the call may try to put information into our variable that will make it overflow.
❑ We can't return a String data type; we have to return a Long that points to a String data type, and use CopyMemory to get that information into a string variable that we can use.

Now that you know there are pitfalls waiting for you, change that employee's salary in the corporate database appropriately.

Reporting API Errors

Well, we've covered a lot of the major data type issues that we can run into when using the Win32 calls. But there's still one more that we should address, and that's error handling.

The majority of API calls will inform you in some way, shape, or form if an error occurred (note, however, that this doesn't include memory exceptions). Most of the time, it takes the form of a return value or some parameter that you pass into the procedure. But virtually all of the calls set some internal OS information that you can obtain using just two API calls. Let's review these calls, and then we'll create a VB function that we can use within our main development application.

```
Declare Function GetLastError Lib "kernel32" _
    Alias "GetLastError" () As Long

Declare Function FormatMessage Lib "kernel32" _
    Alias "FormatMessageA" (ByVal dwFlags As Long, _
    lpSource As Any, ByVal dwMessageId As Long, _
    ByVal dwLanguageId As Long, ByVal lpBuffer As String, _
    ByVal nSize As Long, Arguments As Long) As Long
```

The `GetLastError` function simply returns a number that corresponds to the last error that occurred within a Win32 API call. We can then use this value and pass it into `FormatMessage` to obtain a message that may make more sense than error code 10594. As you can see, that second parameter is already causing me some concern. We'd better look into this further.

> *If you want, you can use the* `SetLastError` *API call to set the error code. I can't think of a reason why you'd need to do this in VB, but it is possible to change this value.*

The first parameter, `dwFlags`, is used to tell the call how it should be used. It's cryptic, I know, but this function gets pretty flexible in a hurry when you start to read the documentation on the call. The only value of `dwFlags` we're concerned about is `FORMAT_MESSAGE_FROM_SYSTEM` (equal to 4096), which will tell the call to look up a description from an internal resource. We can ignore the second parameter for our purposes (thank goodness), since Microsoft's documentation tells us this argument is ignored when we set `dwFlags` equal to 4096. We can pass in the return value from `GetLastError` to `dwMessageId`. We don't care about language issues for now, so we'll set `dwLanguageId` equal to 0. The `lpBuffer` is another case where we need to pass in a pre-allocated string to the call - the length of the string is passed in through `nSize`. We can also ignore the `Arguments` argument as well.

There's a lot more that you can use `FormatMessage` for, but we just want to use it to obtain error information. If you're curious, hop onto Microsoft's web site and look up the documentation on the call. For now, let's just use what we know about the call to create a prototype API error call:

```
Function GetWin32ErrorDescription(ErrorCode _
    as Long) as String

    Dim lngRet as Long
    Dim strAPIError as String

'   Preallocate the buffer.
    strAPIError = String$(2048, " ")

'   Now get the formatted message.
    lngRet = FormatMessage(FORMAT_MESSAGE_FROM_SYSTEM, _
    ByVal 0&, ErrorCode, 0, strAPIError, Len(strAPIError), 0)

'   Reformat the error string.
    strAPIError = Left$(strAPIError, lngRet)

'   Return the error string.
    GetWin32ErrorDescription = strAPIError

End Function
```

We'll improve upon the function in a moment, but I hope you see the point. Whenever you get an error from a Win32 call, run this function to get an error message. It may help you in debugging your applications.

Which DLL Error Code?

Notice that the `GetWin32ErrorDescription` uses an argument to get the error code. This was done for a lot of reasons; such as letting us enter in any value to see what the result would be (not the most exciting thing to do in the world, but it might be somewhat educational). However, it was also done to illustrate the behavior of capturing the error code from a DLL. Let's use a very simple but powerful example to illustrate this fact.

Create a new **Standard EXE** project in VB called `MutexTest`. Add one label to the form. Here's some more specific information about the project:

Object	Name	Caption
Form	frmMutex	Mutex Tester
Label	lblMutex	(leave blank)

Your main form should look something like this:

As with the `TestAPIStringReturn` project, simplicity is the key with this project. We want to focus in on the API calls and keep the UI to a minimum where possible.

Add the `GetWin32ErrorDescription` function that we just looked at to the code window for the form. Now we'll need four API declarations in this project along with one form-level variable and two constants. Add them to the form's `Declarations` section like this:

```
Private mlngHMutex As Long

Private Const ERROR_ALREADY_EXISTS = 183&
Private Const FORMAT_MESSAGE_FROM_SYSTEM = 4096

Private Declare Function GetLastError Lib "kernel32" () As Long

Private Declare Function CreateMutex Lib "kernel32" Alias _
    "CreateMutexA" (ByVal lpMutexAttributes As Long, _
    ByVal bInitialOwner As Long, ByVal lpName As String) As Long

Private Declare Function CloseHandle Lib "kernel32" _
    (ByVal hObject As Long) As Long
```

```
Private Declare Function FormatMessage Lib "kernel32" _
    Alias "FormatMessageA" (ByVal dwFlags As Long, _
    lpSource As Any, ByVal dwMessageId As Long, _
    ByVal dwLanguageId As Long, ByVal lpBuffer As String, _
    ByVal nSize As Long, Arguments As Long) As Long
```

> **Note that we didn't use a module this time. For simple projects like this, we really don't need a module to house the API declaration.**

Now that we've got the project set up, let's back up for a second so I can explain what this project will actually do!

You may run into a situation in your project development where you want to prevent the user from opening up more than one instance of your application. The global `App` object does have a property call `PrevInstance`, which you can use to determine if another instance is running. But I was curious one day, and I started looking into ways to do this myself. As it turns out, you can use a kernel object called a **mutex** (short for **mut**ual **ex**clusion) to make this a very easy task.

Before we get into the details of the code, I should note that we're using a mutex in a way that it probably wasn't intended (of course, that doesn't necessarily make it wrong, either!). Mutexes are commonly used in multithreaded applications, and that's beyond the scope of this book. However, we'll use one nice little feature of a mutex for our problem at hand: it can be accessed from any process in Windows.

So how does this work? Let's add this function to our form:

```
Private Function IsPrevAppRunning() As Boolean

  On Error GoTo error_IsPrevAppRunning

  Dim lngVBRet As Long

  mlngHMutex = CreateMutex(0, 0, "MutexTest.frmMutex")

  lngVBRet = Err.LastDllError

  If lngVBRet = ERROR_ALREADY_EXISTS Then
    ' This app is already running.
    IsPrevAppRunning = True
    MsgBox GetWin32ErrorDescription(lngVBRet)
  End If

  Exit Function

error_IsPrevAppRunning:

  IsPrevAppRunning = False

End Function
```

I'll come back to this function in a moment. For now, assume that this function will return a `True` if the application is already running and `False` if it isn't. In the `Initialize` event of the form, add this code:

```
Private Sub Form_Initialize()

    If IsPrevAppRunning = True Then
     MsgBox "This app is already running.", _
            vbOKOnly + vbExclamation, "App Already In Use"
     Unload Me
     Set frmMutex = Nothing
    Else
     lblMutex.Caption = "Mutex Number = " & CStr(mlngHMutex)
    End If

End Sub
```

And, in the `Terminate` event of the form, add this code:

```
Private Sub Form_Terminate()

    If mlngHMutex <> 0 Then
    '  Close the mutex.
     CloseHandle mlngHMutex
    End If

End Sub
```

Now let's go through how this all works. The first thing we do is create a mutex using the `CreateMutex` API call. The first argument is set to 0 since we don't care about the security attributes of this mutex. The second argument is also set to 0, which means that we don't "own" the mutex if we create it successfully. The last parameter is the one that we're concerned about. If we didn't name the mutex, we'd have to identify it by the return value, which is the handle to the mutex. However, a named mutex can be used by the name given. Furthermore, as I hinted at before, mutexes can be used across processes. Therefore, if another instance of our application has already created this mutex, `CreateMutex` will let us know about it.

The way `CreateMutex` lets us know of this situation is a bit weird, though. The return value is the handle to the mutex on success (i.e. a non-zero value), so we can't use the return value to let us know if the mutex already exists. However, if the mutex already exists, the `GetLastError` function would return a value equal to `ERROR_ALREADY_EXISTS`. In our case, we catch that situation and return a `True`. Note, though, that we **don't** use `GetLastError` - we use `Err.LastDLLError`. This will be important, as we'll see.

If we haven't created the mutex yet, the app will load up just fine. We should get a window that looks like this:

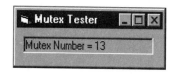

Of course, we should get rid of the mutex when the application is done. This is why we use `CloseHandle` on `mlngHMutex` in the `Terminate` event of the form.

So what does any of this have to do with `GetLastError`? Here's the problem. First, compile the project into an executable (make sure the code is native code, not p-code! To check go to Project | Properties and select the Compile tab.). Then run two instances of the program. The first one should load up fine, but the second one will show the following two message boxes:

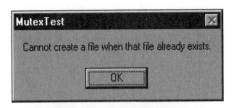

That's the last you'll hear from the second instance.

Now go back into the code and replace this line from within `IsPrevAppRunning`:

```
lngVBRet = Err.LastDllError
```

to this:

```
lngVBRet = GetLastError
```

As before, compile the app and run it twice. Now the app shows up both times! What's the deal?

Internally, VB is making Win32 calls all the time in your application. Sometimes, when you make a Win32 call, this may trigger an event within your application that causes VB to make other Win32 calls (we'll address window messages later on in the book). Well, what happens if your initial call causes an error, but the internal Win32 call made by VB clears out the value of the error? You get the situation that we just saw. `GetLastError` returns a zero, but `Err.LastDllError` returns the correct error code.

In previous versions of VB, the `LastDllError` property didn't exist, and strange situations like the one we just saw popped up again and again. Therefore, the VB designers decided to add the `LastDllError` to the `Err` object. This property should be used when a Win32 call is made that causes an error, because VB will track your Win32 call and make sure that this property reflects any possible error conditions.

But you need to be quick. Grab the value of `LastDllError` after any Win32 calls in question, even before you look at the return value! This is the **only** way to guarantee that any error condition generated by the Win32 call you just made is in `LastDllError`. If you start changing the size of the form, or adding text to a text box, all bets are off, and you've lost the error code (unless you're really, **really**, **REALLY** lucky).

So what's the best situation to be in? Let's leave this discussion of capturing Win32 error codes in VB with this outline. It's no guarantee that we'll report the correct error code all of the time, but this is about as close as we're going to get:

1. Grab the value of `LastDllError` immediately and store it in a variable (call it `lngErrVB`).

2. Grab the value of `GetLastError` and store it in a variable (call it `lngErr32`).

3. If `lngErrVB` is nonzero, then use it to report the error condition.

4. If it's zero, check `lngErr32`. Chances are it's probably zero as well, but if it's nonzero, use it to report the error.

The moral of the story? You should **always** use the value from `LastDllError` whenever possible. VB is making a conscious effort to intervene on your behalf, so this is your best bet for Win32 error codes.

A Quick Review

Let's try to sum up all of the issues we've addressed so far in this chapter concerning API calls:

- ❏ Save your work often
- ❏ Always pass strings `ByVal`
- ❏ Be very careful when using the `Any` keyword
- ❏ Pass in the first element when using arrays as buffers
- ❏ Make sure your `UDT`s map to what the DLL is expecting
- ❏ Never tell a DLL that you've allocated more space than you really have
- ❏ Don't embed null characters in strings if an API call needs it
- ❏ Save your work often
- ❏ And...save your work often

You're bound to run into other subtle "features" when you use the Win32 API. In a way, the Win32 APIs remind me of the English language; it does have structure, but there are a lot of exceptions to the rules. But as long as you try to find out as much as you can about what's going on underneath the scenes, you should be able to solve any problem.

And yes, I did mention the save edict three times. **NEVER** run your code without saving it first, and I mean **NEVER**. You're throwing the safety net away when you tear into the Win32 APIs, so save your work before you try to run your code. A crash may shut down VB or even Windows itself, but if your code was saved, you can always go back and figure out what went wrong after the OS reboots.

The Encryption Program

As we have seen, there's a lot of power in the Win32 APIs. As long as you steer clear of the potential traps, your development will be a smooth process. Throughout the rest of this book, we'll use an application as our main "playground" for API testing and debugging. This application is called **The Encryption Program**. I'll explain why I've decided to use this project in this book, and then we'll take a look at the program itself.

If you don't want to read about the political or social reasons that motivated me to write this program, please skip over the next section. But I would encourage you to do it anyway. Think of it this way: If I was in a business area at the company you worked at, and I came to you with this problem, how would you effectively solve it? You may or may not agree with my arguments or ideas, but I'm coming to you with a problem, I have the money in my budget, and I want you to solve it for me (yesterday, of course). One of the biggest criticisms I've heard about programmers is their inability to relate to business areas, so I'd ask you to set judgment aside and tackle the problem with a technical solution in the back of your mind.

Why This Program?

One issue that you tend to hear about every so often is privacy rights. For example, more and more cameras are showing up in our society every day. Some people claim that these cameras infringe upon our privacy (like when you try on clothes at a department store), while others state that the cameras help minimize criminal activity (like being able to spot a person stuffing a shirt into a bag when they're in the dressing room). This issue is rather complex, and this book is not the place to analyze it in detail, but there is one part of it that, admittedly, annoys me!

A thorny side issue has been raised with employees using e-mail at work. Some employees have used these services to send jokes or pictures that other may consider derogatory or inappropriate. In this day and age of lawsuits and allegations, the last thing a company would want is to be sued by an employee who feels that the content within a message is harmful. Therefore, some companies have set up policies and procedures that allow them to read anyone's e-mail at any time. Content that has been defined as inappropriate and is found within a message can lead to disciplinary action, or even termination.

Granted, this sounds nice, but the reason I want to encrypt a file is that I don't want anyone to see the cookie recipes I'm sending to my parents via e-mail other than my parents! This is where the issue gets personal, so I'll stop at this point. But it motivated me to start investigating cryptography a bit more. I don't claim to be an expert in the field, and the technique I came up with is fairly simplistic, but it required me to break open a lot of API calls to pull it off. So let's take a look at how the algorithm works before we start coding in VB.

If you're interested in learning more about encryption, check out the RSA Data Security, Inc. web page at http://www.rsa.com/. I make no claims that my code will secure the content of your files, since it's a pretty simplistic process compared to RSA. But RSA is very secure, so check out this site if you need tight cryptography.

How the Algorithm Works

Say you have the following message that you'd like to encrypt:

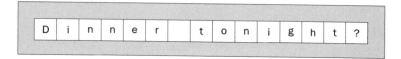

As you can see, the message is broken up such that each character is in its own box. To encrypt this message, we're going to handle each character in the message one at a time. We also have to convert each character into its ASCII character value. Here's what the message looks like in ASCII values:

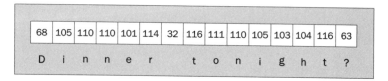

We also need two other parts: the seed value and the key. The **seed value** is to set the starting point in a random sequence, and the key is used as a "filter" on the message. For this example, let's say the key is "XKf7" and the seed value is 24.

Now for the fun stuff. We line up the message's first character against the key's first character value, the message's second character against the key's second character value, and so on. If the message is longer than the key, we just start over. Here's what that looks like:

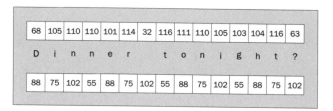

The next step is to simply add the character values up between the two strings, and store the results into another array of characters. Here's what happens during this operation:

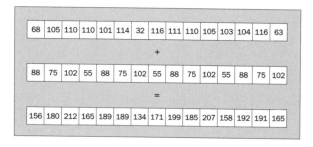

The last step is to introduce some randomness into the picture. If we didn't, our key would stick out like a sore thumb in the resultant array. For example, if we had a message like "ZZZZZZZZZZZZZZZZZ", and our key was "XKf7", here's what would happen:

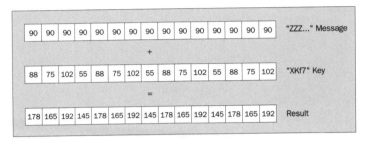

Granted, the exact key value isn't repeated, but that's a glaring hole for any hacker to try and decrypt the message. This gets worse if the file we encrypt has a bunch of null characters in a row. Remember that a null character is equal to 0 in ASCII. Add 0 to the key value, and you get the key value, thereby exposing the key itself! Therefore, we need to mess up the result a little bit. Here's another catch, though: we have to be able to "unmess" the result when we decrypt it. If this isn't possible, the message will be lost forever.

Thankfully, the random number generator in VB helps us out here. If you search for the word `Rnd` in VB's help file, you'll find this sidebar:

> **To repeat sequences of random numbers, call** `Rnd` **with a negative argument immediately before using** `Randomize` **with a numeric argument. Using** `Randomize` **with the same value for number does not repeat the previous sequence.**

`Rnd` is a function that returns a random number. However, without getting into the statistical details, `Rnd` is cyclical. That is, eventually `Rnd` will start to repeat.

It actually takes 16,777,000 iterations, from what I can tell. I've created a project called `RandomSequenceCheck` *that you'll get if you download the code. It has absolutely nothing to with API calls, which is why I don't cover it explicitly in the book; I just wanted to show this interesting little fact in a VB project for the curious reader.*

If you want to start the sequence at a specific point, you use the following code:

```
Rnd (-1)
Randomize (SeedValue)
```

No matter when or where you run this code, your program will produce the same random sequence every single time as long as `SeedValue` is the same. I know that may sound weird - how can you call a sequence random if you know what's going to be generated? - but for our purposes, this is exactly what we need. Now, if we would run this code in VB and call `Rnd` as many times as we need for our message we get:

156	180	212	165	189	189	134	171	199	185	207	158	192	191	165	Added Message

+

116	83	240	90	140	22	204	154	146	244	156	47	3	79	200	Randomness

=

272	263	452	255	329	211	338	325	345	429	363	205	195	270	365	Final Result

If the concept of generating a random number sequence that's predetermined and cyclical sounds like a paradox, you may have to break open a book on statistics and probability to get a thorough explanation on random number generators. One good source that I know of is written by Athanasios Papoulis, entitled "Probability, Random Variables, and Stochastic Processes," but it's definitely not easy on the eyes from a mathematical standpoint!

We still have one minor process to run. The ASCII character set only goes from 0 to 255, so if the resultant value exceeds 255, we simply subtract 256 from the value until it is less than 256. (For all you non-mathematicians out there, we'll skip the group theory analysis.) So here's the final encrypted message:

272	263	452	255	329	211	338	325	345	429	363	205	195	270	365	Final Result

-

256 as needed

=

16	7	196	255	73	211	82	69	89	173	107	205	195	14	109	

In ASCII, this is the message from start to finish: "__ÄÿIÓREY-kÍÃ_m". Pretty messy, isn't it? You'd have to spend a little bit of time to crack this one. Now if we want to decrypt it, we just run the process in reverse. We take the message, subtract each character with the correct number in the random sequence along with the correct value in the key. This time, if the number is less than 0, we add 256 until the value is non-negative. Here's the process in reverse:

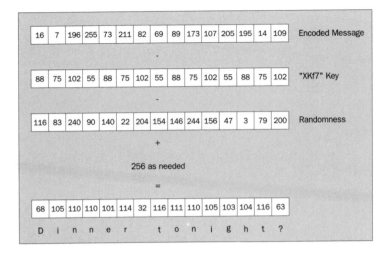

If you look back at the original message in ASCII, we got it back! Also, notice that the randomness is exactly the same sequence as before. If it wasn't, who knows what your friend may be reading on the other end.

It's a simple algorithm, once you get down to it. There are more complex mathematical issues that we didn't delve into, but it does its job. However, you still have the issue of the key and seed value. How do you transmit these components? Well, that's more of a social issue than anything. You may use the key "Stop6Watch" between one group of friends, and simply tell them the seed value in the e-mail along with the attached encrypted file. If anyone intercepted the message, they wouldn't have the key to decrypt the file. However, if someone reveals the key, then the system breaks down.

The VB Project

The Encryption.vbp file is where we'll start incorporating API calls into our code. Here's a screen shot of the main form:

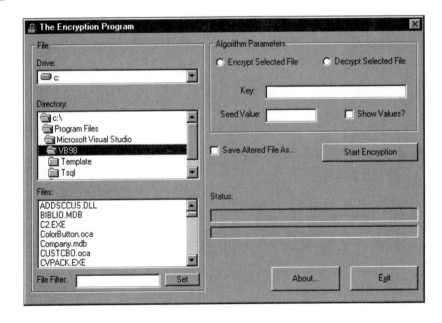

Here's a screenshot of the About form:

Let's cover some of the real basic glue code that we'll need throughout the development of this project. First off, here are some of the basic project information you need to know. Note the **Contained In** entry in the table that designates where the control should go. Because the project has a lot of UI components, this is needed for clarification. Bear with me as we go through the list, but rest assured, this is by far the biggest list of project properties we'll see. Also note that I've left the labels out of the controls list that are used for descriptive purposes only. All the controls can be found in your default Toolbox except for the Progress Bar which is located in `Microsoft Common Controls 6.0`. By looking at the screen shot, you should be able to add them in if you think it's necessary:

Object	Contained In	Property	Value
Form		Name	`frmMain`
		Caption	The Encryption Program
		Borderstyle	3 - Fixed Dialog
Frame	`frmMain`	Name	`fraMain`
		Index	0
		Caption	File:
Frame	`frmMain`	Name	`fraMain`
		Index	1
		Caption	Algorithm Parameters
Drive List Box	`fraMain(0)`	Name	`drvMain`
Directory List Box	`fraMain(0)`	Name	`dirMain`
File List Box	`fraMain(0)`	Name	`filMain`
Text Box	`fraMain(0)`	Name	`txtFileFilter`
		Text	(leave blank)
Command Button	`fraMain(0)`	Name	`cmdSetFilter`
		Caption	Set

Table Continued on Following Page

Object	Contained In	Property	Value
Option Button	fraMain(1)	Name	optEncrypt
		Index	0
		Caption	Encrypt Selected File
Option Button	fraMain(1)	Name	optEncrypt
		Index	1
		Caption	Decrypt Selected File
Text Box	fraMain(1)	Name	txtKey
		Text	(leave blank)
		PasswordChar	*
Text Box	fraMain(1)	Name	txtSeedValue
		Text	(leave blank)
		PasswordChar	*
Check Box	fraMain(1)	Name	chkShowValues
		Caption	Show Values?
Check Box	frmMain	Name	chkSaveAs
		Caption	Save Altered File As...
Command Button	frmMain	Name	cmdRunEncryption
		Caption	Start Encryption
Text Box	frmMain	Name	txtStatus
		Text	(leave blank)
		BackColor	&H00C0C0C0&
Progress Bar	frmMain	Name	ProgressBar
Command Button	frmMain	Name	cmdAbout
		Caption	About...
Command Button	frmMain	Name	cmdExit
		Caption	E&xit
Form		Name	frmAbout
		Caption	About the Encryption Program
Label	frmAbout	Name	lblTitle

Object	Contained In	Property	Value
		Caption	The Encryption Program
Label	frmAbout	Name	lblCreatedBy
		Caption	Created By Victor
Label	frmAbout	Name	lblVersion
		Caption	(leave blank)
Timer	frmAbout	Name	tmrAbout
		Enabled	True
		Interval	5000
Command Button	frmAbout	Name	cmdClose
		Caption	&Close

There's some code we need to add to this skeleton layout before we start adding API calls to the project. We won't spend too much time on them, but they give some basic functionality to the project. Let's start with `frmMain`. The first method is called `SetFilePattern`:

```
Private Sub SetFilePattern()

  If Trim(txtFileFilter.Text) = "" Then
    filMain.Pattern = "*.*"
  Else
    filMain.Pattern = Trim(txtFileFilter.Text)
  End If

End Sub
```

This is called from the `Click` event of `cmdSetPattern`:

```
Private Sub cmdSetPattern_Click()

  SetFilePattern

End Sub
```

`SetFilePattern` sets the `Pattern` property of the file list box to show either all the files or files with a specific pattern given by the user.

The next function we need is called `ValidateInterface`. This function checks entries made in the interface and returns "" on success and something on failure.

```
Private Function ValidateInterface() As String

  On Error Resume Next

  Dim lngCheck As Long
```

```
    If Trim$(txtKey.Text) = "" Then
        ValidateInterface = "Please enter in a key."
        Exit Function
    End If
    If Trim$(txtSeedValue.Text) = "" Then
        ValidateInterface = "Pleae enter in the seed value."
        Exit Function
    Else
        lngCheck = CLng(txtSeedValue.Text)
    If Err.Number <> 0 Then
        ValidateInterface = "The seed value is too large."
        Exit Function
    ElseIf lngCheck < 1 Then
        ValidateInterface = "The seed value must be greater than 0."
        Exit Function
    End If
    End If

End Function
```

This isn't called yet by a control in the project, but we'll need it to verify what the data that the user entered.

The function begins by checking that a key was entered:

```
If Trim$(txtKey.Text) = "" Then
    ValidateInterface = "Please enter in a key."
    Exit Function
End If
```

Then we ensure a seed value was entered:

```
If Trim$(txtSeedValue.Text) = "" Then
    ValidateInterface = "Pleae enter in the seed value."
    Exit Function
```

If a seed value has been entered we check for an overflow:

```
Else
    lngCheck = CLng(txtSeedValue.Text)
    If Err.Number <> 0 Then
        ValidateInterface = "The seed value is too large."
        Exit Function
    ElseIf lngCheck < 1 Then
        ValidateInterface = "The seed value must be greater than 0."
        Exit Function
    End If
End If
```

The Click event of the cmdAbout command button brings up the frmAbout form:

```
Private Sub cmdAbout_Click()

  Screen.MousePointer = vbHourglass
```

```
        frmAbout.Show vbModal

    End Sub
```

The `Click` event of the `cmdExit` command button shuts down the application:

```
Private Sub cmdExit_Click()

    Unload Me
    Set frmMain = Nothing

End Sub
```

The drive, directory, and file list boxes changes are all coordinated using the following lines of code:

```
Private Sub drvMain_Change()

    dirMain.Path = drvMain.Drive

End Sub
```

```
Private Sub dirMain_Change()

    On Error Resume Next

    SetFilePattern
    filMain.Path = dirMain.Path

End Sub
```

The `chkShowValues` check box is used to let the user see what is actually contained in the seed and key text boxes. It does this by calling the `CheckKeyAndSeed` method in its `Click` event:

```
Private Sub chkShowValues_Click()

    CheckKeyAndSeed

End Sub
```

Here's what the `CheckKeyAndSeed` looks like:

```
Private Sub CheckKeyAndSeed()

    On Error Resume Next

    If chkShowValues.Value = vbUnchecked Then
      txtKey.PasswordChar = "*"
      txtSeedValue.PasswordChar = "*"
    Else
      txtKey.PasswordChar = ""
      txtSeedValue.PasswordChar = ""
    End If

End Sub
```

If the user want's to see what's in the boxes, we set `PasswordChar` to an empty string. Otherwise, the text is masked with the `"*"` character.

Now let's move on to `frmAbout`. The first method to look at is `InitializeForm`:

```
Private Sub InitializeForm()

    Screen.MousePointer = vbHourglass
    lblVersion.Caption = "Beta Version " & CStr(App.Major) & _
    "." & CStr(App.Minor) & "." & CStr(App.Revision)
    Randomize
    Screen.MousePointer = vbDefault

End Sub
```

It's called from the `Load` event of the `Form`:

```
Private Sub Form_Load()

    InitializeForm

End Sub
```

The other method is called `AlterLabels`:

```
Private Sub AlterLabels()

End Sub
```

It does nothing yet; trust me, it will! It's called from the `Timer` event of `tmrTimer`:

```
Private Sub tmrAbout_Timer()

    AlterLabels

End Sub
```

Now that the skeleton code is done, let's go over what we **really** have to worry about:

- ❑ Implement the encryption algorithm defined above and show the status of the algorithm to the screen
- ❑ Add a Save As... process
- ❑ Have some fun with the About screen
- ❑ Change each form to look more appealing - gray is getting old

We'll tackle all of these issues along with some other neat tricks in the next three chapters. Whenever we add code that uses the API calls, we'll try to achieve the same functionality using VB code only. We'll compare them from a performance standpoint as well, and see which one "wins".

Summary

I hope you are beginning to see some of the complexity of using API calls and also how they have gained such a poor reputation. However, I would also hope that you can approach API calls with confidence now that you know how to avoid the pitfalls that lie in wait.

In this chapter we:

❑ Saw how many of the data types are communicated between VB and the DLL
❑ Used this knowledge to learn how to avoid other problems with calls we haven't seen yet
❑ Covered how to handle errors when using API calls in VB
❑ Quick overview of some other problems that might occur

We also built the UI for the Encryption application and defined what the encryption algorithm is in readiness for building the real functionality of the application in the next chapter.

In the next three chapters, we'll use calls from the three main Win32 DLLs: kernel32, user32, and gdi32 to begin to examine how we can access some of Windows key programming. We'll also be developing the Encryption program by incorporating calls to these three DLLs to get the program up and running and to spice up the interface.

3

Kernel32 Calls

Now that we understand the basics and are aware of some of the hidden dangers of using API calls we can begin to truly explore the potential of the Win32 programming environment. Therefore, in this chapter we'll examine the first of the three main Win32 DLLs: `kernel32.dll`.

More specifically we'll cover:

- ❑ File operations with API calls
- ❑ Potential problems with `kernel32`
- ❑ Comparison with VB file operations

We'll also add `kernel32.dll` API calls to the Encryption program to handle the file operations necessary to implement the algorithm that we discussed in the previous chapter. In addition, we'll also implement the algorithm using straight VB so that we can compare the two methods. In order to do this we'll build a `Stopwatch` object to time the two mechanisms.

Kernel32 Overview

The first Win32 DLL we're going to look at is `kernel32.dll`. This DLL is primarily responsible for, but not limited to:

- ❑ Memory Management
- ❑ Multithreading
- ❑ File Operations
- ❑ Process Control

Let's take a brief look at these before we continue.

Memory Management

Everything on your PC is dependent upon memory and Windows is no exception. Variables need to be declared, DLLs need to be loaded, and programs need to print reports. If you're looking for an API declaration to allocate a bunch of memory for whatever reason, this is the place to start.

Multithreading

Multithreading is a fairly easy concept to understand, but it's a bear trying to get it to work correctly! All of the calls to create threads exist in this DLL, but unless you've got a fair amount of time, determination, and patience, I wouldn't try this in VB. (Note that I didn't say it was impossible, just a lot harder than setting the `Caption` property of a label.)

File Operations

We'll be using a lot of these calls in this chapter. Everything you ever wanted to do with files - opening, reading, writing, copying, and deleting - are all here.

Process Control

If you need to start up an application, use `CreateProcess`. If you need to load a DLL, use `LoadLibrary`. If you need to increase a process' priority level, use `SetPriorityClass`. If you...well, you get the idea.

API Call Definitions

Let's start out with an overview of the encryption algorithm as it pertains to file manipulation, and then we'll go over each call in detail.

Encrypting Files

In the last chapter, we went over the algorithm using a simple "Dinner tonight?" message. Unfortunately, Windows doesn't store any of its information on paper; we have to get control of the disk in some way in order to accomplish this under Windows. Therefore, let's outline the algorithm using more "computerish" terminology:

1. Open the source file
2. Copy the file's contents to a memory block
3. Encode or decode that memory block per the algorithm's specifications
4. Close the source file
5. Open the destination file (overwriting the existing file is OK)
6. Save the memory block to a file
7. Close the destination file

Sounds easy, right? Just a bunch of file operations. Well, that's true, but nothing's easy with the APIs. Granted, the file operation procedures are not as involved as some that you may run into, but there's room for creativity, so let's make sure we understand every aspect of the calls before we start to use them.

Procedure Declarations

Here are all of the calls we'll need. I'll list the names of the procedures here, and I'll give the full declaration of the function at the beginning of each section:

- ❏ CreateFile
- ❏ GetFileSize
- ❏ ReadFile
- ❏ WriteFile
- ❏ SetFilePointer
- ❏ CloseHandle

When we get to the encryption program, I'll define where these functions should go and how the should be declared. For now, let's review each one in detail.

CreateFile

```
Declare Function CreateFile Lib "kernel32" _
    Alias "CreateFileA" (ByVal lpFileName As String, _
    ByVal dwDesiredAccess As Long, ByVal dwShareMode As Long, _
    ByVal lpSecurityAttributes As Long, _
    ByVal dwCreationDisposition As Long, _
    ByVal dwFlagsAndAttributes As Long, _
    ByVal hTemplateFile As Long) As Long
```

This function is the starting point for any file alterations that you may need. If you noticed, there was no "OpenFile" procedure in the list. Even though there is an API call named OpenFile within kernel32.dll, it's not as flexible as CreateFile, so we've opted for the latter.

If you're curious about what OpenFile *can't do, here's the main list: It can't open pipes and you can't open files with a fully qualified path greater than 128 characters. There are some other very technical limitations that it has, but the limit on the path size is enough of a reason for me to use* CreateFile.

CreateFile has the ability to create other Window objects (like pipes, for example), but for the problem at hand, we'll concentrate on the file objects. Let's take a look at the arguments:

lpFileName

This one's pretty simple. It's the name of the file to create or open - some of the other arguments will determine if the file needs to exist or not before the call is made. I'd suggest giving the complete file path just to eliminate some unnecessary guesswork as to how this call searches for files.

dwDesiredAccess

This argument takes two values defined by the following enumerated type:

```
Enum DesiredAccess
    GENERIC_WRITE = &H40000000
    GENERIC_READ = &H80000000
End Enum
```

If you are wondering why I'm declaring the constants as enumerated types instead of just Long *data type constants, it's just a different way to group together the constant values. Enumerated types are actually long data types, and with VB's* QuickInfo *feature, you can get the entire list of values just by typing the name of the enumeration with the dot (". "), like you would with controls. You don't have to use the enumeration name to use a value within the enumeration, though, and you'll see both declaration styles throughout the book. I like grouping constant values together like this – it's a personal preference that simply makes my coding life a bit easier to manage and maintain.*

If you use GENERIC_READ on the file, you can read from the file, but you can't write to it. Conversely, if you use GENERIC_WRITE, you can write to the file, but you can't read from it. You can combine the two to allow your application read/write access to the file using the Or operator like this:

```
lngRet = CreateFile(..., GENERIC_READ Or GENERIC_WRITE, ...)
```

You can pass in a 0, but this kind of access is for devices only, which we won't cover in this book.

Note that this is **NOT** the same thing as restricting file access for other processes. For example, if you set dwDesiredAccess equal to GENERIC_READ, other processes can still write to the file. In other words, just because you've given yourself read-only privileges through dwDesiredAccess doesn't mean it applies to the rest of the world. We'll find out how to restrict access to the file with the next argument.

dwShareMode

Here are most of the values this parameter can take:

```
Enum FileSharing
    FILE_SHARE_READ = &H1
    FILE_SHARE_WRITE = &H2
End Enum
```

Similar to dwDesiredAccess, FILE_SHARE_READ allows other processes to read the file, while FILE_SHARE_WRITE allows other processes to write to the file. Therefore, if you want to prevent other applications from changing your file, make sure you don't use FILE_SHARE_WRITE. Note that these values can be combined to allow read/write access. If you set this argument equal to 0, no other process can do anything to the file until your process closes the file.

If you're using NT, there's another parameter called FILE_SHARE_DELETE that allows you to read a temporary file that's flagged with the FILE_FLAG_DELETE_ON_CLOSE in dwFlagsAndAttributes. For example, let's say process A has created a file with the FILE_SHARE_DELETE mode specified along with the FILE_FLAG_DELETE_ON_CLOSE value for dwFlagsAndAttributes. Process B tries to open the file using FILE_SHARE_READ, but this request will fail. However, if Process C opens the file with the FILE_SHARE_DELETE attribute, the call will be successful. (Note that the file won't be deleted from the system until all handles to the file have been closed.)

A very interesting application of these delete characteristics was summarized in an "auto-delete" program procedure demonstrated by Jeffrey Richter in an MSJ issue. You can find it in the Q&A section of the January 1998 issue. I should note that readers found that the idea presented didn't always work as planned, but the concept is still very intriguing.

lpSecurityAttributes

This is a pointer to a SECURITY_ATTRIBUTES UDT. This UDT is used to describe...well, the security attributes of kernel objects within Windows. Here's the definition of this UDT:

```
Type SECURITY_ATTRIBUTES
    nLength As Long
    lpSecurityDescriptor As Long
    bInheritHandle As Boolean
End Type
```

The first member, nLength, should contain the size in bytes of the structure, which is always 12. The second member, lpSecurityDescriptor, contains the address of a security descriptor. Basically, security descriptors are used to determine who or what can use whatever you're trying to secure. Security descriptors can get rather complex when you want to use them, plus you can only work with security descriptors via specific API calls (like GetSecurityDescriptorOwner, for example). The last parameter, bInheritHandle, determines whether other processes can inherit these security attributes. This UDT works under both NT and Windows 9x, but the lpSecurityDescriptor value is ignored by 9x systems. We won't bother with using this UDT in our code, so that's why we declared it as a Long data type to allow us to pass in a 0 value later.

dwCreationDisposition

This argument controls how the file should be created:

```
Enum CreationDisposition
    CREATE_NEW = 1
    CREATE_ALWAYS = 2
    OPEN_EXISTING = 3
    OPEN_ALWAYS = 4
    TRUNCATE_EXISTING = 5
End Enum
```

Let's take a look at these values in more detail:

❑ CREATE_NEW states that CreateFile will try to make a new file as defined by lpFileName. If the file already exists, CreateFile will not work.

❑ CREATE_ALWAYS will create a new file. If the file already exists, CreateFile will overwrite the old version of the file, so if you use this value make sure that you don't need the contents of the existing file.

❑ OPEN_EXISTING states that the file specified by lpFileName has to exist for CreateFile to work. If it doesn't, CreateFile will error out. OPEN_ALWAYS will create the file if it doesn't exist and open the file if it does.

❑ TRUNCATE_EXISTING will only work if the file already exists; CreateFile will error out if it doesn't. If it does, CreateFile will open the file and remove all the data from the file, essentially setting the file size to 0 (note that you need to have GENERIC_WRITE as one of the values to dwDesiredAccess. If you haven't given yourself access to change it, TRUNCATE_EXISTING won't work).

Sounds confusing? You bet it is. Read over the descriptions again - it might take a while before the logic underlying `dwCreationDisposition` sinks in. Note that you cannot combine these values in the argument using the `Or` keyword.

dwFlagsAndAttributes

This argument is used to set how the file will be used from a read/write position as well as the attributes of the file. The list of valid constants for this argument looks big at first, but we'll break it down into two enumerated types to make it easier to digest (there are some additional constants you can use for security, but we'll ignore them for now):

```
Enum FileAttributes
    FILE_ATTRIBUTE_ARCHIVE = &H20
    FILE_ATTRIBUTE_COMPRESSED = &H800
    FILE_ATTRIBUTE_HIDDEN = &H2
    FILE_ATTRIBUTE_NORMAL = &H80
    FILE_ATTRIBUTE_READONLY = &H1
    FILE_ATTRIBUTE_SYSTEM = &H4
End Enum
```

```
Enum FileFlags
    FILE_FLAG_WRITE_THROUGH = &H80000000
    FILE_FLAG_NO_BUFFERING = &H20000000
    FILE_FLAG_OVERLAPPED = &H40000000
    FILE_FLAG_RANDOM_ACCESS = &H10000000
    FILE_FLAG_SEQUENTIAL_SCAN = &H8000000
    FILE_FLAG_DELETE_ON_CLOSE = &H4000000
End Enum
```

Let's tackle the attribute parameters first:

❑ `FILE_ATTRIBUTE_ARCHIVE` signals the OS that this file should be archived whenever that archival process is activated.

❑ `FILE_ATTRIBUTE_COMPRESSED` marks the file as compressed.

❑ `FILE_ATTRIBUTE_HIDDEN` marks the file as a hidden file, which means you might not see it in Windows Explorer (depending on the current view settings).

❑ `FILE_ATTRIBUTE_NORMAL` says the file is, well, normal. Basically, this means that the file has none of the file attributes specified by the other file attribute values. If you combine any attributes with this one, it gets overwritten; this value only works on its own.

❑ `FILE_ATTRIBUTE_READONLY` sets the file as read-only. I know that we can do this in `dwShareMode` as well, but remember that this is an attribute - it remains even after we close the file.

❑ `FILE_ATTRIBUTE_SYSTEM` is used to signal that the OS (or at least some part of it) can only use this file.

Note that all of these parameters take effect when the file is created successfully. If you open a file where the attributes differ from what you specified, they change when the file is opened. Now let's look at the flags.

❏ FILE_FLAG_WRITE_THROUGH says that the OS should write any changes to the file directly to disk, bypassing any caches.

❏ FILE_FLAG_NO_BUFFERING requires that the file be written using volume sector blocks. This means that you have to perform I/O operations on the file using integer multiples of the sector size. You can use the GetFreeDiskSpace API call to find out how your drive is set up to accomplish this. If you use this parameter, asynchronous performance speeds up, but I/O tasks will take longer, and you may waste some disk space due to the sector block read/write requirement.

❏ FILE_FLAG_OVERLAPPED allows overlapped, or asynchronous, operations to occur on the file. However, this adds some complexity to any reading or writing operations to the file, since they are not synchronous.

❏ FILE_FLAG_RANDOM_ACCESS optimizes the file for (you guessed it) random access. This means that any file I/O operations are done from different locations in the file at different times. The first file read may be at the beginning, the next one may be at the end, then the next one may in the middle somewhere. Similarly, FILE_FLAG_SEQUENTIAL_SCAN optimizes the file for files that are usually read from or written to in a start-to-finish mode.

❏ FILE_FLAG_DELETE_ON_CLOSE is nice if you just need a temporary file - Windows will delete this file once it's closed.

hTemplateFile

If you want to copy all of a file's attributes to this file, pass in the file's handle to this argument (you must have GENERIC_READ access to do this). This only works under NT. You must pass in a 0 for Win95; otherwise, the function will fail.

Return Value

If the return value equals -1 (or the INVALID_HANDLE_VALUE constant), then an error occurred. Otherwise, you have a handle to the file.

Quick CreateFile Example

Exhausting, isn't it? But you have a lot of flexibility with CreateFile, which, depending upon the problem at hand, may be very useful. Let's go through a brief example to clarify how the arguments work. Say I had the following requirements for a file:

❏ I want to read from it
❏ I don't want to accidentally write to it
❏ I don't want anyone else to have access to the file
❏ It has to already be in existence
❏ I don't want to create it
❏ I'm also going to be reading the file from the first byte to the last

How would I call this function to meet these requirements? Here's the code snippet to show how I would do it:

```
Dim lngFileHandle as Long

lngFileHandle = CreateFile("C:\Windows\myfile.txt", GENERIC_READ, _
                     0, 0, OPEN_EXISTING, FILE_FLAG_SEQUENTIAL_SCAN, 0)
```

We use the `GENERIC_READ` value for `dwDesiredAccess`; the `GENERIC_WRITE` value is not used to prevent us from writing to the file. We set `dwShareMode` to 0, which prevents any other programs from performing any I/O operations on the file except ours. The `OPEN_EXISITING` value is used to ensure that the file must be in existence before we make the `CreateFile` call. Finally, since we know we're going to read the file from the first byte to the last, we set `dwFlagsAndAttributes` to `FILE_FLAG_SEQUENTIAL_SCAN`.

GetFileSize

Now that we have a handle to the file, we need to know how big the file is. `GetFileSize` does just that:

```
Declare Function GetFileSize Lib "kernel32" _
    (ByVal hFile As Long, lpFileSizeHigh As Long) As Long
```

It looks simple, but we'll see that it's got a trick up its sleeve.

hFile

This argument is the file handle, or the return value we get from a successful call to `CreateFile`. Simple enough!

lpFileSizeHigh

This returns the high 32 bits of a 64-bit number that defines the file size. This is similar to the problem we ran into with the `QueryPerformanceCounter` and `QueryPerformanceFrequency` calls discussed in Chapter 2. You'll notice that we're passing this value in by reference - I'll explain why after I go over the return value.

Return Value

This is the confusing part. `GetFileSize` returns the size of the file (the lower 32 bits of the file size to be more exact), but it also returns `&HFFFFFFFF` if an error occurred (we'll call that the `ERROR_FILE_SIZE` constant). The hard part is that this may be a correct value!

Let's back up a minute. Most of us are used to a world where files stay in the megabyte range. However, the Win32 OS can handle files as large as 18 exabytes in size. That's equal to 2^{64}, or 1,152,921,504,606,846,976 bytes! I know that most users of the earlier versions of Windows 95 (myself included) had to partition drives that were larger than 2 gigabytes into separate logical drives that were smaller than 2 gigabytes, so they'll never see files this big. But later versions of Windows 95 and NT don't have this problem. If we want to write robust code, we should try to handle files of that size. But we're limited here by VB. As you'll see, we're going to use arrays to retrieve and save data to files, and we won't be able to allocate more than 2 gigs of memory to do this. Therefore, we're going to make an assumption that if we get `ERROR_FILE_SIZE` as the return value, an error has occurred. Otherwise, we have the file size.

ReadFile

Now that we know the size of the file, we can start to read from it. Here's the declaration for `ReadFile`:

```
Declare Function ReadFile Lib "kernel32" (ByVal hFile As Long, _
    lpBuffer As Any, ByVal nNumberOfBytesToRead As Long, _
    lpNumberOfBytesRead As Long, ByVal lpOverlapped As Long) As Long
```

hFile

This is a handle to a file, just like the first argument to `GetFileSize`.

lpBuffer

This is a buffer to put the data from the file. As you can see, it's declared `As Any`. That should be a warning sign for potential problems ahead, but we'll make sure to pass in our buffer correctly.

nNumberOfBytesToRead

Just like the argument says, this tells `ReadFile` how many bytes we want to read. If you use `Long` arrays to store file information, you'll have to do some conversions here to figure out how much data you really want to read into your buffer.

lpNumberOfBytesRead

This will contain the number of bytes that were actually copied into your buffer. If you asked for 10,000 bytes but you were near the end of the file, `lpNumberOfBytesRead` may equal 234. Since the variable needs to be changed by the DLL, we need to pass in by reference.

lpOverlapped

We won't worry about asynchronous file operations, so we won't pass in the `OVERLAPPED` UDT. However, for the sake of completeness, here's what the structure looks like:

```
Type OVERLAPPED
    Internal As Long
    InternalHigh As Long
    offset As Long
    OffsetHigh As Long
    hEvent As Long
End Type
```

The `Internal` member is used by the OS to return status information. `InternalHigh` is used to return the length of the data transfer. `Offset` and `OffsetHigh` together specify the starting location of the data transfer. Similar to what we saw with `GetFileSize`, `OffsetHigh` is used to specify the high 32 bits of a 64 bit file pointer location. `hEvent` is a handle to an event object. This is used to signal when the data transfer is complete.

I know that most of these descriptions will make little sense, since asynchronous I/O operations won't be discussed in this book. Just remember that it's possible with a little more research.

> *Note that it's not necessary to add this UDT to any of the projects that we'll be working on in this book.*

Return Value

If the return value is non-zero, the file read was a success. Otherwise, we know that an error occurred. We'll use the `GetWin32ErrorDescription` function we wrote in Chapter 2 to give us a message that corresponds to the error codes returned by `ReadFile` (as well as any other error codes returned by any other API call in this book where appropriate).

Quick ReadFile Example

To demonstrate how this call is made, let's go over a brief example. Say that we have a file handle called `lngFileHandle`, and I want to read in 10,523 bytes. This is how I would do it:

```
Dim bytFileInfo() as Byte
Dim lngBytesRead as Long
Dim lngFileHandle as Long
Dim lngRet as Long

'  Do a CreateFile call here.

Redim bytFileInfo(1 to 10523) as Byte

lngRet = ReadFile(lngFileHandle, bytFileInfo(1), 10523, _
                     lngBytesRead, 0)
```

I'm assuming here that a call was made to `CreateFile` and `lngFileHandle` was the return value.

WriteFile

Well, if we can read from a file, we should be able to write to it. Here's the declaration for `WriteFile`:

```
Declare Function WriteFile Lib "kernel32" _
    (ByVal hFile As Long, lpBuffer As Any, _
    ByVal nNumberOfBytesToWrite As Long, _
    lpNumberOfBytesWritten As Long, ByVal lpOverlapped As Long) As Long
```

Since this function is virtually the same as `ReadFile`, I won't go into any specifics over the arguments.

SetFilePointer

We want to make absolutely sure that we read and write information to the correct locations in a file, especially if the source and destination files are one and the same. `SetFilePointer` will help us out with this need:

```
Declare Function SetFilePointer Lib "kernel32" _
    Alias "SetFilePointer" (ByVal hFile As Long, _
    ByVal lDistanceToMove As Long, _
    ByVal lpDistanceToMoveHigh As Long, _
    ByVal dwMoveMethod As Long) As Long
```

hFile

Yep, you guessed it. It's the file handle.

lDistanceToMove

This specifies the offset value in bytes. This value can be either positive to specify a "move-forward" operation, or negative to indicate a "move-backward" operation. This becomes important depending upon the value of `dwMoveMethod`.

lpDistanceToMoveHigh

If this were declared `ByRef`, this would specify the high 32 bits of a 64-bit file size. We're going to ignore this parameter, so we have to declare it `ByVal` and pass in a zero (or NULL) value as the documentation specifies for this function.

dwMoveMethod

There are only three values that this argument will accept:

```
Public Enum FileMoveMethods
    FILE_BEGIN = 0
    FILE_CURRENT = 1
    FILE_END = 2
End Enum
```

If we set it equal to `FILE_BEGIN`, we offset the file `lDistanceToMove` bytes from the beginning of the file. Conversely, if we use `FILE_END`, we move `lDistanceToMove` bytes from the end of the file. If we use `FILE_CURRENT`, we move `lDistanceToMove` bytes from the current position in the file. Depending upon the value for `lDistanceToMove`, we can either go forward or backward from the position specified by `dwMoveMethod`. Of course, if we tried to move backwards when `dwMoveMethod` is set to `FILE_BEGIN`, the file pointer won't move.

Return Value

If the return value equals `HFILE_ERROR`, an error occurred. Otherwise, we get the new position of the file pointer. This allows us to use this function as a "GetFilePointer" function as well. We simply set `lDistanceToMove` equal to zero and `dwMoveMethod` equal to `FILE_CURRENT`. We'll use this little trick later in this chapter.

CloseHandle

Once we're done with the file, we need to get rid of our hold on the file. This is very important, especially if we have any read/write locks on the file. If we don't do this, the file may stay in a locked state, even after our program terminated. `CloseHandle` does this for us:

```
Declare Function CloseHandle Lib "kernel32" _
    (ByVal hObject As Long) As Long
```

hObject

This is the handle that we want to close. Note that this function can close the handle to other system objects, like threads and processes.

Return Value

If the return value is non-zero, the handle is closed, or, in our case, the file is closed. Otherwise, an error occurred.

Win32 Implementation of the Encryption Algorithm

Now that we've defined all of the functions we're going to use in detail, let's start coding the algorithm. We'll begin by defining the procedural rules of the algorithm, and then implement the rules into the VB project.

Procedural Rules of the Algorithm

Following is a list of all the rules that we want our code to reflect:

- ❑ No one should be able to perform any read/write operations to the files while we are manipulating them
- ❑ The source file must exist
- ❑ If the destination file exists, we should not change the file unless the user allows us to
- ❑ The source and destination files can be the same

As you can see, there aren't a lot of rules associated with the algorithm. Some of them are simple common sense, like the second one (how can you encrypt or decrypt a file that doesn't exist?), but it always helps to be as thorough as you can. We may run into others when we start coding, but for now this list will suffice.

Win32 Implementation

Finally, we get to code! We know we need to have a function to handle the algorithm, and we need to pass in some parameters to let it know where the files are, what the key is, etc. Furthermore, as we saw in Chapter 2, the algorithm is very similar when we encrypt as well as decrypt a file. Therefore, we'll make one function called `FileCrypt` that takes in a UDT, which holds all of the information it needs to run the encryption algorithm on a specified file. First, open up the Encryption project we started working on in Chapter 2. Then, add a new code module and call it **EncryptionLib**. Now add the following items to this module:

- ❑ **All** of the functions and enumerations defined above, and make sure they have `Public` scope
- ❑ Add the `GetWin32ErrorDescription` function we defined in Chapter 2 along with the `FormatMessage` API call to this module, and make sure they have `Public` scope as well

We have some constants that need defined as well:

```
Public Const FORMAT_MESSAGE_FROM_SYSTEM = 4096
Public Const HFILE_ERROR = &HFFFFFFFF
Public Const INVALID_HANDLE_VALUE = -1
Public Const MAX_BUFFER_SIZE = 32768
Public Const MAX_PATH = 260
Public Const MOD_BY = 256
```

Some of these constants we've seen before; the other ones will pop up later in the chapter. Now let's define the interface for `FileCrypt` along with some other enumerations and types. You should add this information to the module:

```
Public Enum CodingParam
    Encrypt
    Decrypt
End Enum
```

```
Public Type EncryptionParameters
    SourceFile As String
    DestinationFile As String
    Key As String
    Seed As Long
    CodingType As CodingParam
    ErrorDescription As String
End Type
```

```
Public Function FileCrypt(Params As EncryptionParameters) _
    As Boolean

End Function
```

The `CodingParam` enums define the two possibilities of the algorithm: either you encrypt or decrypt the source file. The `EncryptionParameters` houses all of the data that the algorithm will need. As we'll see, `FileCrypt` will be making some assumptions about the data that's stored in the UDT, but as long as we document this behavior, we'll be fine.

FileCrypt

I'll give you the entire function in full, and then we'll go over it step-by-step. I'll admit it's pretty big, so read through it carefully before you read the explanation. Essentially the function accepts a `Params` UDT containing the relevant information and uses it to either encrypt or decrypt the source file and place the results into the destination file. The function will return `True` if successful and `False` if an error occurs (The error will be stored in `Params.ErrorDescription`):

```
Public Function FileCrypt(Params As EncryptionParameters) _
    As Boolean

    On Error GoTo error_FileCrypt

    Dim lngDestFile As Long
    Dim lngError As Long
    Dim lngRet As Long
    Dim lngSourceFile As Long
    Dim strTempFile As String

    With Params
      ' Clear out any information in ErrorDescription
        .ErrorDescription = ""
      ' Check to make sure that the source file exists.
        If DoesFileExist(.SourceFile) = False Then
          ' Return a FALSE.
            FileCrypt = False
            .ErrorDescription = "The source file does not exist."
        Else
          ' Try to open the file such that
          ' no one else has access to it.
            lngSourceFile = CreateFile(.SourceFile, _
                    GENERIC_READ Or GENERIC_WRITE, _
                    0, 0, OPEN_EXISTING, _
```

```
                          FILE_FLAG_RANDOM_ACCESS, 0)
    '  Grab the error code!
        lngError = Err.LastDllError
        If lngSourceFile = INVALID_HANDLE_VALUE Then
         '  We couldn't open the file
            .ErrorDescription = _
                    GetWin32ErrorDescription(lngError)
            FileCrypt = False
        Else
            If .SourceFile = .DestinationFile Then
                lngDestFile = lngSourceFile
            Else
                lngDestFile = CreateFile(.DestinationFile, _
                            GENERIC_READ _
                            Or GENERIC_WRITE, _
                            0, 0, CREATE_ALWAYS, _
                            FILE_FLAG_RANDOM_ACCESS, 0)
            End If
         '  Grab the error code!
            lngError = Err.LastDllError
            If lngDestFile = INVALID_HANDLE_VALUE Then
             '  We couldn't open the file
                .ErrorDescription = _
                        GetWin32ErrorDescription(lngError)
                FileCrypt = False
            Else

             '  OK!  Onto encrypting.
                EncryptionAlgorithm lngSourceFile, _
                            lngDestFile, Params
             '  Return a TRUE.
                FileCrypt = True
            End If
        End If
    End If
    End With

    If lngSourceFile <> INVALID_HANDLE_VALUE Then
        CloseHandle lngSourceFile
    End If

    If lngDestFile <> INVALID_HANDLE_VALUE And _
        lngDestFile <> lngSourceFile Then
           CloseHandle lngDestFile
    End If

    Exit Function

error_FileCrypt:

'  Report the program error.
    Params.ErrorDescription = "PROCEDURE ERROR:  " & Err.Description
    FileCrypt = False

'  Close any open file handles
    If lngSourceFile <> INVALID_HANDLE_VALUE Then
        CloseHandle lngSourceFile
    End If

    If lngDestFile <> INVALID_HANDLE_VALUE And _
```

```
        lngDestFile <> lngSourceFile Then
            CloseHandle lngDestFile
    End If

End Function
```

First, we clear out anything that's in `ErrorDescription` to make sure we start off with a clear slate. Then we check to make sure that the source file exists by calling the `DoesFileExist` function (I'll explain how this one works in a moment). If it does, we open the file such that no one else can use it:

```
lngSourceFile = CreateFile(.SourceFile, _
                    GENERIC_READ Or GENERIC_WRITE, _
                    0, 0, OPEN_EXISTING, _
                    FILE_FLAG_RANDOM_ACCESS, 0)
```

If the file opens successfully, we then look at the destination file. If it's the same as the source file, we set the source file handle variable equal to the destination file handle variable. Otherwise, we open up the destination file - it doesn't matter if it already exists or not.

```
If .SourceFile = .DestinationFile Then
                lngDestFile = lngSourceFile
Else
    lngDestFile = CreateFile(.SourceFile, GENERIC_READ _
                        Or GENERIC_WRITE, 0, 0, _
CREATE_ALWAYS, _
                        FILE_FLAG_RANDOM_ACCESS, 0)
```

If we have valid file handles, we call `EncryptionAlgorithm` and close up the files once the algorithm is done. Any errors that occur are reported by returning a `FALSE` and filling `ErrorDescription` with the appropriate information.

Note that whenever we make an API call we check the return value for an error by grabbing the value from `Err.LastDLLError` and storing it in `lngError`. I can already feel the wrath coming from some readers who will (rightly) point out to me that I'm not following my own directions in Chapter 2 about grabbing DLL error codes. I'm only grabbing the value from `LastDllError`, and I'm doing this in the interest of space. Most of the time, only checking the value for `LastDllError` will work. At the very least, we won't get an error message from `GetWin32ErrorDescription` if we pass a 0, but we will know that an error occurred.

FindFirstFile and FileClose

Before we move on to the `EncryptionAlgorithm` function, let's explain what that `DoesFileExist` does. It simply accepts the path for the file to check and returns `True` if the file exists:

```
Public Function DoesFileExist(FullFilePath As String) As Boolean

    On Error Resume Next

    Dim lngFile As Long
    Dim lngRet As Long
    Dim udtFindData As WIN32_FIND_DATA

    ' See if the file exists.
    lngFile = FindFirstFile(FullFilePath, udtFindData)
```

```
'   Check to make sure that the handle isn't invalid.
    If lngFile <> INVALID_HANDLE_VALUE Then
        DoesFileExist = True
    Else
        DoesFileExist = False
    End If

'   Close the handle.
    lngRet = FindClose(lngFile)

End Function
```

It's pretty straightforward, but there are a couple of new API calls that we'll need to go over. We simply pass in a file path that's complete, like C:\thispath\righthere.txt. Then we call the FindFirstFile API call to determine if it really does exist. If we don't get an INVALID_HANDLE_VALUE back, we know that the file exists, so we return a TRUE. Otherwise, we return a FALSE. In either case, we make sure that the file is closed by calling FindClose.

So what do the FindFirstFile and FindClose API calls look like? I'm glad you asked:

```
Declare Function FindFirstFile Lib "kernel32" _
    Alias "FindFirstFileA" (ByVal lpFileName As String, _
    lpFindFileData As WIN32_FIND_DATA) As Long
```

```
Declare Function FindClose Lib "kernel32" _
    (ByVal hFindFile As Long) As Long
```

The FindFirstFile's first argument holds the file to search for. In our case, we want an entire path, but it can take wildcard characters to allow for the search to find more than one file (if you're interesting in doing a search like this, you'll need to use another API call named FindNextFile). The second argument uses the WIN32_FIND_DATA UDT to return information about the file - here's what that data type looks like:

```
Type WIN32_FIND_DATA
    dwFileAttributes As Long
    ftCreationTime As FILETIME
    ftLastAccessTime As FILETIME
    ftLastWriteTime As FILETIME
    nFileSizeHigh As Long
    nFileSizeLow As Long
    dwReserved0 As Long
    dwReserved1 As Long
    cFileName As String * MAX_PATH
    cAlternate As String * 14
End Type
```

The observant eye will notice that there's another UDT that's needed for this UDT called FILETIME. Although we won't use it for anything, we need to define it to use WIN32_FIND_DATA, so here it is:

```
Type FILETIME
    dwLowDateTime As Long
    dwHighDateTime As Long
End Type
```

I won't go into any detail over this UDT (you can probably figure out what most of the values stand for just by looking at them); all we're worried about is the return value of `FindFirstFile`. If that value doesn't equal `INVALID_HANDLE_VALUE` the file exists. Once we're done with the search, we call `FindClose` and set `hFindFile` equal to the file handle we got back from `FindFirstFile`.

Now that we've gone through these APIs and UDTs, add them to `EncryptionLib.bas`. As before, make sure that they all have `Public` scope.

EncryptionAlgorithm

We've confirmed that everything is OK using the `DoesFileExist` and `FileCrypt` functions. Now we actually have to secure or open up the file. Here's `EncryptionAlgorithm` - I know it's a beast, but I've broken it up to make it easier to swallow and we'll go over it in detail. (You'll notice that there is no error handling. This is because it's assumed that `FileCrypt` is calling this function):

```
Private Sub EncryptionAlgorithm(SourceFileHandle As Long, _
    DestFileHandle As Long, FileParams As EncryptionParameters)

    Dim blnEOF As Boolean
    Dim bytFileInfo() As Byte
    Dim lngBufferSize As Long
    Dim lngBytesRead As Long
    Dim lngCount As Long
    Dim lngDestPosition As Long
    Dim lngError As Long
    Dim lngFileSize As Long
    Dim lngHighValue As Long
    Dim lngKeyLength As Long
    Dim lngKeyLocation As Long
    Dim lngKeyValue As Long
    Dim lngRet As Long
    Dim lngRnd As Long
    Dim lngSourcePosition As Long
    Dim lngTempByte As Long

    With FileParams
    '   Get the key's length.
        lngKeyLength = Len(.Key)
    '   Get the source's size.
        lngFileSize = GetFileSize(SourceFileHandle, lngHighValue)
    '   Set the buffer size - the maximum will be 32K.
        If lngFileSize < MAX_BUFFER_SIZE Then
            lngBufferSize = lngFileSize
        Else
            lngBufferSize = MAX_BUFFER_SIZE
        End If
```

Let's start from the beginning. We get two file handles and the `EncryptionParameters` UDT that we got in `FileCrypt`. Then we get the length of the `Key` value and the source file size - we'll be using those two parameters a lot later on. We also check to see if the file is larger than `MAX_BUFFER_SIZE`, which is a constant I arbitrarily set to 32768. This ensures that we never read a chunk of data from the file larger than 32K. Some files can be megabytes in size, and I really don't want to load that much information into memory, because this could be too much for some PCs to handle.

```
' Now read the source file in chunks until we're done.
    blnEOF = False
  ' Set the file pointers to the start of the files
    lngSourcePosition = SetFilePointer(SourceFileHandle, _
                                 0, 0, FILE_BEGIN)
    lngDestPosition = SetFilePointer(DestFileHandle, _
                                 0, 0, FILE_BEGIN)
  ' Seed the randomize sequence
    Rnd (-1)
    Randomize (.Seed)
  ' Dimension the array.
    ReDim bytFileInfo(1 To lngBufferSize) As Byte
```

We then set the file pointers in each file to the beginning using the `SetFilePointer` call.
Remember that the source and destination files can be the same. If we read the first 10 bytes out of
source file and then tried to write to it to the same file, the file pointer will be located at the 11th
byte. This would really mess things up, so we have to keep track of the file pointers ourselves. By
doing this, we will ensure that the `ReadFile` and `WriteFile` operations always occur at the correct
locations in the file(s).

```
    Do
      ' Move the file pointer as needed.
        lngRet = SetFilePointer(SourceFileHandle, _
                          lngSourcePosition, 0, FILE_BEGIN)
        lngRet = ReadFile(SourceFileHandle, bytFileInfo(1), _
                     lngBufferSize, lngBytesRead, 0)
        lngError = Err.LastDllError
        If lngRet = 0 Then
          ' Raise an error - couldn't read the file
            Err.Raise lngError, "", _
                    "Could not read from the source file - " & _
GetWin32ErrorDescription(lngError)
        Else
            If lngBytesRead = 0 Then
              ' We're done
                blnEOF = True
            Else
                If lngBytesRead < lngBufferSize Then
                  ' I'll shrink the array down -
                  ' also, this is the last read we
                  ' have to do.
                    blnEOF = True
                    ReDim Preserve _
                            bytFileInfo(1 To lngBytesRead)
                End If
              ' Increment the file pointer
                lngSourcePosition = lngSourcePosition + _
                                    lngBytesRead
                For lngCount = 1 To lngBytesRead
                  ' Figure out where we are in the key.
                    lngKeyLocation = ((lngCount - 1) Mod _
                                lngKeyLength) + 1
                  ' Get that character's ASCII value.
                    lngKeyValue = Asc(Mid$(.Key, _
```

```
                                       lngKeyLocation, 1))
                    lngRnd = Int((MOD_BY - 1) * Rnd)
                    If .CodingType = Encrypt Then
                        bytFileInfo(lngCount) = (lngKeyValue _
                               + lngRnd + bytFileInfo(lngCount)) _
                            Mod MOD_BY
                    Else
                        lngTempByte = (bytFileInfo(lngCount) _
                                - lngKeyValue - lngRnd)
                        Do Until lngTempByte >= 0
                            lngTempByte = lngTempByte + MOD_BY
                        Loop
                        bytFileInfo(lngCount) = _
                                        CByte(lngTempByte)
                    End If
                Next lngCount
        ' Write the file to the destination file.
        ' Make sure the file pointer is set.
                lngRet = SetFilePointer(DestFileHandle, _
                        lngDestPosition, 0, FILE_BEGIN)
                lngRet = WriteFile(DestFileHandle, _
                        bytFileInfo(1), _
                        UBound(bytFileInfo), _
                        lngBytesRead, 0)
                lngError = Err.LastDllError
                If lngRet = 0 Then
                ' Raise an error - couldn't write the file
                    Err.Raise lngError, "", "Could not write" _
                        & " to the destination file - " & _
                            GetWin32ErrorDescription(lngError)
                End If
        ' Increment the file pointer.
                lngDestPosition = lngDestPosition + _
                                        lngBytesRead
            End If
    End If
    Loop Until blnEOF = True
        End With

    End Sub
```

Now we enter into a `Do...Loop`, which will terminate once we've read all of the data from the source file and translated it appropriately to the destination file. Each time we get a chunk of data from the source file using the `ReadFile` call, we enter a `For...Next` loop where we change that chunk of file data according the value of `CodingType`.

Let's go over this part in detail, because we have to get it right - it's what the whole program is based around. First of all, we have to ensure that we match up each byte in the file with the correct character in the key. That's what the following line of code does:

```
lngKeyLocation = ((lngCount - 1) Mod lngKeyLength) + 1
```

`lngCount` is the current location in the buffer and `lngKeyLength` is the length of the key calculated before. It looks a little confusing, but an example should make it clear. Let's say that we're at the 17th byte in the buffer, and our key is 5 characters long. Therefore, we get:

```
lngKeyLocation = ((17 - 1) Mod 5) + 1
lngKeyLocation = (16 Mod 5) + 1
lngKeyLocation = 1 + 1
lngKeyLocation = 2
```

Recall that the `Mod` operator gives us the remainder of dividing x by y. As you can see, we should look at the 2nd character of the key to encode or decode this byte in the file. We can then use the `Asc` and `Mid` functions to retrieve the ASCII value for that character.

We also have to add in some randomness to the process. That's what the following lines of code do:

```
Rnd (-1)
Randomize (.Seed)
```

This will insure that any time we call `Rnd` inside the `For...Next` loop we will get the same sequence as long as `Seed` is the same. However, we only want to generate a random value between 0 and 255 - the valid values in the ASCII character set. The following code does that for us:

```
lngRnd = Int((MOD_BY - 1) * Rnd)
```

where `MOD_BY` is a constant set to 256. This works because `Rnd` generates a floating-point value between 0 and 1. By multiplying that value by 255 and truncating the result using the `Int` function, we're guaranteed to get a value between 0 and 255.

Now that we know how we get the characters from the key and add randomness into the process, let's look at how we encrypt the source file first. As we saw in Chapter 2, we add the current byte of the file to the correct ASCII value of the character in the key along with a random value, which is what the following code does:

```
bytFileInfo(lngCount) = (lngKeyValue + lngRnd + _
                         bytFileInfo(lngCount)) Mod MOD_BY
```

As you can see, we use the file buffer to store the result. We also use the `Mod` operator to ensure that the value stays between 0 and 255.

As easy as the encoding implementation is, the decoding is somewhat trickier. We have to subtract the key character value along with the randomness from the source file's byte value, but this time we can't use the `Mod` operator to ensure that the result stays between 0 and 255. Why? Because the result from the calculation may be negative, and using the `Mod` operator on a negative number returns a negative number. This will overflow the `Byte` data type, which is something that would cause the whole process to come crashing to its knees.

So how do we get around this? We have to use a temporary variable, and keep on adding `MOD_BY` to it until the value is non-negative. Here's how we do it:

```
lngTempByte = (bytFileInfo(lngCount) - lngKeyValue - lngRnd)

Do Until lngTempByte >= 0
    lngTempByte = lngTempByte + MOD_BY
Loop

bytFileInfo(lngCount) = CByte(lngTempByte)
```

We use a Long variable to hold the temporary result. Once we know that we have a non-negative number, we store the result into the buffer using the CByte data type conversion function. Once we've completely read through the buffer, we use the WriteFile command to write to the destination file:

```
lngRet = WriteFile(DestFileHandle, _
                            bytFileInfo(1), _
                            UBound(bytFileInfo), _
                            lngBytesRead, 0)
```

We keep looping through these stages until the process is complete.

Potential Problems

However, do you see one glaring big hole here? There's no error trapping! Well, I did this on purpose because I know that FileCrypt will catch any errors raised by EncryptionAlgorithm. However, if the source and destination files are the same and the process ran into an error halfway through, the source file is completely corrupted. That's not good, and the right way to rectify it is to create a temporary source file before the process starts when the source is the same as the destination (you can always use this one as a backup) or to simply delete the destination file when an error occurs. The correct place to do this is in FileCrypt, and we'll use three API calls to help us out: GetTempFileName, CopyFile and DeleteFile (note: As we've done before, please add these calls to EncryptionLib.bas with Public scope).

GetTempFileName

If we're going to make a temporary file, we have to worry about creating a file that may collide with a file that already exists on the hard drive. Fortunately, we can let Windows do all of the work for us by calling GetTempFileName:

```
Declare Function GetTempFileName Lib "kernel32" _
    Alias "GetTempFileNameA" (ByVal lpszPath As String, _
    ByVal lpPrefixString As String, ByVal wUnique As Long, _
    ByVal lpTempFileName As String) As Long
```

The first argument, lpszPath, is used to tell the OS where you want to store the temporary file. lpPrefixString allows you to set a prefix for the file name, but only the first three characters are used. You can use wUnique as a "starting point" that GetTempFileName will use to create the file name, but I would set it to 0 unless you care about controlling the sequence yourself. The last argument, lpTempFileName, will be used by GetTempFileName to let you know the name of the new file. If the function returns a non-zero value, the call was successful and the temporary file was created. You're responsible for the file after Windows is done creating it; so make sure you clean up any of these files when the application closes.

Here's the catch. The `lpTempFileName` value has to be pre-allocated with enough space to prevent a memory exception occurring. I'm surprised that the designers of this call didn't add on another argument that would specify the size of the buffer, but we're stuck with a kind of guessing game. The documentation recommends that you allocate a string that's longer than the value specified by `MAX_PATH`. Personally, I'm not for cutting corners when a potential memory exception lurks in the darkness, so whenever I use this function, I'll allocate the string like this:

```
Dim strTempPath as String

strTempPath = String$(4 * MAX_PATH, " ")
```

Since `MAX_PATH` is equal to 260, our string is around 1K in size. I'm comfortable with that.

CopyFile

Now that we know how to create a temporary file, we need to copy our source file's contents to this file. Here's the `CopyFile` declaration:

```
Declare Function CopyFile Lib "kernel32" Alias "CopyFileA" _
    (ByVal lpExistingFileName As String, _
    ByVal lpNewFileName As String, _
    ByVal bFailIfExists As Long) As Long
```

It's pretty easy. The first argument, `lpExistingFileName`, is the source file, and the second argument, `lpNewFileName`, is the destination. If you don't want to copy to a file that already exists, set `bFailIfExists` equal to a non-zero value - `CopyFile` will then fail. Otherwise, set `bFailIfExists` equal to zero, and `CopyFile` will overwrite the destination file. The function returns a non-zero value on success and zero if an error occurred.

DeleteFile

If we made a temporary file to store our source file's information or if we need to get rid of our destination file, we need to delete it. We can use `DeleteFile` to do this:

```
Declare Function DeleteFile Lib "kernel32" _
    Alias "DeleteFileA" (ByVal lpFileName As String) As Long
```

The only argument, `lpFileName`, lets `DeleteFile` know which file you want to remove from disk. The only issue with this call is that under Windows 95 `DeleteFile` will remove a file even if it's currently opened by an application. NT will not let you do this.

Filling the Hole

We now understand the three functions we need to prevent a serious error from occurring within our algorithm implementation. Now, let's use them in `FileCrypt`. We have two cases: Either the source and destination files are the same or they're different. The last case is easy - we just delete the destination file if an error occurred. To handle the first case, we'll add a `String` variable called `strTempFile` and create a temporary file right before we open the source file. Because we lock the source file such that nothing else can modify it, we need to copy the contents before we lock it down. This is how I changed the code:

```
If DoesFileExist(.SourceFile) = False Then
'  Return a FALSE.
    FileCrypt = False
```

```
    .ErrorDescription = "The source file does not exist."
Else
'  Make a backup copy of the file if needed.
    If .SourceFile = .DestinationFile Then
        strTempFile = String$(4 * MAX_PATH, " ")
        lngRet = GetTempFileName(App.Path, "", _
                        0, strTempFile)
        lngError = Err.LastDllError
        If lngRet <> 0 Then
            strTempFile = Trim$(Left$(strTempFile, _
                    InStr(strTempFile, vbNullChar) - 1))
            lngRet = CopyFile(.SourceFile, strTempFile, 0)
            lngError = Err.LastDllError
            If lngRet = 0 Then
                Err.Raise lngError, "", _
                        GetWin32ErrorDescription(lngError)
            End If
        Else
            Err.Raise lngError, "", _
                    GetWin32ErrorDescription(lngError)
        End If
    End If
'  Try to open the file such that
'  no one else has access to it.
    lngSourceFile = CreateFile(.SourceFile, _
                    GENERIC_READ Or GENERIC_WRITE, _
                    0, 0, OPEN_EXISTING, _
                    FILE_FLAG_RANDOM_ACCESS, 0)
```

Now that we've taken care of the temporary file, we need to clean up our act. Right before we exit the function, add this code:

```
    If Trim$(strTempFile) <> "" Then
'  We made a temp file - kill it.
        DeleteFile strTempFile
    End If
```

```
Exit Function
```

Of course, if an error occurred, the mess is bigger. We have to copy the temporary file back to the source file, but we can't do it until the file is closed, so we have to add this after the `CloseHandle` call on the source file. Also, we have to delete the destination file after the handle is closed as well. Here's how I implemented this in the error section of `FileCrypt`:

```
error_FileCrypt:

'  Report the program error.
    Params.ErrorDescription = "PROCEDURE ERROR:  " & _
                        Err.Description
    FileCrypt = False

'  Close any open file handles
    If lngSourceFile <> INVALID_HANDLE_VALUE Then
        CloseHandle lngSourceFile
    End If
```

```
        If lngDestFile <> INVALID_HANDLE_VALUE And _
           lngDestFile <> lngSourceFile Then
           CloseHandle lngDestFile
        End If
```

```
        If lngSourceFile = lngDestFile Then
           If Trim$(strTempFile) <> "" Then
              '  We made a temp file. Copy the
              '  contents back to the source file
              '  and kill the temp file.
              CopyFile strTempFile, Params.SourceFile, 0
              DeleteFile strTempFile
           End If
        Else
           '  Delete the destination file.
              DeleteFile Params.DestinationFile
        End If
```

```
    End Function
```

That's it! We've prevented a big problem from occurring with a few lines of code. If we had corrupted a source file after we reported an error, the users would've been waiting outside our places of residence with baseball bats.

> *To tighten the code even more, we should create a temporary file for the destination file if the source and destination files are different regardless of the destination file's existence. That way, we don't change the destination file's content until all of the changes are complete. If you want to add this, check out the* GetDiskFreeSpace *function to make sure that you have enough room to make the temporary file. However, this leads down another contingency path that we don't have the space to cover here, but I'd encourage you to try and add this code on your own.*

By the way, if you want to test this contingency plan out, just add the following line of code in the EncryptionAlgorithm method right after you write information to the destination file:

```
    Err.Raise 32
```

What error we raise doesn't matter - we just want to see if the error handling works.

Tying it All Together

We've got the algorithm in code, now we just have to add code to our UI to encrypt or decrypt files. To do this, we have to add one text box under the **Save Altered File As...** check box in case the user wants to save the results in a different file. It's called txtSaveAsFile. Here's what the new screen looks like:

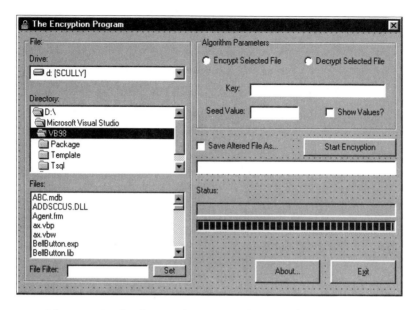

There are no special properties for this text box, just make sure it's under the check box. Now add the following method to the **Declarations** section of `frmMain` (It simply asks the user of any possible mistakes and then calls the algorithm):

```
Private Sub EncodeFiles()

    Dim blnRet As Boolean
    Dim lngRet As Long
    Dim udtInfo As EncryptionParameters

    On Error GoTo error_EncodeFiles

    Screen.MousePointer = vbHourglass

'   Set the source and destination files.
    udtInfo.SourceFile = dirMain.Path & "\" & filMain.filename

    If chkSaveAs.Value = vbUnchecked _
        Or (chkSaveAs.Value = vbChecked _
            And UCase$(udtInfo.SourceFile) = _
                UCase$(Trim$(txtSaveAsFile.Text))) = True Then
'       The source and destination are the same,
'       but make sure the user really want to do this.
        Screen.MousePointer = vbDefault
        lngRet = MsgBox("The source and destination files are " & _
                    "the same. Do you want to overwrite " & _
                    "the source file?", vbYesNo + vbQuestion, _
                    "Source File Overwrite")
        If lngRet = vbNo Then
'           Stop the process.
            Exit Sub
        End If
        udtInfo.DestinationFile = udtInfo.SourceFile
    Else
'       Save to a different file.
```

```
                udtInfo.DestinationFile = Trim$(txtSaveAsFile.Text)
        End If
    '   Set the key and the seed value.
    udtInfo.Key = Trim$(txtKey.Text)
        udtInfo.Seed = CLng(txtSeedValue.Text)
    If optEncrypt(0).Value = True Then
            udtInfo.CodingType = Encrypt
        Else
    udtInfo.CodingType = Decrypt
        End If

        Screen.MousePointer = vbHourglass

        blnRet = FileCrypt(udtInfo)

        Screen.MousePointer = vbDefault

        If blnRet = False Then
            MsgBox "An error occurred during the algorithm:  " & _
                    udtInfo.ErrorDescription, _
                    vbExclamation + vbOKOnly, "File Error"
        End If

        Exit Sub

    error_EncodeFiles:

        Screen.MousePointer = vbDefault
        MsgBox "EncodeFiles Error:  " & CStr(Err.Number) & "  " & _
                    Err.Description, vbExclamation + vbOKOnly, _
                    "Program Error"

    End Sub
```

Most of what this code does is simple data validation, so we won't go over it here. You can call this method from any event in the form - in our case, let's call it from the Click event of cmdRunEncryption:

```
    Private Sub cmdRunEncryption_Click()

        EncodeFiles

    End Sub
```

To test that you have everything working as planned, I've included some test files to play with - they're located in the Test Files directory that you can download from the Wrox Press website (www.wrox.com). For example, if you encrypt the executable file, you'll notice that the icon will change in Windows Explorer like this:

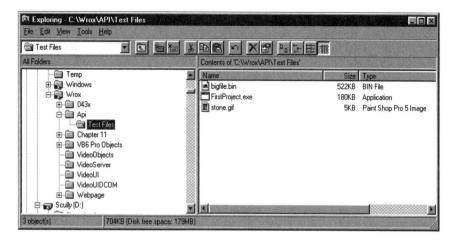

Like most file formats that Windows uses, they need to follow the format rules to perfection; otherwise, they simply won't run. In this case, Windows can't extract the icon that's embedded in your executable, so you get a general icon. Furthermore, if you try to run the encrypted file, you will get unpredictable results depending upon your key and seed values.

VB Implementation of the Encryption Algorithm

Now that we've got the algorithm working using API calls, let's try to get the algorithm to work using pure VB code. Since we'll be comparing the two implementations later on, we'll try to match what we did with the API implementation to make sure we're comparing apples to apples. Also, since we've gone through most of the file translation issues, I won't go into too much detail here, but I will point out where some of the differences between the two lie.

VB Functions

As with the API implementation, I've created three functions to handle the processing: `VBFileCrypt`, `VBDoesFileExist`, and `VBEncryptionAlgorithm`. Let's take a look at `VBFileCrypt` first. It behaves in a similar way to the API version returning `True` or `False` and accepting a UDT parameter:

```
Public Function VBFileCrypt(Params As EncryptionParameters) As _
    Boolean

    On Error GoTo error_VBFileCrypt

    Dim lngDestFile As Long
    Dim lngRet As Long
    Dim lngSourceFile As Long
    Dim strTempFile As String

    With Params
    '   Clear out any information in ErrorDescription
        .ErrorDescription = ""
    '   Check to make sure that the source file exists.
        If VBDoesFileExist(.SourceFile) = False Then
```

```
                   '  Return a FALSE.
                      VBFileCrypt = False
                      .ErrorDescription = "The source file does not exist."
                Else
                    If .SourceFile = .DestinationFile Then
                    '  Make a backup copy.
                        strTempFile = App.Path & "\temp.tmp"
                        If Dir$(strTempFile) <> "" Then
                            Kill strTempFile
                        End If
                        FileCopy .SourceFile, strTempFile
                    End If
                '  Try to open the file such that
                '  no one else has access to it.
                    lngSourceFile = FreeFile
                    Open .SourceFile For Binary Access Read Write _
                        Lock Read Write As lngSourceFile
                '  We also have to open the destination file.
                    If .SourceFile = .DestinationFile Then
lngDestFile = lngSourceFile
Else
                        lngDestFile = FreeFile
                        Open .DestinationFile For Binary _
                            Access Read Write _
                            Lock Read Write As lngDestFile
                    End If
                '  OK!  Onto encrypting.
                    VBEncryptionAlgorithm lngSourceFile, lngDestFile, Params
                '  Return a TRUE.
                    VBFileCrypt = True
            End If
        End With

        If lngSourceFile > 0 Then
            Close lngSourceFile
        End If

        If lngDestFile > 0 And _
            lngDestFile <> lngSourceFile Then
            Close lngDestFile
        End If

        If Trim$(strTempFile) <> "" Then
        '  We made a temp file - kill it.
            Kill strTempFile
        End If

        Exit Function

error_VBFileCrypt:

    '  Report the program error.
        Params.ErrorDescription = "PROCEDURE ERROR:  " & _
                            Err.Description
        VBFileCrypt = False

    '  Close any open file handles
        If lngSourceFile > 0 Then
            Close lngSourceFile
        End If
```

```
      If lngDestFile > 0 And _
          lngDestFile <> lngSourceFile Then
          Close lngDestFile
      End If

      If Params.SourceFile = Params.DestinationFile Then
          If Trim$(strTempFile) <> "" Then
              FileCopy strTempFile, Params.SourceFile
              Kill strTempFile
          End If
      Else
      '   Delete the destination file.
          Kill Params.DestinationFile
      End If

  End Function
```

Let's see what's different about this one. The obvious thing is that we're using the VB functions `FreeFile`, `Open`, `Get`, `Put`, `Close`, `FileCopy`, and `Kill` to handle all of the file operations. There are some subtle differences between what VB has to offer and what the API calls can do, but for the most part we get the functionality we need.

However, we have to make the temporary file ourselves. VB doesn't have anything to help us out, so we'd have to let the user know that they should create a file called `temp.tmp` in the application's directory. We could be more robust and create a `VBCreateTempFile` function similar to the `GetTempFileName` API call, but I'll live with this implementation for now.

To check for a file's existence, I created a function called `VBDoesFileExist`:

```
  Public Function VBDoesFileExist(FullFilePath As String) As Boolean
      On Error Resume Next

      Dim strRet As String

  '   See if the file exists.
      strRet = Dir$(FullFilePath, vbNormal Or vbSystem Or _
                    vbHidden Or vbReadOnly)

  '   Check to make sure that the handle isn't invalid.
      If strRet <> "" Then
          VBDoesFileExist = True
      Else
          VBDoesFileExist = False
      End If

  End Function
```

I used the `Dir` function to verify that the file given exists. However, be warned that if you call this function to check for a file that is located on a floppy drive and nothing is in the drive, you'll get a message box notifying you of this error. But this is one of the few ways to do it in VB.

Finally, we have the `VBEncryptionAlgorithm` function:

```
  Private Sub VBEncryptionAlgorithm(SourceFileHandle As Long, _
      DestFileHandle As Long, FileParams As EncryptionParameters)
```

```
Dim blnEOF As Boolean
Dim bytFileInfo() As Byte
    Dim lngBufferSize As Long
    Dim lngBytesRead As Long
Dim lngCheck As Long
    Dim lngCount As Long
    Dim lngDestPosition As Long
    Dim lngFileSize As Long
    Dim lngKeyLength As Long
    Dim lngKeyLocation As Long
    Dim lngKeyValue As Long
    Dim lngRnd As Long
    Dim lngSourcePosition As Long
    Dim lngTempByte As Long

With FileParams
'   Get the key's length.
        lngKeyLength = Len(.Key)
    '   Get the source's size.
        lngFileSize = LOF(SourceFileHandle)
    '   Set the buffer size - the maximum will be 32K.
        If lngFileSize < MAX_BUFFER_SIZE Then
            lngBufferSize = lngFileSize
        Else
            lngBufferSize = MAX_BUFFER_SIZE
        End If
'   Now read the source file in chunks until we're done.
        blnEOF = False
'   Set the file pointers to the start of the files
        lngSourcePosition = 1
        lngDestPosition = 1
'   Seed the randomize sequence
        Rnd (-1)
        Randomize (.Seed)
'   Dimension the array.
        ReDim bytFileInfo(1 To lngBufferSize) As Byte
        Do
            lngCheck = (lngFileSize - lngSourcePosition) + 1
            If lngCheck <= 0 Then
            '   We've read through the file.
                blnEOF = True
            Else
                If lngCheck <= lngBufferSize Then
                '   This is the final read.
                '   Resize down if necessary.
                    If lngCheck < lngBufferSize Then
                        ReDim bytFileInfo(1 To lngCheck) As Byte
                    End If
                    blnEOF = True
                End If
                Get #SourceFileHandle, lngSourcePosition, _
                        bytFileInfo
                lngBytesRead = UBound(bytFileInfo)
            '   Increment the file pointer
                lngSourcePosition = lngSourcePosition + _
                                    lngBytesRead
                For lngCount = 1 To lngBytesRead
```

```
                              ' Figure out where we are in the key.
                              lngKeyLocation = ((lngCount - 1) Mod _
                                                 lngKeyLength) + 1
                        ' Get that character's ASCII value.
                              lngKeyValue = Asc(Mid$(.Key, lngKeyLocation, _
                                                 1))
                              lngRnd = Int((MOD_BY - 1) * Rnd)
                              If .CodingType = Encrypt Then
                                  bytFileInfo(lngCount) = (lngKeyValue + _
                                          lngRnd + bytFileInfo(lngCount)) _
                                                       Mod MOD_BY
                              Else
                                  lngTempByte = (bytFileInfo(lngCount) - _
                                          lngKeyValue - lngRnd)
                                  Do Until lngTempByte >= 0
                                      lngTempByte = lngTempByte + MOD_BY
                                  Loop
                                  bytFileInfo(lngCount) = CByte(lngTempByte)
                              End If
                          Next lngCount
                      ' Write the file to the destination file.
                      ' Make sure the file pointer is set.
                          Put #DestFileHandle, lngDestPosition, bytFileInfo
                      ' Increment the file pointer.
                          lngDestPosition = lngDestPosition + lngBytesRead
                      End If
                  Loop Until blnEOF = True
              End With

      End Sub
```

One of the main differences here is that the `Get` and `Put` functions do not tell us how many bytes were read. If our buffer was 10K in size and `Get` only read the last 5K of the file, we have no way of knowing this. Therefore, I had to add some logic using the file pointer locations along with the buffer size to keep track of what the size of the read was going to be. Also, notice that we use the `Get` and `Put` functions to set the file pointer; there's no equivalent to `SetFilePointer` in VB.

All in all, the VB functions are very similar to the API functions. In fact, after I wrote the API calls (which took a lot of time), it only took me about an hour to convert the functions and test them out because the functions are not that different.

Calling the VB Functions from the UI

To call the VB functions, all I did was add a check box called `chkPureVB` that the user could select which implementation they wanted. Here's what the screen looks like now:

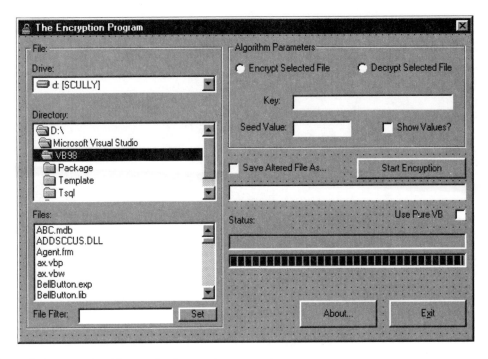

The code in `EncodeFiles` only changes in one spot:

```
    Screen.MousePointer = vbHourglass
```

```
    If chkPureVB.Value = vbChecked Then
        blnRet = VBFileCrypt(udtInfo)
    Else
blnRet = FileCrypt(udtInfo)
    End If
```

```
    Screen.MousePointer = vbDefault
```

This is a good example of why I don't like putting code into events. By having this functionality located in one place, any other control that calls this function now has the change. I admit that it's very easy to add code in your events, and if I need to test something out really fast, I do it. And some events, like the `Initialize` *and* `Terminate` *events of a form, will only be called once during the lifetime of the form. In those events, it's probably not a bad idea to put the code in the event. But I force myself not to when I code on a project for virtually all other events, and I would encourage you to do the same if you're not already using this technique.*

Comparing the Two Implementations

We now have two ways to encrypt and decrypt our files. So which one's better? There's so many ways to determine what's "better" in code, and we could be here for a long time trying to decide that. However, for our comparison purposes, we'll concentrate on speed, since that's one of the biggest reasons programmers give to use the APIs.

The Stopwatch Class

In Chapter 8, we'll look at creating a component in VB, but since we're going to be doing a lot of performance benchmarks in this book, I decided to add a `Stopwatch` class to the project to help us out. To add this class to our project, simply choose <u>P</u>roject I Add <u>C</u>lass Module..., and add a new class to the project. Name the class `Stopwatch`, and use the default properties that VB gives for the class. Also, make sure the file is called `Stopwatch.cls`. Since we'll go over classes and objects in more detail in Chapter 8, I'll only cover how we want to use this class from a general implementation perspective. However, feel free to look at the code in the class if you're not familiar with classes to give you some insight as to what classes are all about.

First, add these constants, enumerations, and variables to the Declarations section of the class:

```
Private Const HIGH_32_BITS As Double = 2 ^ 32
Private Const MS_CONVERSION As Double = 1000#

Private m_blnRunning As Boolean
Private m_enmQuality As ClockQuality
Private m_lngEnd As Long
Private m_lngStart As Long
Private m_udtEnd As LARGE_INTEGER
Private m_udtFreq As LARGE_INTEGER
Private m_udtStart As LARGE_INTEGER

Public Enum ClockQuality
    High
    Low
End Enum
```

The `Stopwatch` class has three methods: `StartClock`, `StopClock`, and `ResetClock`. Here's the code for all three methods:

```
Public Sub StartClock()

    m_blnRunning = True

    If m_enmQuality = High Then
      Call QueryPerformanceCounter(m_udtStart)
    Else
      m_lngStart = GetTickCount
    End If

End Sub
```

```
Public Sub StopClock()

    m_blnRunning = False
If m_enmQuality = High Then
      Call QueryPerformanceCounter(m_udtEnd)
    Else
      m_lngEnd = GetTickCount
    End If

End Sub
```

```
Public Sub ResetClock()

   m_blnRunning = False

   If m_enmQuality = High Then
      m_udtStart.HighPart = 0
      m_udtStart.LowPart = 0
      m_udtEnd.HighPart = 0
      m_udtEnd.LowPart = 0
   Else
      m_lngStart = 0
      m_lngEnd = 0
   End If

End Sub
```

They're pretty much self-explanatory, so I won't go into any detail about them. There are also two properties: View and Quality:

```
Public Function View() As Double

   Dim dblDiff As Double
   Dim lngCurrent As Long
   Dim udtCurrent As LARGE_INTEGER

If m_blnRunning = True Then
      If m_enmQuality = High Then
           Call QueryPerformanceCounter(udtCurrent)
           dblDiff = ConvertLIToDouble(udtCurrent) - _
               ConvertLIToDouble(m_udtStart)
           View = dblDiff / ConvertLIToDouble(m_udtFreq)
      Else

           lngCurrent = GetTickCount
           View = CDbl(lngCurrent - m_lngStart) / MS_CONVERSION
      End If
   Else
      If m_enmQuality = High Then
           dblDiff = ConvertLIToDouble(m_udtEnd) - _
               ConvertLIToDouble(m_udtStart)
           View = dblDiff / ConvertLIToDouble(m_udtFreq)
      Else
           View = CDbl(m_lngEnd - m_lngStart) / MS_CONVERSION
      End If
   End If

End Function
```

```
Public Property Get Quality() As ClockQuality

    Quality = m_enmQuality

End Property
```

```
Private Property Let Quality(Val As ClockQuality)

    m_enmQuality = Val

End Property
```

View allows you to see the current running time, while Quality tells you if the timer has a high or low resolution. Note that View calls another function called ConvertLIToDouble, which takes a LARGE_INTEGER UDT and converts it into a Double data type:

```
Private Function ConvertLIToDouble(LargeValue As LARGE_INTEGER) _
    As Double

    With LargeValue
        ConvertLIToDouble = HIGH_32_BITS * CDbl(.HighPart) + _
                            CDbl(.LowPart)
    End With

End Function
```

If you look at the internals of the class, we use either the QueryPerformanceCounter or GetTickCount functions depending upon if the hardware supports a high-resolution timer. Therefore, you'll need to add these two API calls to EncryptionLib's **Declaration** section (with Public scope). Also, you'll need to add the LARGE_INTEGER UDT to the module as well. Note that you can't set the kind of counter you want to use; the Initialize event of the class determines that for you:

```
Private Sub Class_Initialize()

    Dim lngRet As Long

    lngRet = QueryPerformanceFrequency(m_udtFreq)

    If lngRet <> 0 Then
        m_enmQuality = High
    Else
        m_enmQuality = Low
    End If

End Sub
```

We'll use this class in the EncodeFiles method to determine which function is faster: FileCrypt or VBFileCrypt. We'll set it by using its StartClock method right before the function is invoked, and then we'll call StopClock to get a total time reading. Here's the code in EncodeFiles to do it:

```
    Set objWatch = New Stopwatch

If chkPureVB.Value = vbChecked Then
    objWatch.StartClock
    blnRet = VBFileCrypt(udtInfo)
    objWatch.StopClock
Else
    objWatch.StartClock
    blnRet = FileCrypt(udtInfo)
    objWatch.StopClock
End If

Screen.MousePointer = vbDefault

MsgBox "Total processing time:  " & CStr(objWatch.View) & _
        "seconds."
```

The objWatch object was declared as a Stopwatch object where all of the other variables are dimensions. Now that we're ready to benchmark the two implementations, let's see how they do.

Benchmark Results

To test each implementation, I encrypted and decrypted each file in the Test Files directory using both methods 5 times. I used the key "h3k5**3f" and the seed value 5942. I also ran the code in an executable and not from VB's IDE. Here are the results:

File Name + Operation	FileCrypt	VBFileCrypt	Winner
Stone.gif (encrypt)	0.0257	0.0256	Too close.
Stone.gif (decrypt)	0.0254	0.0256	Too close.
FirstProject.exe (encrypt)	0.9846	0.8924	VB code.
FirstProject.exe (decrypt)	0.9411	0.9223	Close, but it's the VB code.
Bigfile.bin (encrypt)	2.3865	2.1792	VB code.
Bigfile.bin (decrypt)	2.3088	2.2352	VB code.

Are you shocked? Yes, the pure VB implementation seems faster! It's not by much – the VB implementation is about 3% faster - but there is a noticeable difference when the files increase in size.

Where Do We Go from Here?

Before you start wondering how the VB code beat out the API code, remember that this test is one of many that we should do. Maybe we need to re-evaluate how we're moving the file pointers around in the API implementation. Or maybe we should increase the file buffer size to minimize the number of reads. Using memory-mapped files may make a big difference as well. Furthermore, the API calls given can be made to make the I/O asynchronous. This would add more complexity to the algorithm, but it would "free" the UI from waiting on the algorithm's completion. The VB calls have no such option.

Also, remember that the API implementation has more flexibility than the VB code does. Remember, the initial test was done strictly from a performance standpoint. Granted, that's a factor that is usually very important in program design, but it shouldn't be the only one. We can let Windows make a temporary file for us via the API, the test for existence of a file is less error-prone, we can manipulate other system objects other than just files, and so on. So don't get discouraged that the API implementation is initially slower. Using an API call *does not* guarantee that we'll get faster code - we have to do some more digging to figure out where we can increase the performance.

Summary

In this chapter, we took our first real look at using some of the core Win32 API calls from the `kernel32.dll`. The key focus of the chapter, however, was to code the encryption algorithm using file operation API calls as well as pure VB.

```
Therefore in this chapter we covered:
```

- ❏   File operations with API
- ❏   The same file operations with VB
- ❏   The `Stopwatch` class
- ❏   Comparison of VB and API calls

Now that we have a functional Encryption program we'll take a look as some calls from `user32.dll`, in the next chapter, to enhance some of the common controls and menu items as well as using the "real" message box.

4

User32 Calls

In the last chapter, we looked at calls related to file operations from `kernel32.dll`. We created two implementations of the encryption algorithm, one using pure VB code and the other using API calls, and compared the two. In this chapter, we'll continue with this trend by looking at some of the calls from `user32.dll`, and seeing if we can mirror the techniques in VB.

In this chapter you will learn how to:

Use the `MessageBox` API call as an alternative to the VB `Msgbox` command

- ❑ Alter the appearance and functionality of a standard Tree View control using various API calls
- ❑ Explore the great flexibility of the `SendMessage` API call
- ❑ Add images to menus in your apps using API calls

User32 Overview

The second Win32 DLL we're going to look at is `user32.dll`. This DLL is primarily responsible for, but not limited to:

- ❑ Window Management
- ❑ Menus
- ❑ Controls

Let's take a look at these before we continue.

Window Management

Most of the applications that you run on your PC are visual. That is, you have some kind of graphical interface to communicate to the program what you want to do. In Windows, this is done through (drum roll please) a window. The user32.dll's functions are responsible for creating and maintaining windows along with modifying them.

Menus

Although menus are usually contained within a window, they seem to pop up (no pun intended) all over the place. If you need to do anything that you've seen menus do in other applications, the user32.dll is where to look. You can really extend your own VB menus by making some API calls.

Controls

Buttons, drop-down lists, tree view controls...there are a lot of UI controls that you can use in VB. However, it seems like there are always things that you would like to do with controls in VB but can't (for example, until version 5.0 you couldn't add a picture to a button). With knowledge of a few APIs, you can greatly open up what is possible with controls.

An Easy Start: The MessageBox API Call

In the last chapter, we saw a fair amount of similarities between the pure VB and the API implementations of the Encryption algorithm. Although the calls were somewhat different in style, the code looked almost identical in flow and appearance. The first call we are going to look at from user32.dll, MessageBox, looks so much like its VB counterpart, MsgBox, you may wonder why I'm going to talk about it in the first place. However, because it's so familiar, I thought it would be a good call to use to introduce the concept of a window handle. Furthermore, there are some subtle differences between the two calls, so let's start by going over the API call in detail.

The MessageBox Declaration

Here's the declaration for the MessageBox call:

```
Declare Function MessageBox Lib "user32" Alias "MessageBoxA" _
    (ByVal hwnd As Long, ByVal lpText As String, _
    ByVal lpCaption As String, ByVal wType As Long) As Long
```

Now, let's go over each argument of this call in detail.

hwnd

This indicates the owner of the new message box. If this is set to 0, the message box isn't owned by anything. We'll cover window handles in a moment.

lpText

This is the message to be displayed in the message box.

lpCaption

This is the title caption of the message box. If you pass in vbNullString, you'll get the default caption: "Error".

wType

This argument can take a boatload of parameters. I've grouped them together into the following four enumerations:

```
Public Enum MBButtons
    MB_ABORTRETRYIGNORE = &H2
    MB_OK = &H0
    MB_OKCANCEL = &H1
    MB_RETRYCANCEL = &H5
    MB_YESNO = &H4
    MB_YESNOCANCEL = &H3
End Enum
```

```
Public Enum MBIcons
    MB_ICONEXCLAMATION = &H30
    MB_ICONASTERISK = &H40
    MB_ICONQUESTION = &H20
    MB_ICONHAND = &H10
End Enum
```

```
Public Enum MBDefaultButton
    MB_DEFBUTTON1 = &H0
    MB_DEFBUTTON2 = &H100
    MB_DEFBUTTON3 = &H200
End Enum
```

```
Public Enum MBModality
    MB_APPLMODAL = &H0
    MB_SYSTEMMODAL = &H1000
    MB_TASKMODAL = &H2000
End Enum
```

Note that you can only use one parameter from each enumeration, but values can be combined using the Or operator. For example, you could set wType equal to MB_OK Or MB_ICONQUESTION, but setting wType equal to MB_OK Or MB_ICONQUESTION Or MB_ICONEXCLAMATION would not work as the message box window can only display one icon at a time.

The MBButtons enumeration controls the buttons that will be displayed. Following is a table that lists which buttons are displayed for each value:

Constant	Buttons Displayed
MB_ABORTRETRYIGNORE	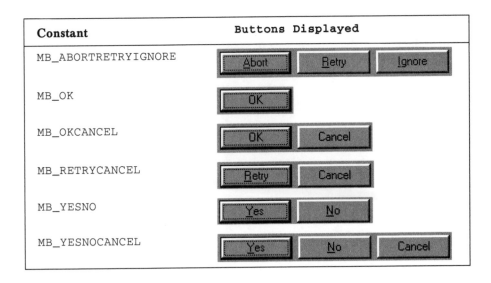
MB_OK	
MB_OKCANCEL	
MB_RETRYCANCEL	
MB_YESNO	
MB_YESNOCANCEL	

The MBIcons enumeration determines which icon should show up in the message box. We'll use a table again to describe the different kinds of icons:

Constant	Icon Displayed
MB_ICONEXCLAMATION	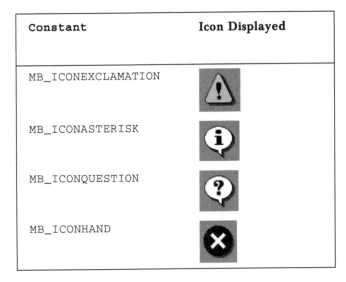
MB_ICONASTERISK	
MB_ICONQUESTION	
MB_ICONHAND	

The MBDefaultButton enumeration simply determines which button gets the focus when the message box is created.

The MBModality enumeration, however, can lead to problems if not used correctly. For example, the MB_APPLMODAL value will not allow any input to the window identified by hWnd, but will allow interaction with any other window either in the application or in another application.

MB_SYSTEMMODAL should only be used when a serious, system-wide failure may occur, such as a total loss of disk space or memory. The user is required to respond to the message box before control is given back to the other applications.

MB_TASKMODAL will disable all top-level windows within the current application if hWnd is null. Therefore, depending upon the MBModality value you use, you might prevent a user from using any other applications until they respond to the box.

Return Value

If the OS can't make the message box for any reason, the return value will be zero and the message box won't be displayed. Otherwise, you can use the following enumerated type to determine which button was pressed in the message box:

```
Public Enum MBReturn
    IDABORT = 3
    IDCANCEL = 2
    IDIGNORE = 5
    IDNO = 7
    IDOK = 1
    IDRETRY = 4
    IDYES = 6
End Enum
```

The names pretty much describe which value to use to check for a particular button, so I won't go into that here.

Win32 Handles

We touched on the concept of using handles indirectly in Chapter 3 when we opened a file. If the CreateFile call was successful, we got a handle to the file that we could use to perform read/write operations on that file. Let's take a more detailed look at what a handle actually is.

A handle is simply an identifier. It's a 32-bit number that is used to identify an object. It serves as a way to refer to an object stored in memory.

A file handle is just one of many handles that exist in Windows. There's a long list of objects that have handles, like a bitmap, or a font, or a menu, or a window, and so on. If you ever run into an API call that has an argument that starts with the letter "h", it's probably a handle of some sort.

> *You may have noticed that the forms in VB have a property called* hWnd. *This is the window handle for that form (after all, a form is more or less a window in disguise – more on this in Chapter 8).*

You have to be a little careful when you use a handle. Each kind of handle has different rules that you must follow in order to prevent memory leaks or exceptions. For example, we'll see in the next chapter that you have to use your graphical handles with care; certain operations soon start to eat up memory.

All that said, using handles is pretty benign compared to the pitfalls that usually nail us when we start using API calls, so I wouldn't worry too much about the handles. Just make sure you use them correctly, and don't try to mix them together. That would really be asking for it!

Using *MessageBox* in the Encryption Algorithm

Let's use the `MessageBox` API call in the Encryption project. Open the code window for the `EncryptionLib.bas` module and add the `MessageBox` API call:

```
Declare Function MessageBox Lib "user32" Alias "MessageBoxA" _
    (ByVal hwnd As Long, ByVal lpText As String, _
    ByVal lpCaption As String, ByVal wType As Long) As Long
```

Now you need to define all those enumerations that we have just discussed:

```
Public Enum MBButtons
    MB_ABORTRETRYIGNORE = &H2
    MB_OK = &H0
    MB_OKCANCEL = &H1
    MB_RETRYCANCEL = &H5
    MB_YESNO = &H4
    MB_YESNOCANCEL = &H3
End Enum
```

```
Public Enum MBIcons
    MB_ICONEXCLAMATION = &H30
    MB_ICONASTERISK = &H40
    MB_ICONQUESTION = &H20
    MB_ICONHAND = &H10
End Enum
```

```
Public Enum MBDefaultButton
    MB_DEFBUTTON1 = &H0
    MB_DEFBUTTON2 = &H100
    MB_DEFBUTTON3 = &H200
End Enum
```

```
Public Enum MBModality
    MB_APPLMODAL = &H0
    MB_SYSTEMMODAL = &H1000
    MB_TASKMODAL = &H2000
End Enum
```

```
Public Enum MBReturn
    IDABORT = 3
    IDCANCEL = 2
    IDIGNORE = 5
    IDNO = 7
    IDOK = 1
    IDRETRY = 4
    IDYES = 6
End Enum
```

Take a look at the `EncodeFiles` method in `frmMain`. There's one location in the code that warns the user of overwriting the source file:

```
lngRet = MsgBox("The source and destination files are " & _
                "the same.  Do you want to overwrite " & _
                "the source file?", vbYesNo + vbQuestion, _
                "Source File Overwrite")

If lngRet = vbNo Then
    '  Stop the process.
    Exit Sub
End If
```

Now let's rewrite it using the `MessageBox` function:

```
lngRet = MessageBox(Me.hwnd, "The source and destination files are " & _
                    "the same. Do you want to overwrite the source " & _
                    "file?", "Source File Overwrite", _
                    MB_YESNO + MB_ICONQUESTION)
If lngRet = IDNO Then
    '  Stop the process.
    Exit Sub
End If
```

As you can see, it's almost identical to the code we had before! In fact, the values for the constant that I grouped together as enumerated types are exactly the same as the ones you use in VB. So why would I even bother using the `MessageBox` call as opposed to `MsgBox`? Well, there are some constants that we didn't go over in this discussion that you may find useful, but that's not the only reason why I wanted to introduce you to this function. Along with it being a fairly easy call from `user32`, it shows that if you do a little bit of investigation, you may save yourself from some ugly results.

When you use the `Msgbox` command, other commands in your app are effectively put on hold until the presence of the Message Box is acknowledged by the user. As we shall see in the next chapter, where we'll start to do some graphical manipulation to our forms, using `MsgBox` can affect the graphical performance of your application. *Then* you'll see how beneficial the added flexibility of `MessageBox` can be.

Altering the Tree View Control

We're really going to shift gears here by jumping into the tree view control and developing it from the basic that VB gives you. We'll add another form to our application that displays file information in a tree view control. This will require us to add some other file APIs, so I'll show them to you and briefly explain what they do. I'll also describe the `SendMessage` API call, a call that is simple to use and can be used in a number of places.

Creating the File Information Form

Begin by adding a new form to the project and naming it `frmFileInfo`. You will need to add a tree view control named `treFileInfo` onto the form. If you don't have the tree view icon in your ToolBox window, then select Project | Components, and make sure that the Microsoft Windows Common Controls 6.0 list item is selected, as is shown in the following screen shot:

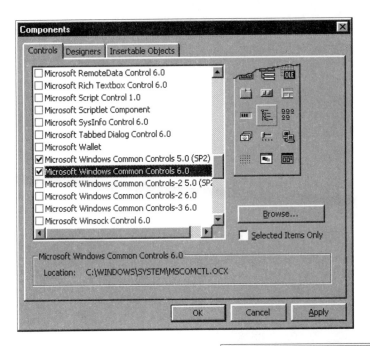

Now add a label called `lblFileName`, and one command button named `cmdOK`. (you can accept all of the default values for these controls, but change the `Caption` property for the command button to `&OK`). Arrange the controls to make your form look something like this:

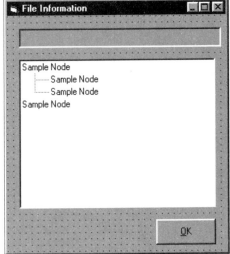

Populating the File Information Form

First of all, let's go over the two new API calls we'll use to retrieve file information. You need to add both these calls to the `EncryptionLib` module.

The first of these calls is called `GetFileTime`.

GetFileTime

As the name states, this call retrieves time information about the file specified by its handle, hFile. It is defined as follows:

```
Declare Function GetFileTime Lib "kernel32" _
    (ByVal hFile As Long, lpCreationTime As FILETIME, _
    lpLastAccessTime As FILETIME, lpLastWriteTime As FILETIME) As Long
```

You should define the above call in your EncryptionLib module.

The following table summarizes the rest of the arguments for this call:

Argument	Description
lpCreationTime	The time when the file was created.
lpLastAccessTime	The last time the file was opened.
lpLastWriteTime	The last time the file was modified.

But what is this FILETIME UDT? It's a representation of a 64-bit number that specifies the elapsed time since January 1st, 1601, in 100 nanosecond increments. (If you notice, we already have this UDT defined since the WIN32_FIND_DATA UDT that FindFirstFile uses also requires the FILETIME structure.) Judging by this definition, it looks like we're going to be writing some data conversion code to get this UDT into something something that makes sense to us.

Fortunately we can use the FileTimeToSystemTime API call to convert this UDT into a SYSTEMTIME UDT. Define SYSTEMTIME in your EncryptionLib module with Public scope:

```
Type SYSTEMTIME
    wYear As Integer
    wMonth As Integer
    wDayOfWeek As Integer
    wDay As Integer
    wHour As Integer
    wMinute As Integer
    wSecond As Integer
    wMilliseconds As Integer
End Type
```

Then declare the API call:

```
Declare Function FileTimeToSystemTime Lib "kernel32" _
    (lpFileTime As FILETIME, lpSystemTime As SYSTEMTIME) As Long
```

As you can see by looking at the format for SYSTEMTIME, using this structure makes the conversion to a Date data type much easier than trying to convert the information in FILETIME. We'll create a function later on in the chapter that will handle the conversion from a FILETIME UDT to a Date data type.

GetFileAttributes

Now we can declare the other API call that is used to get file information for the frmFileInfo form. Again, this should be defined in the EncryptionLib module:

```
Declare Function GetFileAttributes Lib "kernel32" _
    Alias "GetFileAttributesA" (ByVal lpFileName As String) As Long
```

This function returns a value that contains in its bits the different kind of file attributes for the file defined by lpFileName (note that this function does not require a handle to the file). Soon we shall see how we can use the AND operation in VB to go through each value in our FileAttributes enumeration that we defined in Chapter 3 and see what attributes the file has.

Redesigning the Main Form

We need to change the main form around by adding some menus options - not only will this clean up the form a bit, but it will allow us to work with other user32.dll API calls.

Using the **VB Menu Editor**, create a menu for frmMain with the following menu items:

Menu Name	SubMenu of	Caption
MnuOptions		&Options
MnuOStartEncryption	mnuOptions	&Start Encryption
MnuOFileInformation	mnuOptions	&File Information...
MnuODash	mnuOptions	-
MnuOExit	mnuOptions	E&xit
MnuHelp		&Help
MnuHAbout	mnuHelp	&About...

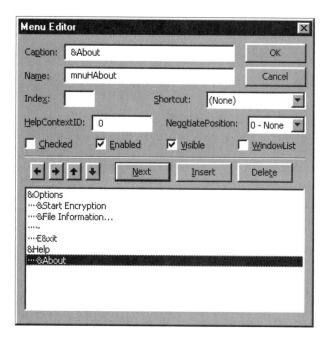

Now we are able to remove the About, Exit and Start Encryption command buttons, as we have replaced them with corresponding menu items. Here's a screenshot of what the modified `frmMain` screen should look like now:

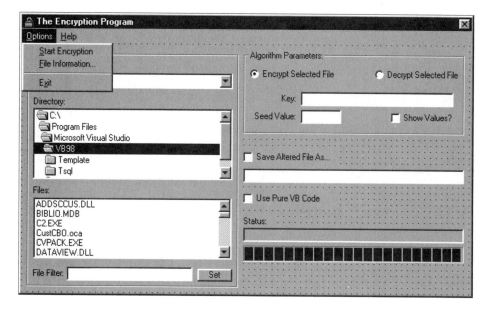

Since we got rid of some command buttons, we have to add some code to the `Click` events of `mnuOStartEncryption`, `mnuOExit` and `mnuHAbout`:

```
Private Sub mnuOStartEncryption_Click()

   EncodeFiles

End Sub


Private Sub mnuOExit_Click()

   Unload Me
   Set frmMain = Nothing

End Sub


Private Sub mnuHAbout_Click()

   Screen.MousePointer = vbHourglass
   frmAbout.Show vbModal

End Sub
```

OK, we're done with the main form for now. It still needs work, but we're getting there. Let's concentrate on the code to display the file's information.

Displaying the File's Information

Add the following method to `frmMain`'s **Declaration** section. This method simply shows the file information window and displays information about the current highlighted file.

```
Private Sub ShowFileInformation()

   On Error GoTo error_ShowFileInformation

   If fleMain.ListIndex <> -1 Then
   ' Something is selected.

      Screen.MousePointer = vbHourglass
      Load frmFileInfo
      frmFileInfo.FindFileInfo dirMain.Path & "\" & fleMain.filename
      Screen.MousePointer = vbDefault
      frmFileInfo.Show vbModal

   End If

   Exit Sub

error_ShowFileInformation:

   Screen.MousePointer = vbDefault
   MsgBox "The file information screen could not be loaded." & _
```

```
        vbCrLf & "Error: " & Err.Description, vbOKOnly + vbExclamation, _
        "Screen Error"

End Sub
```

Now we need to call the method from the `Click` event of `mnuOFileInformation`:

```
Private Sub mnuOFileInformation_Click()

    ShowFileInformation

End Sub
```

As you can see, the `ShowFileInformation` method calls a method called `FindFileInfo` that is contained on `frmFileInfo`, passing in the file that on which we want to get information. In this case, we're using the directory and file list box controls from `frmMain` to determine the file that we want. Here's the code for the `FindFileInfo` method. This method needs to be defined in `frmFileInfo`:

```
Public Sub FindFileInfo(FullFilePath As String)

    Dim lngFileHandle As Long
    Dim lngRet As Long

    On Error GoTo error_FindFileInfo

    If DoesFileExist(FullFilePath) = True Then
        lngFileHandle = CreateFile(CStr(FullFilePath), GENERIC_READ, _
                            FILE_SHARE_READ Or FILE_SHARE_WRITE, _
                            0, OPEN_EXISTING, 0, 0)
        lblFileName.Caption = FullFilePath
        AddFileSize lngFileHandle
        AddFileAttributes lngFileHandle
        CloseHandle lngFileHandle
    End If

    Exit Sub

error_FindFileInfo:

    Screen.MousePointer = vbDefault
    MsgBox "The file information could not be loaded." & vbCrLf & _
        "Error:  " & Err.Description, vbOKOnly + vbExclamation, _
        "File Load Error"

    If lngFileHandle <> INVALID_HANDLE_VALUE Then
        CloseHandle lngFileHandle
    End If

End Sub
```

All this function does is look for a file along the file path the user has chosen (by using the `DoesFileExist` function defined in the last chapter). If the file does exist, it then creates a handle to this file:

```
        If DoesFileExist(FullFilePath) = True Then
            lngFileHandle = CreateFile(CStr(FullFilePath), GENERIC_READ, _
                                   FILE_SHARE_READ Or FILE_SHARE_WRITE, _
                                   0, OPEN_EXISTING, 0, 0)
```

The `AddFileSize` and `AddFileAttributes` procedures (which we shall define in a moment) are
then called using this handle:

```
        AddFileSize lngFileHandle
        AddFileAttributes lngFileHandle
        CloseHandle lngFileHandle
```

If the file is not found at the specified path an error is raised:

```
        MsgBox "The file information could not be loaded." & vbCrLf & _
               "Error:  " & Err.Description, vbOKOnly + vbExclamation, _
               "File Load Error"
```

Adding Information to the Tree View Control

To display file information to the user, we shall use the `AddFileAttributes` and `AddFileSize`
methods to add the appropriate file information to the tree view control. Let's start with the
`AddFileAttributes` method.

AddFileAttributes

This method adds a node to the tree specifying if the file has certain attributes or not. You should
define this method in the code window of `frmFormInfo`. There is quite a large procedure, so bear
with me, and I'll explain what it does after:

```
    Private Sub AddFileAttributes(FileHandle As Long)

        Dim blnAttr As Boolean
        Dim lngRet As Long
        Dim dtmTime As Date
        Dim objNodeAttr As Node
        Dim objNodeDates As Node
        Dim strDate As String
        Dim udtAtts As BY_HANDLE_FILE_INFORMATION

        On Error GoTo error_AddFileAttributes

        lngRet = GetFileInformationByHandle(FileHandle, udtAtts)

        If lngRet <> 0 Then
            Set objNodeDates = treFileInfo.Nodes.Add(, , _
                                       "FILEINFO", "File Dates")
          With udtAtts
            dtmTime = ConvertUTCToDate(.ftCreationTime)
            strDate = Format$(dtmTime, "mm/dd/yyyy hh:nn:ss AM/PM")
            treFileInfo.Nodes.Add objNodeDates.Key, tvwChild, , _
                               "Creation Date: " & strDate
            dtmTime = ConvertUTCToDate(.ftLastAccessTime)
            strDate = Format$(dtmTime, "mm/dd/yyyy hh:nn:ss AM/PM")
            treFileInfo.Nodes.Add objNodeDates.Key, tvwChild, , _
```

```
                        "Last Access Date:   " & strDate
        dtmTime = ConvertUTCToDate(.ftLastWriteTime)
        strDate = Format$(dtmTime, "mm/dd/yyyy hh:nn:ss AM/PM")
        treFileInfo.Nodes.Add objNodeDates.Key, tvwChild, , _
                        "Last Modification Date:   " & strDate
    End With

    objNodeDates.Selected = True
    lngRet = SetTVSelectedItemBold(treFileInfo, True)
    objNodeDates.Selected = False

    Set objNodeAttr = treFileInfo.Nodes.Add(, , "ATTR", "Attributes")

    With udtAtts
        If .dwFileAttributes And FILE_ATTRIBUTE_ARCHIVE Then
            blnAttr = True
        Else
            blnAttr = False
        End If
        treFileInfo.Nodes.Add objNodeAttr.Key, tvwChild, , _
                        "Archived = " & CStr(blnAttr)

        If .dwFileAttributes And FILE_ATTRIBUTE_COMPRESSED Then
            blnAttr = True
        Else
            blnAttr = False
        End If
        treFileInfo.Nodes.Add objNodeAttr.Key, tvwChild, , _
                        "Compressed = " & CStr(blnAttr)

        If .dwFileAttributes And FILE_ATTRIBUTE_HIDDEN Then
            blnAttr = True
        Else
            blnAttr = False
        End If
        treFileInfo.Nodes.Add objNodeAttr.Key, tvwChild, , _
                        "Hidden = " & CStr(blnAttr)

        If .dwFileAttributes And FILE_ATTRIBUTE_NORMAL Then
            blnAttr = True
        Else
            blnAttr = False
        End If
        treFileInfo.Nodes.Add objNodeAttr.Key, tvwChild, , _
                        "Normal = " & CStr(blnAttr)

        If .dwFileAttributes And FILE_ATTRIBUTE_READONLY Then
            blnAttr = True
        Else
            blnAttr = False
        End If
        treFileInfo.Nodes.Add objNodeAttr.Key, tvwChild, , _
                        "Read-Only = " & CStr(blnAttr)

        If .dwFileAttributes And FILE_ATTRIBUTE_SYSTEM Then
            blnAttr = True
        Else
            blnAttr = False
        End If
        treFileInfo.Nodes.Add objNodeAttr.Key, tvwChild, , _
```

```
                                    "System = " & CStr(blnAttr)
        End With

        objNodeAttr.Selected = True
        lngRet = SetTVSelectedItemBold(treFileInfo, True)
        objNodeAttr.Selected = False
    End If

    Exit Sub

    error_AddFileAttributes:

        If Not objNodeDates Is Nothing Then
                treFileInfo.Nodes.Remove objNodeDates.Index
                treFileInfo.Nodes.Add , , , "Unknown File Dates"
        End If

        If Not objNodeAttr Is Nothing Then
                treFileInfo.Nodes.Remove objNodeAttr.Index
                treFileInfo.Nodes.Add , , , "Unknown File Attributes"
        End If

    End Sub
```

How It Works: AddFileAttributes

Right, what does all this do then?

As normal, there are some definitions to begin with:

```
Private Sub AddFileAttributes(FileHandle As Long)

Dim blnAttr As Boolean
Dim lngRet As Long
Dim dtmTime As Date
Dim objNodeAttr As Node
Dim objNodeDates As Node
Dim strDate As String
Dim udtAtts As BY_HANDLE_FILE_INFORMATION

On Error GoTo error_AddFileAttributes

lngRet = GetFileInformationByHandle(FileHandle, udtAtts)
```

These definitions are mainly self-explanatory, but what is the mysterious
BY_HANDLE_FILE_INFORMATION? It is simply another UDT, which we shall define in a moment.
And what is GetFileInformationByHandle? Yes, you guessed it, it's another API call. Again, we
will define this very shortly.

What happens next? Well, if `lngRet` has a value, then the procedure adds the date information to the tree:

```
If lngRet <> 0 Then
    Set objNodeDates = treFileInfo.Nodes.Add(, , _
                                    "FILEINFO", "File Dates")
```

And then, converts the times to the correct format:

```
With udtAtts
    dtmTime = ConvertUTCToDate(.ftCreationTime)
    strDate = Format$(dtmTime, "mm/dd/yyyy hh:nn:ss AM/PM")
    treFileInfo.Nodes.Add objNodeDates.Key, tvwChild, , _
                    "Creation Date:   " & strDate
    dtmTime = ConvertUTCToDate(.ftLastAccessTime)
    strDate = Format$(dtmTime, "mm/dd/yyyy hh:nn:ss AM/PM")
    treFileInfo.Nodes.Add objNodeDates.Key, tvwChild, , _
                    "Last Access Date:   " & strDate
    dtmTime = ConvertUTCToDate(.ftLastWriteTime)
    strDate = Format$(dtmTime, "mm/dd/yyyy hh:nn:ss AM/PM")
    treFileInfo.Nodes.Add objNodeDates.Key, tvwChild, , _
                    "Last Modification Date:   " & strDate
End With
```

Now the `objNodeDates` are made bold, and the attributes are set:

```
objNodeDates.Selected = True
lngRet = SetTVSelectedItemBold(treFileInfo, True)
objNodeDates.Selected = False

'  Now set the attributes.
Set objNodeAttr = treFileInfo.Nodes.Add(, , "ATTR", "Attributes")
With udtAtts
    If .dwFileAttributes And FILE_ATTRIBUTE_ARCHIVE Then
        blnAttr = True
    Else
        blnAttr = False
    End If
    treFileInfo.Nodes.Add objNodeAttr.Key, tvwChild, , _
                    "Archived = " & CStr(blnAttr)

    If .dwFileAttributes And FILE_ATTRIBUTE_COMPRESSED Then
        blnAttr = True
    Else
        blnAttr = False
    End If
    treFileInfo.Nodes.Add objNodeAttr.Key, tvwChild, , _
                    "Compressed = " & CStr(blnAttr)

    If .dwFileAttributes And FILE_ATTRIBUTE_HIDDEN Then
        blnAttr = True
    Else
        blnAttr = False
```

```
          End If
          treFileInfo.Nodes.Add objNodeAttr.Key, tvwChild, , _
                             "Hidden = " & CStr(blnAttr)

          If .dwFileAttributes And FILE_ATTRIBUTE_NORMAL Then
              blnAttr = True
          Else
              blnAttr = False
          End If
          treFileInfo.Nodes.Add objNodeAttr.Key, tvwChild, , _
                             "Normal = " & CStr(blnAttr)

          If .dwFileAttributes And FILE_ATTRIBUTE_READONLY Then
              blnAttr = True
          Else
              blnAttr = False
          End If
          treFileInfo.Nodes.Add objNodeAttr.Key, tvwChild, , _
                             "Read-Only = " & CStr(blnAttr)

          If .dwFileAttributes And FILE_ATTRIBUTE_SYSTEM Then
              blnAttr = True
          Else
              blnAttr = False
          End If
          treFileInfo.Nodes.Add objNodeAttr.Key, tvwChild, , _
                             "System = " & CStr(blnAttr)

      End With
```

Finally, the selected attributes are bolded. There is also some basic error handling code.

```
    '   Let's also bold objNodeAttr
    objNodeAttr.Selected = True
    lngRet = SetTVSelectedItemBold(treFileInfo, True)
    objNodeAttr.Selected = False
End If

Exit Sub

error_AddFileAttributes:

    If Not objNodeDates Is Nothing Then
          treFileInfo.Nodes.Remove objNodeDates.Index
          treFileInfo.Nodes.Add , , , "Unknown File Dates"
    End If

    If Not objNodeAttr Is Nothing Then
          treFileInfo.Nodes.Remove objNodeAttr.Index
          treFileInfo.Nodes.Add , , , "Unknown File Attributes"
    End If

End Sub
```

So, as we have just discovered, we need to define the `GetFileInformationByHandle` API call and the `BY_HANDLE_FILE_INFORMATION` UDT.

The `GetFileInformationByHandle` API call is used to get attribute and file time information about the selected file, and should be defined as follows in the `EncryptionLib` module:

```
Declare Function GetFileInformationByHandle Lib "kernel32" (ByVal hFile As
    Long, lpFileInformation As BY_HANDLE_FILE_INFORMATION) As Long
```

As for the UDT, it reads as follows, and should also be defined in the `EncryptionLib` module:

```
Public Type BY_HANDLE_FILE_INFORMATION
    dwFileAttributes As Long
    ftCreationTime As FILETIME
    ftLastAccessTime As FILETIME
    ftLastWriteTime As FILETIME
    dwVolumeSerialNumber As Long
    nFileSizeHigh As Long
    nFileSizeLow As Long
    nNumberOfLinks As Long
    nFileIndexHigh As Long
    nFileIndexLow As Long
End Type
```

Although not every parameter in `BY_HANDLE_FILE_INFORMATION` is needed in `GetFileAttributes`, let's go through a quick run-down of the UDT's parameters.

`dwFileAttributes` directly corresponds to the `FileAttributes` enumeration we saw in Chapter 3. You can use the OR operator with `dwFileAttributes` and values from `FileAttributes` to determine which attributes the file has.

`ftCreationTime`, `ftLastAccessTime`, and `ftLastWriteTime` are all FILETIME UDTs - we'll create a `ConvertUTCToDate` function in a moment to convert this structure into a `Date` data type.

`dwVolumeSerialNumber` is the serial number of the volume on disk that contains the file. The `nFileSizeHigh` and `nFileSizeLow` parameters define the file size as a 64-bit number, similar to what we saw with `GetFileSize`. `nNumberOfLinks` let you know how many links there are to the file. Finally, `nFileIndexHigh` and `nFileIndexLow` create a 64-bit unique identifier for the file.

Now, we've finished that, let's define the other method I mentioned earlier:

AddFileSize

This method simply adds the file size information to the tree view and bolds the object node. Again, type this definition into the code window of `frmFileInfo`.

```
Private Sub AddFileSize(FileHandle As Long)

    On Error GoTo error_AddFileSize

    Dim lngRet As Long
    Dim lngSize As Long
    Dim objNode As Node

    lngSize = GetFileSize(FileHandle, 0)

    If lngSize <> HFILE_ERROR Then
        Set objNode = treFileInfo.Nodes.Add(, , , _
                                   ' "File Size = " & _
                                   CStr(lngSize) & " Bytes")
    Else
        Set objNode = treFileInfo.Nodes.Add(, , , _
                                   "Unknown File Size")
    End If

    objNode.Selected = True
    lngRet = SetTVSelectedItemBold(treFileInfo, True)
    objNode.Selected = False

Exit Sub

error_AddFileSize:

    treFileInfo.Nodes.Add , , , "Unknown File Size"

End Sub
```

You may have noticed that a reference is made to a method called `SetTVSelectedItemBold`. We shall be covering the `SetTVSelectedItemBold` method later on in the chapter. For now, you can declare the function like this:

```
Public Function SetTVSelectedItemBold _
    (TreeViewControl As TreeView, ChangeToBold As Boolean) As Long

    SetTVSelectedItemBold = 1

End Function
```

There's one more function that we need to define: We mentioned it earlier - `ConvertUTCToDate`. This function is used to convert the information in a `FILETIME` UDT to a `Date` data type. The UTC time is defined at the number of ticks since January 1st, 1601, in 100 nanosecond increments.

```
Public Function ConvertUTCToDate(UTCType As FILETIME) As Date

    On Error Resume Next

    Dim lngRet As Long
    Dim strDate As String
    Dim udtSystem As SYSTEMTIME
```

```
    lngRet = FileTimeToSystemTime(UTCType, udtSystem)

    With udtSystem
        strDate = CStr(.wMonth) & "/" & CStr(.wDay) & "/" & _
            CStr(.wYear) & " " & CStr(.wHour) & "" & _
            CStr(.wMinute) & "" & CStr(.wSecond)
    End With

    ConvertUTCToDate = CDate(strDate)

End Function
```

Again, you should add this function to the `EncryptionLib` module.

Just before we finish, you can tidy up the behavior of your form by adding these three simple events to the code for `frmFileInfo`:

```
Private Sub cmdOK_Click()

    Unload Me

End Sub
```

```
Private Sub Form_Load()

    Screen.MousePointer = vbDefault

End Sub
```

```
Private Sub Form_Unload(Cancel As Integer)

    Set frmFileInfo = Nothing

End Sub
```

Finally! We actually have the form set up! Of course, on the grand scheme of things, we're far from done, but we have some base procedures written. Here's what a populated tree view control looks likes when we select a test file. I have chosen one of the standard Windows bitmaps:

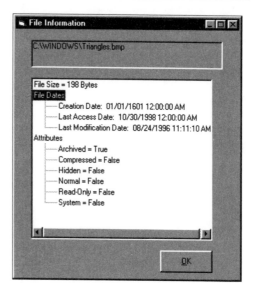

I really like the tree view control for a number of reasons. The main one is that you can categorize your data into groups very easily. With a list box, grouping data is not as easy in my opinion.

Also, you can load and unload data lines (or nodes) whenever you see fit, so if a user closes a parent node, you could remove all the child nodes to save on space if the parent node is not visited frequently.

However, one really glaring omission that I've noticed about the tree view is the lack of color control. You can't change its background color! Since this control is a common Windows control, and I know that it does really allow you to change colors, we should look at the API layer to see what there's to help us out. What we'll see in a moment is that there's one call that does a lot of the work for us, and that call's name is SendMessage.

Using the SendMessage API Call

The SendMessage API call is a very powerful and versatile call indeed. This call is used to send a message to a window or a set of windows (hence its name). What makes this call so flexible is the great variety of messages that can be sent. Let's look at this call's definition first:

```
Declare Function SendMessage Lib "user32" Alias "SendMessageA" _
    (ByVal hwnd As Long, ByVal wMsg As Long, ByVal wParam As Long, _
    lParam As Any) As Long
```

hwnd

Just as we talked about before, this is a handle to a window i.e. this argument identifies the window that will receive the message. Indeed, if you were to set hwnd equal to HWND_BROADCAST (&HFFFF), the message would be sent to all top-level windows currently in the system. This is nice if you are running applications to receive your message (although they may not know what to do with it), but we'll usually be interested in sending a message to just one window.

wMsg

This argument tells the receiving window what you are asking it to do. Note that this also applies to the VB controls as well, since they are also windows. There are a bunch of constants that you can use in this argument to manipulate anything that the window is capable of doing.

For example, WM_GETFONT can be used to get font information from any control that displays text. Another message value is WM_GETTEXT, which will retrieve the caption of a window specified by hwnd. However, the results of this value will depend upon where the message is being sent. For example, using this value for a command button will return the value of the button's caption. For a combo box, however, this will return the static-text portion of the control.

Depending upon the value for wMsg, the usage of wParam and lParam will change. They can be used to either send information to the window, or they can be used as buffers that the window will fill with information.

For a complete list of the valid window messages, check out
http://premium.microsoft.com/msdn/library/sdkdoc/winui/windows_2v8z.htm.

wParam and lParam

These arguments allow you to send and/or retrieve information to and/or from the destination window. This may sound a bit confusing, because `SendMessage` can be used to get descriptive information about a window as well as simply tell the window to do something. Again, depending upon the value of `wMsg`, the meaning of these arguments will change.

Note that some messages require that `lParam` pass in a `String` data type, so you might want to make another declaration named `SendMessageString` that declares the last argument as a `String` data type (passed in by value, of course). However, for our purposes, we'll make sure that we pass in `String` data types `ByVal` to `SendMessage`.

> *Although we won't be using it in this book, you can also send messages using the* `PostMessage` *API call. This call does not let you know if the message was processed by the receiving window(s) or not, since it simply posts the message into the window(s)'s message queue, and immediately returns control back to the sender. This may be useful for some situations, but it's also somewhat dangerous.*
>
> *For example, if you use* `PostMessage` *to send information contained in a string, that string may not exist on the stack after the procedure that called* `PostMessage` *is done. In general, don't use* `PostMessage` *if any of its arguments are pointing to some kind of value, which, as we saw in Chapter 2, is exactly what is happening when we pass strings into API functions.*

Sending Messages and the Return Value

When the receiving window gets the message, it will try and process the message. If it understands the value for `wMsg` and the two arguments, it will attempt to process the message, and return a value notifying the caller of the results.

Some messages will return a zero, which means the call was successful. Other calls may return a non-zero value to let the sender know if the message was processed successfully or not. Therefore, depending upon the message being sent, the return value's meaning will change from call to call. Make sure you read up on each message's documentation before you use it so you understand what the return value is telling you. Also, depending upon what you want the target window to do, you have to send the messages in the correct order.

> If a window receives a message that it doesn't understand, it will send that message to another internal function called `DefWindowProc`. This allows a window to handle developer-defined messages. However, this is beyond the scope of our discussion here, but we'll see what window procedures are all about in Chapter 8.

Processing window messages may be a difficult concept to pick up for VB developers. VB is handling all of the messages for you underneath the scenes, masking them with events and properties that are easier to understand and use. When you use a technique called subclassing, you suddenly become responsible for all of the messages that the window is receiving. This can make your application crash in a most grotesque fashion, but you also can process all of the messages that Windows is sending to your window. We won't need to do any subclassing with the tree view control to change any colors, so let's start to see what kind of messages we can send.

*Subclassing will be defined in Chapter 8. We'll **eventually** get there! .*

Sending Messages to the Tree View Control

Each control responds not only to the standard window messages (their values range from 1 to 1024), but can also respond to other messages defined outside this range. The tree view control is no exception. For starters, let's take a look at the parameters that we'll be using to determine what node we want to change:

```
Public Enum TVItemMove
    TVGN_ROOT = &H0
    TVGN_NEXT = &H1
    TVGN_PREVIOUS = &H2
    TVGN_PARENT = &H3
    TVGN_CHILD = &H4
    TVGN_FIRSTVISIBLE = &H5
    TVGN_NEXTVISIBLE = &H6
    TVGN_PREVIOUSVISIBLE = &H7
    TVGN_DROPHILITE = &H8
    TVGN_CARET = &H9
End Enum
```

Unfortunately, you're not going to find these constants in the **API Text Viewer** program. However, if you have the Win32 SDK or access to Microsoft's search site, you should be able to find control message values there. Also, the MSDN Help files that come with Visual Studio 6 contain this information.

As you can see, we have a fair amount of flexibility in moving through the nodes. All of the names make the values self-explanatory, except for TVGN_CARET. When I first did some research on this at Microsoft's web site, I found out that you use this value to get information on the current node selected. That may be obvious to some, but you'd think something like TVGN_CURRENT would have made it clearer. Oh well...

You also have to use the following message enumeration to control which item you're getting or changing:

```
Public Enum TVMItemProps
    TVM_GETNEXTITEM = 4362
    TVM_GETITEM = 4364
    TVM_SETITEM = 4365
End Enum
```

TVM_GETNEXTITEM is used to retrieve a specific node in a tree view. Usually, values defined in the TMItemMove are used with this value in SendMessage calls to determine which item should be retrieved. TVM_GETITEM and TVM_SETITEM are used to retrieve and set item attributes. Believe me, I know it might be getting a bit confusing. Examples will be coming up soon, so please hang on!

Anyway, we now have the values of the message to navigate through our items. Next we need the message values to actually change some properties of the items:

```
Public Enum TVMColorProps
    TVM_GETBKCOLOR = 4383
    TVM_GETTEXTCOLOR = 4384
    TVM_SETBKCOLOR = 4381
    TVM_SETTEXTCOLOR = 4382
End Enum
```

When I first looked at extending the tree view control, I saw all of these values and shook my head. This is really making no sense at all! The names make sense, but how do you get all of these values to change colors on the tree view control? It didn't look like it would be possible to use `SendMessage` by itself to get and save the information that I wanted (and as we'll see, we'll have to use some other API calls as well as a UDT that defines tree view items to make the color change work).

It takes a lot of careful reading and stumbling before you can get things to work correctly when sending messages to controls, so the suggestion to save your code should be adhered to. However, let's start by using `SendMessage` simply changing the background color of the tree view, which is pretty easy compared to some other things we're going to do to the control!

Changing the Background Color

First of all, let's add all of the API calls and constants that we've been talking about to our project. Since our `EncryptionLib.bas` file is getting pretty big so let's make another module called `TreeViewLib` to keep the calls in. So, we need to define our API call:

```
Declare Function SendMessage Lib "user32" Alias "SendMessageA" _
    (ByVal hwnd As Long, ByVal wMsg As Long, ByVal wParam As Long, _
    lParam As Any) As Long
```

And the enumerations:

```
Public Enum TVItemMove
    TVGN_ROOT = &H0
    TVGN_NEXT = &H1
    TVGN_PREVIOUS = &H2
    TVGN_PARENT = &H3
    TVGN_CHILD = &H4
    TVGN_FIRSTVISIBLE = &H5
    TVGN_NEXTVISIBLE = &H6
    TVGN_PREVIOUSVISIBLE = &H7
    TVGN_DROPHILITE = &H8
    TVGN_CARET = &H9
End Enum
```

```
Public Enum TVMItemProps
    TVM_GETNEXTITEM = 4362
    TVM_GETITEM = 4364
    TVM_SETITEM = 4365
End Enum
```

```
Public Enum TVMColorProps
    TVM_GETBKCOLOR = 4383
    TVM_GETTEXTCOLOR = 4384
```

```
        TVM_SETBKCOLOR = 4381
        TVM_SETTEXTCOLOR = 4382
End Enum
```

Also, we need to define the following four constants in `TreeViewLib`:

```
Public Const GWL_STYLE As Long = -16
Public Const TVIS_BOLD As Long = 16
Public Const TVIF_STATE As Long = 8
Public Const TVS_HASLINES As Long = 2
```

You may be wondering where I got this information. I found `GWL_STYLE` using the **API Text Viewer**, and I got the `TV..` constants from the common control's C header file. If you have VC++ installed you should be able to find this file. It will be installed on a path like

…`Vc98\include\Commonctrl.h`.

SetTVBackgroundColor

Now, we're going to add a function called `SetTVBackgroundColor` to our `TreeViewLib` module. This function takes a `ColorValue` argument which defines what the new color should be. We can use the `RGB` function in VB to figure out what this value should be. Here's what the implementation looks like:

```
Public Function SetTVBackgroundColor _
    (ColorValue As Long, TreeViewControl As TreeView) As Long


    On Error GoTo error_SetTVBackgroundColor

    Dim lngLineStyle As Long
    Dim lngRet As Long

    With TreeViewControl
        lngRet = SendMessage(.hwnd, TVM_SETBKCOLOR, 0, _
                ByVal ColorValue)
        lngLineStyle = GetWindowLong(.hwnd, GWL_STYLE)

        If (lngLineStyle And TVS_HASLINES) = True Then

            lngRet = SetWindowLong(.hwnd, GWL_STYLE, _
                                lngLineStyle Xor TVS_HASLINES)
            lngRet = SetWindowLong(.hwnd, GWL_STYLE, _
                                lngLineStyle)
        End If

        SetTVBackgroundColor = 1
    End With

    Exit Function

error_SetTVBackgroundColor:

    SetTVBackgroundColor = 0

End Function
```

You may have noticed that calls were made to undeclared functions. These are the following two API calls (which need to be defined in `TreeViewLib`):

```
Declare Function GetWindowLong Lib "user32" _
    Alias "GetWindowLongA" (ByVal hwnd As Long, _
    ByVal nIndex As Long) As Long
```

```
Declare Function SetWindowLong Lib "user32" _
    Alias "SetWindowLongA" (ByVal hwnd As Long, _
    ByVal nIndex As Long, ByVal dwNewLong As Long) As Long
```

How it Works: SetTVBackgroundColor

So, how does this function work?

First, we `TVM_SETBKCOLOR` as the message to tell the specific tree view ctrl (defined by the `hwnd` value) to change its color to the value specified by `ColorValue`. Note that we have to pass this value in `ByVal`; if you don't do this, the OS won't change the color to what you have specified. In this case, `SendMessage` returns the previous color value before the change. If the return value is equal to -1, then the control was using the default system color.

```
lngRet = SendMessage(.hwnd, TVM_SETBKCOLOR, 0, _
    ByVal ColorValue)
```

Now, we have to make sure that we redraw any lines that were there before the background color was changed. There are many styles that be defined for any particular window; for the tree view control, you can define what the tree should look like, which includes whether or not connecting lines should be used between nodes.

```
lngLineStyle = GetWindowLong(.hwnd, GWL_STYLE)

If (lngLineStyle And TVS_HASLINES) = True Then

    lngRet = SetWindowLong(.hwnd, GWL_STYLE, _
                         lngLineStyle Xor TVS_HASLINES)
    lngRet = SetWindowLong(.hwnd, GWL_STYLE, _
                         lngLineStyle)
End If
```

To find out what styles are currently defined, we use the `GetWindowLong` API call to return the style information. Conversely, to change something about the window, we can use the `SetWindowLong` API call, which we have defined as follows:

```
Declare Function GetWindowLong Lib "user32" _
    Alias "GetWindowLongA" (ByVal hwnd As Long, _
    ByVal nIndex As Long) As Long

Declare Function SetWindowLong Lib "user32" _
    Alias "SetWindowLongA" (ByVal hwnd As Long, _
    ByVal nIndex As Long, ByVal dwNewLong As Long) As Long
```

The first argument, `hwnd`, defines the window to evaluate. The second argument, `nIndex`, determines what kind of information you want to return, and the last argument in `GetWindowLong`, `dwNewLong`, specifies the changes that you want to make.

As we can see in our `SetTVBackgroundColor` function, we use the `SetWindowLong` with the `GWL_STYLE` constant, which returns information about the styles of the window. We then check the return value to see if the tree view control is using lines to connect the nodes (`TVS_HASLINES`). If it is, we use the `SetWindowLong` call to first remove the lines, and then redraw them. Note that the first `SetWindowLong` uses the `Xor` operation to remove the lines style value in `lngStyleReturn` because we want to keep any other style in the control the same - we only want to remove the line style. The next call redraws the lines.

> *This line style "refresh" code is a good example of what I described before about* `SendMessage`. *When I was creating this example, I thought I had to make only one* `SendMessage` *call to change the color, and that would be it. But I noticed that the connecting lines were not being redrawn. After spending some time looking through Microsoft's web site, I finally came across the article http://support.microsoft.com/support/kb/articles/q178/4/91.asp, which simply stated that you had to add the* `GetWindowLong` *and* `SetWindowLong` *calls to redraw the node lines. I tried to find out if this is a bug or not, but to no avail. My guess is that it isn't a bug and that this behavior is by design, but I hope this illustrates that using* `SendMessage` *to change a control's state may start you down another path to other API calls.*

Now, to change the color of your tree view control, you need to add the following line of code to the `FindFileInfo` method. Note that it must be added after the file information is added to the control:

```
    AddFileSize lngFileHandle
    AddFileAttributes lngFileHandle
    CloseHandle lngFileHandle
End If

lngRet = SetTVBackgroundColor(RGB(0, 200, 255), treFileInfo)

Exit Sub

error_FindFileInfo:
```

As you can see, we have used the `RGB` function to pass in a color value that changes the tree view control's background color to a light shade of blue. Even though you can't see the blue color in this screen shot, you'll notice that it's definitely not white:

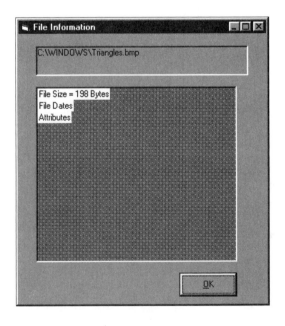

First, Suppose that you are interested in getting the current background color value. You can do this with a rather handy API call, GetSysColor.

```
Declare Function GetSysColor Lib "user32" _
    (ByVal nIndex As Long) As Long
```

We don't actually need to use this call in our particular application, but I want to show it to you as it can come in very handy. The nIndex argument is used to specify what system color we want to get. In our case, we will use the COLOR_WINDOW constant to return the default window color.

In order to use In this API call, we need to create a function called GetTVBackgroundColor, which looks like this:

```
Public Function GetTVBackgroundColor(TreeViewControl As TreeView) As Long

'   Returns:
'               Non-zero on success.
'               Zero on failure.

    On Error GoTo error_GetTVBackgroundColor

    Dim lngRet As Long

'   First, try to get the color of the control.
    lngRet = SendMessage(TreeViewControl.hwnd, _
            TVM_GETBKCOLOR, 0, 0&)

    If lngRet = -1 Then
    '   The tree view is using the default
    '   system background color, so we need
    '   to get what that is.
    '   For a tree view control, that's
    '   COLOR_WINDOW
        lngRet = GetSysColor(COLOR_WINDOW)
    End If

'   Return lngRet
    GetTVBackgroundColor = lngRet

    Exit Function

error_GetTVBackgroundColor:

    GetTVBackgroundColor = 0

End Function
```

Let's take a look at how this function works. We first get the current value of the tree view control by sending the TVM_GETBKCOLOR message to the control using the SendMessage call. If we don't get a -1 back, we can simply return the return value from SendMessage. However, as we saw in the SetTVBackgroundColor call, a -1 return value signifies that the tree view control is using the default background color as its color. Therefore, we have to find out what that color is, which is what the GetSysColor API call does rather nicely for us.

The VB Implementation (or Lack Thereof)

Just like the title says, there's no way in VB that we can do what we have just done with the API calls to change the background color. We're stuck, stymied, hung out to dry, finished, etc., etc. This example clearly illustrates the power that the APIs can have over VB.

It is Microsoft's choice to decide what they do and do not expose to you in any of their controls through properties and methods. Therefore you need to know how to tap into Windows and harness the power of the API. This gives you much more freedom of choice in your programming.

Now that we know how to change the background color of our tree view control at will, let's move on to changing the node's appearances.

Changing an Item's Appearance

In this section, we are going to find out how to bold each first-level node in our file information tree view control to make them stand out from the other nodes. To do this, we need to reference (or get a handle for) the node from the tree view control that we want to change. We can do this by making the following call to `SendMessage`:

```
lngItemHandle = SendMessage(TreeView1.hwnd, _
                TVM_GETNEXTITEM, TVGN_CARET, 0&)
```

The `TreeView1` name is purely arbitrary – I'm only using it to illustrate that the first argument for `SendMessage` must be the tree view's `hwnd` value. Remember that the `TVM_GETNEXTITEM` message says that we're going to get a specific item in the control. By using the `TVGN_CARET` value, we're telling the OS to get the handle to the currently selected node. As we saw in the `TVItemMove` enumeration, we could use a bunch of other values to move around in the tree, but we'll use `TVGN_CARET` for our purposes because we want to change the bold attribute of the item that is currently selected.

If `lngItemHandle` equals a nonzero value after `SendMessage` returns, we have a handle to the selected item in the tree view control. Well, we actually don't have a handle in the window handle in that sense; it only defines the item with a window handle within the tree view control (or window) and isn't valid elsewhere. Therefore, whenever we want to do something to this item, we still have to pass in the control's `hwnd` value to `SendMessage`, but we also have to use a UDT to define the item's state. This is what that UDT looks like:

```
Public Type TVITEM
    mask As Long
    hItem As Long
    state As Long
    stateMask As Long
    pszText As String
    cchTextMax As Long
    iImage As Long
    iSelectedImage As Long
    cChildren As Long
    lParam As Long
End Type
```

We actually won't be using all of the parameters defined in TVITEM for our purposes. Some of them hint at what they can be used for (like pszText - do you think it's used to set or retrieve the item's text?), but we'll be using the first four for our purposes.

The first one, mask, lets us define what kind of information is valid in the structure when we want to retrieve information about a tree view item. The following table lists the valid values for this parameter and what other parameters they validate:

Mask Names	Valid Paramater(s)
TVIF_CHILDREN	CChildren
TVIF_HANDLE	HItem
TVIF_IMAGE	IImage
TVIF_PARAM	LParam
TVIF_SELECTEDIMAGE	ISelectedImage
TVIF_STATE	state and stateMask
TVIF_TEXT	pszText and cchTextMax

For example, if we set mask equal to TVIF_HANDLE, then the value in hItem would correspond to the item's handle.

We use hItem as a handle to set which node we're interested in. (Note: The value we got from the SendMessage code snippet given above is the identifier to this item.) The state parameter is a set of bit values that indicate what state the item is in. This parameter is tied rather tightly to the stateMask parameter, which indicates which states in the state parameter are valid.

Is Windows ever easy? If that last paragraph made any sense to you, you really deserve some kind of reward, and that's not meant to be sarcastic. The documentation on the tree view control does clear it up a bit if you look it up, but I don't blame you if you're stumped right now. Let's look at the code to set the bold state on a tree view item to try and clear things up.

Bolding the Top-Level Nodes

Recall that we created a function called SetTVSelectedItemBold, and placed it in frmFileInfo without any code. Well, now we need to make this function actually do what it "says" it will do, which is to bold or unbold the currently selected item in the tree view control. To keep everything together, move this function to the TreeViewLib module.

Before we code up this function, you should also include the UDT that we were just talking about:

```
Public Type TVITEM
    mask As Long
    hItem As Long
    state As Long
    stateMask As Long
    pszText As String
    cchTextMax As Long
    iImage As Long
```

```
        iSelectedImage As Long
        cChildren As Long
        lParam As Long
    End Type
```

Now you can type the following code into the `SetTVSelectedItemBold` function and we'll go through it afterwards.

```
Public Function SetTVSelectedItemBold(TreeViewControl As TreeView, _
    ChangeToBold As Boolean) As Long

    On Error GoTo error_SetTVSelectedItemBold

    Dim lngItemHandle As Long
    Dim lngRet As Long
    Dim udtItem As TVITEM

    SetTVSelectedItemBold = 1

    With TreeViewControl
        lngItemHandle = SendMessage(.hwnd, TVM_GETNEXTITEM, _
                                TVGN_CARET, 0&)

        If lngItemHandle = 0 Then
            SetTVSelectedItemBold = 0
        Else
            udtItem.hItem = lngItemHandle
            udtItem.mask = TVIF_STATE
            udtItem.stateMask = TVIS_BOLD
            lngRet = SendMessage(.hwnd, TVM_GETITEM, 0, _
                                udtItem)

            If ChangeToBold = True Then
                ' Now check to make sure it isn't bold yet.

                If udtItem.state And TVIS_BOLD > 0 Then
                    ' Change the state.
                    udtItem.state = TVIS_BOLD
                    lngRet = SendMessage(.hwnd, TVM_SETITEM, 0, _
                                        udtItem)
                End If

            Else
                ' Now check to make sure it isn't bold yet.

                If udtItem.state And TVIS_BOLD > 0 Then
                    ' Change the state.
                    udtItem.state = udtItem.state Xor TVIS_BOLD
                    lngRet = SendMessage(.hwnd, TVM_SETITEM, 0, _
                                        udtItem)
                End If

            End If

        End If

    End With
```

```
   Exit Function

error_SetTVSelectedItemBold:

  SetTVSelectedItemBold = 0

End Function
```

How it Works: SetTVSelectedItemBold

The first thing we try to do is get the item handle from the tree view control using the `SendMessage` call. If we get a non-zero value back, then we can start to manipulate that item:

```
lngItemHandle = SendMessage(.hwnd, TVM_GETNEXTITEM, _
                            TVGN_CARET, 0&)
If lngItemHandle = 0 Then
    SetTVSelectedItemBold = 0
Else
    udtItem.hItem = lngItemHandle
    udtItem.mask = TVIF_STATE
    udtItem.stateMask = TVIS_BOLD
```

We set the `hItem` value equal to the return value from `SendMessage` along with setting the `mask` parameter equal to `TVIF_STATE`, which makes the `state` and `stateMask` parameters valid. Since we want to find out whether or not the item is in a bold state, we set the `stateMask` parameter equal to `TVIS_BOLD`. As none of the other parameters are valid due to our setting of `mask` equal to `TVIF_STATE`, we'll leave those parameters be.

Now that we have the UDT defined correctly, we'll see what state the item is in. We use the `SendMessage` command along with the `TVM_GETITEM` value to get information about an item, but note that we pass in the `hwnd` value of the control into the first argument, and `udtItem` as the last argument. Note also that here we want the UDT to be passed in by reference.

```
lngRet = SendMessage(.hwnd, TVM_GETITEM, 0, _
                     udtItem)
```

Again, the item's `hItem` is not a window handle; it is simply an identifying value for the tree view item, so we can't expect `SendMessage` to be able to do anything with `hItem`. Therefore, we have to pass in the entire UDT in the last value.

Finally, we check the value of `state` to see if the item is bolded or not. If we want it bolded and it isn't, we set the value of `state` appropriately to bold it. If we want it unbolded, we have to use the `Xor` function to turn off the bolded bit.

```
If ChangeToBold = True Then
    If udtItem.state And TVIS_BOLD > 0 Then
        udtItem.state = TVIS_BOLD
        lngRet = SendMessage(.hwnd, TVM_SETITEM, 0, _
                             udtItem)
    End If
Else
    If udtItem.state And TVIS_BOLD > 0 Then
        udtItem.state = udtItem.state Xor TVIS_BOLD
        lngRet = SendMessage(.hwnd, TVM_SETITEM, 0, _
                             udtItem)
```

```
        End If
    End If
```

Then we pass in the modified `udtItem` into `SendMessage` using the `TVM_SETITEM`.

If you now look at the code for `AddFileSize`, we always call `SetTVSelectedItemBold` for the top-level nodes in our tree view control. Here's a picture of the tree view with each of the parent nodes bolded:

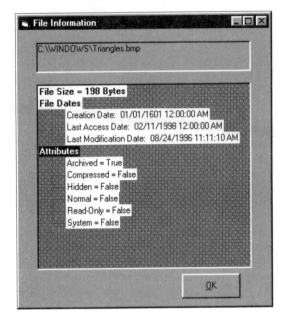

It now makes the parent nodes stand out from the child nodes.

As you'll find out when you start to investigate the innards of the controls that VB gives, it's not a pretty world. However, because VB doesn't always expose all of the functionality available in the controls, you sometimes have to go to this level to see if you can pull off some of the things that users ask for. There's a lot more to the tree view control than what we have just gone over, if you want to know more, you'll have to spend some time hunting around some of the resources I mentioned earlier.

Bolding Nodes Using VB Only

Well, we've seen how to bold nodes using API, but can we mirror this technique using VB?

Well, pre VB6, we could not. However, in VB6, a `Bold` property was added to the `Node` object. This effectively means that you can actually bold nodes using code as simple as this:

```
TreeView1.Nodes(2).Bold = True
```

So, you may be wondering why we went through this whole exercise to achieve something that can be done with one line of code! I did this for two reasons. The first one is to show you how we can achieve functionality in a control through API calls.

The second, and in my opinion, more important reason is to demonstrate the ever-changing world of VB. You know that a certain control can perform a certain action, but for some reason, VB doesn't have any mechanism available that exposes this functionality. Therefore, you dig through web sites and SDKs before you finally figure out how to do it through API calls. However, future versions of VB may extend the control in question to provide you with the desired functionality through a property or method. Unfortunately, that's just the way things are in VB. If you want to do certain things in VB before the VB Developers have got round to coding in the mechanism, then the only way to do it is to use API calls.

I wouldn't consider such exercises a waste of time and effort, though. You gain a lot of knowledge about the inner workings of the control, and in doing so, you might find other behaviors that the control can achieve which the current of VB still doesn't support. Knowing what window messages are needed to affect a control is powerful knowledge to have.

Altering the Menus

We'll end this chapter on the topic of menus. By now, you've probably included menus in your applications (whether you wanted to or not), so you've become well acquainted with VB Menu Editor. For those who have not had the honor to see what it looks like, look under Tools | Menu Editor... to see the following window:

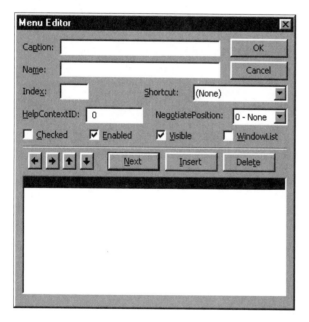

Some people have complained about it, simply because it hasn't changed since its inception. Personally, I've used it without a hitch in all of the applications I've used, and most of the API calls I've seen that deal with menus are exposed here. However, just like the tree view control, it's purposely limited in terms of what you can do. For example, if you look at the File menu in VB, you'll see images next to some of the submenu options. Here's a partial screen shot of the Visual Basic File menu:

For example, the <u>O</u>pen Project... menu option has an opening folder image next to the words. Since we know we can't add this in VB, we're off to the API world to do this.

Adding a Bitmap Image

Next, we take a look at the API calls needed to change a menu, we need to add an image to our form. Add a picture box to `frmMain` that contains the `Info16.bmp` image. This image is available from the Wrox website along with the source code for this book. Alternatively, you can create a bitmap using the Paint program that comes with Windows. Just make sure it's not bigger than 13 by 13 pixels, and don't use more than 256 colors.

Name the picture box `picInfo`, since we'll be adding this image to the <u>F</u>ile Information... menu option. Also, make sure that it's `Visible` property is set to `False`, since we don't want this image showing up anywhere on the form.

Now, let's take a look at the API declarations we'll need to add this image to the menu (which you should add in a separate module called `MenuLib.bas`):

```
Declare Function GetMenu Lib "user32" _
    (ByVal hwnd As Long) As Long
```

```
Declare Function GetMenuItemID Lib "user32" _
    (ByVal hMenu As Long, ByVal nPos As Long) As Long
```

```
Declare Function GetSubMenu Lib "user32" _
    (ByVal hMenu As Long, ByVal nPos As Long) As Long
```

```
Declare Function SetMenuItemBitmaps Lib "user32" _
    (ByVal hMenu As Long, ByVal nPosition As Long, _
     ByVal wFlags As Long, ByVal hBitmapUnchecked As Long, _
     ByVal hBitmapChecked As Long) As Long
```

GetMenu

This function takes only one argument, `hwnd`, which specifies which window you want to work with. If the window has menus, you'll get a nonzero value back (the handle to the menu); otherwise, you'll get a zero if no menus exist.

GetMenuItemID

This function returns the menu identifier of the menu specified by `nPos`. If `nPos` is set to zero, you'll get the first menu option available. The `hMenu` argument specifies which menu you want to take a look at. As with `GetMenu`, you'll get a non-zero value back if a menu exists where you think it does. Note that if the return values equals `&HFFFFFFFF`, the menu item is actually opens up a submenu.

GetSubMenu

This one is pretty descriptive, and it's very similar to `GetMenuItemID`. You get a menu handle back for a menu option located within a menu. You set `hMenu` to the menu you want to search in, and `nPos` to set which submenu you want get a handle on. If the value is non-zero, you've got a handle.

The difference between this function and `GetMenuItemID` is that you use the `GetSubMenu` function to get menu handles that have submenus; `GetMenuItemID` simply returns menu handles for menu options that exist within the defined menu. We'll see the difference in a moment.

SetMenuItemBitmaps

You use this function to add a bitmap image to a menu. The image can't be too big; otherwise the OS won't add the image to your menu (see the `GetMenuCheckMarkDimensions` or `GetSystemMetrics` calls if you want to add some size checking to your code).

If you know that the bitmap image is smaller than 13 by 13, then you're fine. The first parameter specifies which menu you're going after. The second, `nPosition`, defines which menu option will get the bitmap. The third, `wFlags`, is usually used to determine how `nPosition` defines the menu to change, but we'll use it in a slightly different fashion. The last two arguments allow us to set the enabled and disabled bitmaps in one call. Then, whenever the enabled state of the menu item changes, the image will correspondingly change.

Implementing the API Calls to Display a Bitmap

We have the bitmap loaded in our picture box, so now we have to add it to the appropriate menu item. Before we continue, add the following constant to the `MenuLib` module:

```
Public Const MF_BITMAP = &H4&
```

Here's the `AddPictureToFileInfo` method that will add the image to `mnuFileInformation`. You need to define this function in `frmMain`.

```
Private Sub AddPictureToFileInfo()

    On Error Resume Next

    Dim lngMenu As Long
    Dim lngMenuItemID As Long
    Dim lngRet As Long
    Dim lngSubMenu As Long
```

```
        lngMenu = GetMenu(Me.hwnd)

        lngSubMenu = GetSubMenu(lngMenu, 0)

        lngMenuItemID = GetMenuItemID(lngSubMenu, 1)

        lngRet = SetMenuItemBitmaps(lngMenu, lngMenuItemID, _
                            MF_BITMAP, picInfo.Picture, _
                            picInfo.Picture)

    End Sub
```

Let's take a look at how this method works:

The first thing we do is get the menu handle for the entire form:

```
    lngMenu = GetMenu(Me.hwnd)
```

After that's done, we get a menu handle to the first submenu (Options) in frmMain (encryption program):

```
    lngSubMenu = GetSubMenu(lngMenu, 0)
```

Depending on your background, you may be used to saying that element one is located at the zero position in a set. If you're not, be aware that most API calls expect that you count in this manner.

Anyway, after we get this menu handle, we have to get the identifier for the File Information... item, which is done using the GetMenuItemID call:

```
    lngMenuItemID = GetMenuItemID(lngSubMenu, 1)
```

Finally, we use SetMenuItemBitmaps to set the funny-looking "I" letter next to the menu item:

```
    lngRet = SetMenuItemBitmaps(lngMenu, lngMenuItemID, _
                        MF_BITMAP, picInfo.Picture, _
                        picInfo.Picture)
```

This is much easier than the tree view control, right? But there's something that may have caught your eye. Notice that in the last two arguments of SetMenuItemBitmap, we're passing in the value of the Picture property, and not the hwnd value, for the picture control. This may appear to be somewhat odd. Why would we do this when the documentation clearly asks for a handle?

Well, the Picture property contains the handle to the image currently loaded in the control. Getting the handle for the control itself doesn't do us any good, so that's why we use the Picture property value.

Now if you add a call to this method in the Load event of the frmMain like this:

```
Private Sub Form_Load()

    CheckKeyAndSeed
    AddPictureToFileInfo

End Sub
```

you'll see the "I" next to the menu item just like this screen shot shows:

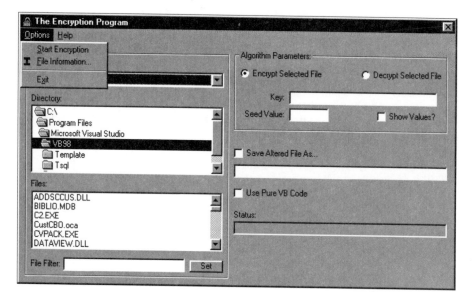

No VB Implementation (Again...)

We're not doing very well in this chapter for VB code, are we? The menu items do not have a property or method that we could use to add images. This could change in the future, but, again, VB is lacking in the implementation department. Furthermore, I wouldn't hold my breath for the VB designers to change the menu editor in VB any time soon. The way it looks in the 6.0 version looks identical to the one I saw in version 4.0.

Summary

In this chapter, we saw where we could extend controls and menus using the API. We added color to our tree view control and images to our menu items, and generally discovered how an understanding of API calls can allow you much greater flexibility in your programming.

You should now know how to:

Use the `MessageBox` API call as an alternative to the VB `MsgBox` command.

- ❏ Alter the appearance and functionality of a standard Tree View control using various API calls
- ❏ Manipulate controls using the `SendMessage` API call
- ❏ Add images to menus in your apps using API calls

We also saw that we could not reproduce most of this functionality using pure VB code, which further strengthened the argument to learn as much about the Windows environment as possible. In the next chapter, we'll start to add some much-needed character to our application using calls from `gdi32.dll`.

5

Gdi32 Calls

Now that we're getting pretty comfortable using API calls, it's time to have some fun and investigate the graphical aspect of Windows using calls from `gdi32.dll`. Windows is all about presenting the user with a graphical user interface and so you would expect Windows to have a great many tricks up its sleeve in this regard. In this chapter we're going expose some of these tricks so that we might use them in our own apps.

More specifically we'll cover:

❑ Creating gradients in Windows
❑ Tiling images across a form
❑ Rotating Text
❑ Creating differently shaped windows

We'll implement all these functions in our Encryption program and we'll also compare the performance of these functions with API calls and straight VB.

Gdi32 Overview

The third Win32 DLL we're going to look at is `gdi32.dll`. This DLL is primarily responsible for, but not limited to, graphical manipulations. If you want to change text in terms of its size and/or position, look here. If you want to alter the look of your windows, this is the place to start. Really, anything that you could think of that you'd want to do visually in Windows is found in this DLL. Let's spend some time going over just how Windows actually displays the information we want to the screen.

The POINT and RECT UDTs

If you remember from your geometry classes (sorry if this will bring up horrific memories of proofs that never made sense), we can always define where a point exists on a 2D plane using a simple coordinate system. For example, this is what the Cartesian coordinate system looks like:

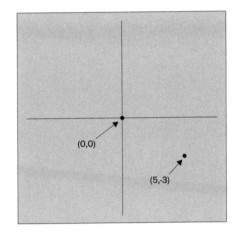

As the picture shows, the point is located at the coordinates (5, -3) in the system. Note that by convention we always give the x coordinate first.

However, in the Windows world, things are a bit different. A coordinate system is used that is very similar to the Cartesian system, but in practice only one plane is usually in use. Here's a layout of what this looks like:

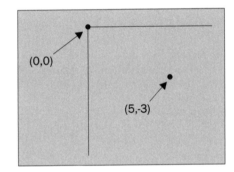

Whenever you put a control on a form in VB, the tool is handling the placement of the control for you. However, if you want to move controls around (for example, when a form is resized) you can use the `Move` method to reposition the control. Recall the arguments for the `Move` method:

```
Move Left, [Top], [Width], [Height]
```

where the last three parameters are optional. However, the argument values to `Move` are relative to the upper-left hand corner of the window. For example, if you had a button named `Command1` on a form named `Form1` like this:

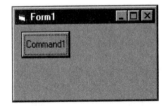

and you wanted to move it 450 units to the right of where it currently is whenever you press the button, you would add the following line code in its `Click` event:

```
Command1.Move Command1.Left + 450
```

After two button clicks, this is where the button is:

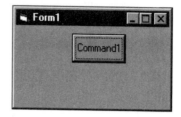

As you can see, the button moved to the right. This is because we told VB to move it 900 units to the right from where it originated.

In the API world, two UDTs are used to define points and rectangular regions like buttons. They're called RECT and POINTAPI (the API is added on to resolve a conflict with the Point keyword in VB):

```
Type RECT
    Left As Long
    Top As Long
    Right As Long
    Bottom As Long
End Type

Type POINTAPI
    x As Long
    y As Long
End Type
```

As you can see, they're pretty self-explanatory. We could define a rectangle that's 200 units long in the x direction and 400 units long in the y direction located 15 units from the top and 25 units from the left of a window in the following manner:

```
Dim udtRect As RECT

With udtRect
    .Top = 15
    .Left = 25
    .Bottom = 415
    .Right = 225
End With
```

In our first example in using calls from the gdi32.dll, we'll use the RECT UDT a lot. However, before we start running blindly down that path, we need to go over another concept: the **device context**.

The Device Context

Whenever you need to draw something in Windows, whether it's a picture on the screen or to the printer, you need to define attributes of that picture. For example, you may set the color of the text in a picture box equal to red. However, the printer that you're using to print the picture box may not be a color printer. Therefore, what Windows does is set up a **device context** (or DC) that allows you to define these attributes independent of the hardware that will eventually render your commands. Therefore, even if you specify red text to a black and white printer, the OS will handle the discrepancy for you.

Every form in VB and some of its controls (like the picture box) already have a hDC property that we can use to manipulate its graphical appearance. Furthermore, there are API calls that allow you to create your own DCs. However, care must be taken when using the two within VB.

> DCs used through a form or control property must never be destroyed using the DeleteDC API call, as these DCs are allocated through a pool that Windows maintains. If you create your own DC, though, you must delete it using DeleteDC to prevent memory leaks from occurring.

As is the theme in this book, we'll use two examples in our encryption project to illustrate the UDTs and how one should use a DC properly.

Adding a Gradient to the Main Form

If you've ever used the Package and Deployment Wizard that comes with VB to ship your applications, you'll notice that the background color has a nice color transition from blue to black. This is typically called a gradient, and it's much nicer to look at than the usual gray color we're used to seeing. In this section, we'll add a gradient to our main form using both an API and VB implementation.

API Implementation

First of all, we need to understand the calls that we'll use to pull something like this off. Here are the four calls necessary to add a gradient to our form:

CreateSolidBrush

```
Declare Function CreateSolidBrush Lib "gdi32" _
    (ByVal crColor As Long) As Long
```

First off, what is a brush in Windows? It's an object that defines how an area should be painted, or filled. You can use solid brushes (like this API call does) or hatched brushes (these can be created using the CreateHatchBrush call). If you want to define your own filling pattern, you can use CreatePatternBrush that takes a handle to a bitmap image to fill a defined area.

Anyway, we're only concerned with boring (i.e. one color) brushes for the gradient example. To define the color of the brush we want, we pass in a RGB color value to crColor. If we get a zero return value, an error occurred; otherwise, we get a handle to the brush (note that we do not get a DC back - this is important to know for the next call).

DeleteObject

```
Declare Function DeleteObject Lib "gdi32" _
    (ByVal hObject As Long) As Long
```

Once we're done using a GDI object like a brush, we need to destroy any memory allocated to create it. DeleteObject does just that. We simply set hObject equal to the GDI object handle. If we get a nonzero value back, we successfully deleted the object.

FillRect

```
Declare Function FillRect Lib "user32" (ByVal hdc As Long, _
    lpRect As RECT, ByVal hBrush As Long) As Long
```

The function name says it all - it's used to fill a rectangular region. The area that we want to fill is defined by `lpRect`, which is a `RECT` UDT. The `hBrush` parameter takes a handle to a brush to define how the region should be filled. Finally, the first parameter, `hdc`, defines in what DC this operation should take place. As usual, a nonzero return value signifies success.

GetDeviceCaps

```
Declare Function GetDeviceCaps Lib "gdi32" _
    (ByVal hdc As Long, ByVal nIndex As Long) As Long
```

This function is used to retrieve information about the given DC. The `nIndex` argument is used to tell the OS exactly what you're looking for. As with some of the API calls we've seen, we won't go over all of the values, but we will use two constants to retrieve color information about the computer.

The CreateGradient Function

Now that we have all of the API functions defined, let's discuss the `CreateGradient` function. Before we do that, make sure that you add the four API calls given above to the encryption project. Any module will do, but to keep things separate, let's add them to a module called `GradientLib` with `Public` scope. Also, add the `POINT_API` and `RECT` structures as well (again, with `Public` scope). We're also going to need a variation of the `RECT` UDT called `RECT_DOUBLE` defined as follows:

```
Public Type RECT_DOUBLE
    Left As Double
    Top As Double
    Right As Double
    Bottom As Double
End Type
```

This is needed to handle some precision problems with the gradient - you'll see what I mean in a moment. Finally, add the following constants:

```
Public Const BITSPIXEL = 12
Public Const PLANES = 14
Public Const RED_BITS As Long = 255
Public Const GREEN_BITS As Long = 65280
Public Const BLUE_BITS As Long = 16711680
Public Const BLUE_COLOR As Long = &H10000
Public Const GREEN_COLOR As Long = &H100
Public Const SRCCOPY = &HCC0020
```

We'll use all of these constants eventually. Now let's take a look at the `CreateGradient` function, which should be added to the `GradientLib` module. I know it's long, but we'll go over it in detail:

```
Public Function CreateGradient(RefForm As Form, Direction As Long, _
    StartingColor As Long, EndingColor As Long) As Boolean

On Error GoTo error_CreateGradient

Dim dblCurrentRed As Double
Dim dblCurrentBlue As Double
Dim dblCurrentGreen As Double
Dim dblBlueInc As Double
Dim dblGreenInc As Double
Dim dblRedInc As Double
Dim dblX As Double
Dim dblY As Double
Dim lngBitsPerPixel As Long
Dim lngBrushHandle As Long
Dim lngColorBits As Long
Dim lngColorDiff As Long
Dim lngCurrentRed As Long
Dim lngCurrentBlue As Long
Dim lngCurrentGreen As Long
Dim lngCurrentScale As Long
Dim lngEndColor As Long
Dim lngFormHeight As Long
Dim lngFormWidth As Long
Dim lngPlanes As Long
Dim lngRegionCount As Long
Dim lngRet As Long
Dim lngStartColor As Long
Dim lngC As Long
Dim udtAreaLng As RECT
Dim udtAreaDbl As RECT_DOUBLE

If Not RefForm Is Nothing Then

    lngStartColor = EndingColor
    lngEndColor = StartingColor

    lngBitsPerPixel = GetDeviceCaps(RefForm.hDC, BITSPIXEL)
    lngPlanes = GetDeviceCaps(RefForm.hDC, PLANES)
    lngColorBits = (lngBitsPerPixel * lngPlanes)
    If lngColorBits > 15 Then
        lngRegionCount = 256
    Else
        lngRegionCount = 32
    End If

    With RefForm

        lngCurrentScale = .ScaleMode
        .ScaleMode = vbPixels
        lngFormHeight = .ScaleHeight
        lngFormWidth = .ScaleWidth
        .ScaleMode = lngCurrentScale

    End With

    dblRedInc = CDbl((-1 * ((lngEndColor And RED_BITS) - _
        (lngStartColor And RED_BITS))) / lngRegionCount)
    dblGreenInc = CDbl((-1 * (((lngEndColor And _
        GREEN_BITS) / RED_BITS) - ((lngStartColor And GREEN_BITS) / _
```

```
        RED_BITS))) / lngRegionCount
    dblBlueInc = CDbl((-1 * (((lngEndColor And BLUE_BITS) / _
        GREEN_BITS) - ((lngStartColor And BLUE_BITS) / _
        GREEN_BITS))) / lngRegionCount)

    dblCurrentRed = lngEndColor And RED_BITS
    lngCurrentRed = IIf(dblCurrentRed > 255, 255, _
        IIf(dblCurrentRed < 0, 0, CLng(dblCurrentRed)))
    dblCurrentGreen = (lngEndColor And GREEN_BITS) / RED_BITS
    lngCurrentGreen = IIf(dblCurrentGreen > 255, 255, _
        IIf(dblCurrentGreen < 0, 0, CLng(dblCurrentGreen)))
    dblCurrentBlue = (lngEndColor And BLUE_BITS) / GREEN_BITS
    lngCurrentBlue = IIf(dblCurrentBlue > 255, 255, _
        IIf(dblCurrentBlue < 0, 0, CLng(dblCurrentBlue)))

    dblX = lngFormWidth / lngRegionCount
    dblY = lngFormHeight / lngRegionCount

    udtAreaLng.Left = 0
    udtAreaDbl.Left = 0
    udtAreaLng.Top = 0
    udtAreaDbl.Top = 0
    udtAreaLng.Right = lngFormWidth
    udtAreaDbl.Right = lngFormWidth
    udtAreaLng.Bottom = lngFormHeight
    udtAreaDbl.Bottom = lngFormHeight

    For lngC = 0 To (lngRegionCount - 1)
        lngBrushHandle = CreateSolidBrush(RGB _
            (lngCurrentRed, lngCurrentGreen, lngCurrentBlue))
        If Direction = 0 Then

            '   Diagonal.
            udtAreaDbl.Top = udtAreaDbl.Bottom - dblY
            udtAreaLng.Top = CLng(udtAreaDbl.Top)
            udtAreaDbl.Left = 0
            udtAreaLng.Left = 0
            lngRet = FillRect(RefForm.hDC, udtAreaLng, _
                lngBrushHandle)
            udtAreaDbl.Top = 0
            udtAreaLng.Top = 0
            udtAreaDbl.Left = udtAreaDbl.Right - dblX
            udtAreaLng.Left = CLng(udtAreaDbl.Left)
            lngRet = FillRect(RefForm.hDC, udtAreaLng, _
                lngBrushHandle)
            udtAreaDbl.Bottom = udtAreaDbl.Bottom - dblY
            udtAreaLng.Bottom = CLng(udtAreaDbl.Bottom)
            udtAreaDbl.Right = udtAreaDbl.Right - dblX
            udtAreaLng.Right = CLng(udtAreaDbl.Right)

        ElseIf Direction = 1 Then

            '   Vertical.
            udtAreaDbl.Top = udtAreaDbl.Bottom - dblY
            udtAreaLng.Top = CLng(udtAreaDbl.Top)
            lngRet = FillRect(RefForm.hDC, udtAreaLng, _
                lngBrushHandle)
            udtAreaDbl.Bottom = udtAreaDbl.Bottom - dblY
            udtAreaLng.Bottom = CLng(udtAreaDbl.Bottom)
```

```vb
    ElseIf Direction = 2 Then

            ' Horizontal
            udtAreaDbl.Left = udtAreaDbl.Right - dblX
            udtAreaLng.Left = CLng(udtAreaDbl.Left)
            lngRet = FillRect(RefForm.hDC, udtAreaLng, _
                lngBrushHandle)
            udtAreaDbl.Right = udtAreaDbl.Right - dblX
            udtAreaLng.Right = CLng(udtAreaDbl.Right)

        Else

        End If

        lngRet = DeleteObject(lngBrushHandle)

        dblCurrentRed = dblCurrentRed + dblRedInc
        lngCurrentRed = IIf(dblCurrentRed > 255, 255, _
            IIf(dblCurrentRed < 0, 0, CLng(dblCurrentRed)))
        dblCurrentGreen = dblCurrentGreen + dblGreenInc
        lngCurrentGreen = IIf(dblCurrentGreen > 255, 255, _
            IIf(dblCurrentGreen < 0, 0, CLng(dblCurrentGreen)))
        dblCurrentBlue = dblCurrentBlue + dblBlueInc
        lngCurrentBlue = IIf(dblCurrentBlue > 255, 255, _
            IIf(dblCurrentBlue < 0, 0, CLng(dblCurrentBlue)))

    Next lngC

    udtAreaLng.Top = 0
    udtAreaLng.Left = 0
    lngBrushHandle = CreateSolidBrush(RGB _
        (lngCurrentRed, lngCurrentGreen, lngCurrentBlue))
    lngRet = FillRect(RefForm.hDC, udtAreaLng, lngBrushHandle)
    lngRet = DeleteObject(lngBrushHandle)
    CreateGradient = True

Else

    CreateGradient = False

End If

Exit Function


error_CreateGradient:

  CreateGradient = False

  If Not RefForm Is Nothing Then
      RefForm.Tag = Err.Number & "  " & Err.Description
  End If

End Function
```

Again, it looks like a lot, so let's start from the top - with the arguments to `CreateGradient`. `RefForm` is the form that we want to add a gradient to. The second one, `Direction`, determines which way we want the gradient to go (0 for a diagonal, 1 for a right to left, and 2 for a bottom to top). The last two, `StartingColor` and `EndingColor`, are RGB color values that determine which colors the gradient should start and end at.

Note that we reverse the colors when we enter the function. This is done to help us visually differentiate this function from the VB one we'll write later.

```
lngStartColor = EndingColor
lngEndColor = StartingColor
```

If you use this function to create a gradient for your business applications, you might want to alter the color reversal!

Now let's start dissecting the function.

We begin by determining the number of color bits supported:

```
lngBitsPerPixel = GetDeviceCaps(RefForm.hDC, BITSPIXEL)
lngPlanes = GetDeviceCaps(RefForm.hDC, PLANES)
lngColorBits = (lngBitsPerPixel * lngPlanes)
```

If the value of `lngColorBits` is greater than 15 we tile for 256 regions. Alternatively, if `lngColorBits` is smaller than or equal to 15 the color count is low so we only tile 32 regions.

```
If lngColorBits > 15 Then
    lngRegionCount = 256
Else
    lngRegionCount = 32
End If
```

After saving the current value of the `ScaleMode` property of the form into `lngCurrentScale`, we change the `ScaleMode` property to figure out its `ScaleHeight` and `ScaleWidth` values in pixels (don't use the `Height` and `Width` properties here - they're not relative to what the `ScaleMode` is):

```
With RefForm

    lngCurrentScale = .ScaleMode
    .ScaleMode = vbPixels
    lngFormHeight = .ScaleHeight
    lngFormWidth = .ScaleWidth
    .ScaleMode = lngCurrentScale

End With
```

Depending upon your application's needs, you might set the scaling factor for your forms to be relative to the screen's dimensions, or you might want the form size to be fixed by a specific pixel value. This is what the `ScaleHeight` and `ScaleWidth` properties are used for. In our case, we need the exact dimensions of the form in pixels to add the gradient to the form. However, to leave things the way we started, we reset `ScaleMode` after we have these values.

The next thing we do is determine how much the red, green and blue values will change from the starting color to the ending color:

```
dblRedInc = CDbl((-1 * ((lngEndColor And RED_BITS) - _
    (lngStartColor And RED_BITS))) / lngRegionCount)
dblGreenInc = CDbl((-1 * (((lngEndColor And _
    GREEN_BITS) / RED_BITS) - ((lngStartColor And GREEN_BITS) / _
    RED_BITS))) / lngRegionCount)
dblBlueInc = CDbl((-1 * (((lngEndColor And BLUE_BITS) / _
    GREEN_BITS) - ((lngStartColor And BLUE_BITS) / _
    GREEN_BITS))) / lngRegionCount)
```

It looks complicated, but there are two reasons why we do this. First, we simply can't take the ending color from the starting color and figure out how much we should vary the gradient from region to region. Remember that the RGB color value is actually made up of three 8-bit values. Using hexadecimal notation, it looks like this:

&H00bbggrr

The last byte holds the red bits, the next byte holds the green bits, and the third byte holds the red bits (the most significant bit is unused in the RGB format). Therefore, we have to figure out what these values are for both the starting and ending colors, and then determine what the difference is between each part. That's what all the And operators are for. We're simply shifting and moving the bits around to get at the bits that we need for each component of the RGB format.

The second thing to note is that we're using Double data types to store these incremental values. In fact, we use Double data types everywhere in this function! If we used Long data types to hold the incremental values, we'd lose some information, and the gradient might not show up correctly. Let me illustrate this with a quick example. Say our starting red value was 128, and our ending red value was 100 (we won't use any of the other colors for this example). The function determined that we should color 256 regions, so we get:

```
dblRedInc = CDbl((-1 * ((lngEndColor And RED_BITS) - _
    (lngStartColor And RED_BITS))) / lngRegionCount)
dblRedInc = CDbl ((-1 * ((100 And 255) - (128 And 255))) / 256)
dblRedInc = CDbl ((-1 * (100 - 128)) / 256)
dblRedInc = CDbl (28/256)
dblRedInc = 0.109375
```

Now, if we would used Long data types to hold the incremental values, the result would be truncated down to 0. That's not good! The red color in the gradient would never change, and we'd be left with a form that was colored dark red. We can't afford to lose that kind of information, so that's why Double data types are used.

> The same holds true for the RECT_DOUBLE **UDT. If the form's width and/or height is less than double the region count, we may not even color the form at all. Again, the differential's fractional part would be lost with** Long **data types, so we have to use a** RECT **UDT that's defined with** Double **data types to maintain the correct position on the form. Granted, when we make a call to** FillRect**, we have to convert the** RECT_DOUBLE **UDT's values to a** RECT **UDT, so we will lose some precision in the call. However, we will maintain the correct location values with the** RECT_DOUBLE **UDT.**

In the following section of code we set up the starting values:

```
dblCurrentRed = lngEndColor And RED_BITS
lngCurrentRed = IIf(dblCurrentRed > 255, 255, _
    IIf(dblCurrentRed < 0, 0, CLng(dblCurrentRed)))
dblCurrentGreen = (lngEndColor And GREEN_BITS) / RED_BITS
lngCurrentGreen = IIf(dblCurrentGreen > 255, 255, _
    IIf(dblCurrentGreen < 0, 0, CLng(dblCurrentGreen)))
dblCurrentBlue = (lngEndColor And BLUE_BITS) / GREEN_BITS
lngCurrentBlue = IIf(dblCurrentBlue > 255, 255, _
    IIf(dblCurrentBlue < 0, 0, CLng(dblCurrentBlue)))
```

Next, we use the region count to figure out what our length (db1Y) and width (db1X) differentials are relative to lngRegionCount.

```
dblX = lngFormWidth / lngRegionCount
dblY = lngFormHeight / lngRegionCount
```

What's a region count? It's the number of rectangular regions that we will break our form up into. This value is dependent upon the number of bits per pixel and the number of planes that the display monitor has. That's why we needed the GetDeviceCaps API call - it allows us to retrieve these values. Now the color bits value is equal to the bits per pixel multiplied by the planes. Therefore, if the current monitor settings support more than 15 color bits, we'll use 256 regions. Otherwise, we'll only color 32 regions. This is an optimization of sorts, because there's no reason to color so many regions if the monitor can't support that many shades of color.

Anyway, enough with the conversion code! Let's get to the fun part. We set our udtAreaLng and udtAreaDbl size equal to the current size of the form - we'll use some values that I got during a test run:

```
udtAreaLng.Left = 0
udtAreaDbl.Left = 0
udtAreaLng.Top = 0
udtAreaDbl.Top = 0
udtAreaLng.Right = lngFormWidth
udtAreaDbl.Right = lngFormWidth
udtAreaLng.Bottom = lngFormHeight
udtAreaDbl.Bottom = lngFormHeight
```

Then, we enter a For...Next loop that creates the gradient. Let's take a look at the horizontal gradient code in detail to see just how this is done.

```
ElseIf Direction = 2 Then

    ' Horizontal
    udtAreaDbl.Left = udtAreaDbl.Right - dblX
    udtAreaLng.Left = CLng(udtAreaDbl.Left)
    lngRet = FillRect(RefForm.hDC, udtAreaLng, _
        lngBrushHandle)
    udtAreaDbl.Right = udtAreaDbl.Right - dblX
    udtAreaLng.Right = CLng(udtAreaDbl.Right)

Else
```

The first time we enter the loop, we set the `Left` parameter equal to the `Right` parameter offset by `dblX` (in my test, `dblX` was equal to 4). This, in effect, shifts the `udtAreaLng` rectangle all the way over to the right with a width of 4. The following diagram illustrates this:

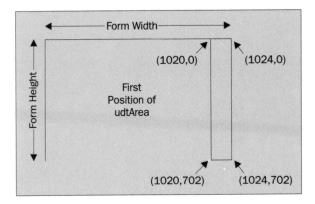

Now we fill in the rectangle with the starting color by calling `FillRect`:

```
lngRet = FillRect(RefForm.hDC, udtAreaLng, _
            lngBrushHandle)
```

After this is done, we decrement the `Right` parameter by `dblX`:

```
udtAreaDbl.Right = udtAreaDbl.Right - dblX
```

We now have a line, since our `Left` parameter is equal to the `Right` parameter - they're both now equal to the original value of the `Right` parameter minus `dblX`.

However, the second time we color the rectangle, we reset `Left` equal to `Right` minus `dblX`:

```
udtAreaDbl.Left = udtAreaDbl.Right - dblX
```

This shifts the rectangle over from where it previously was by 4 pixels, as is shown in the following diagram:

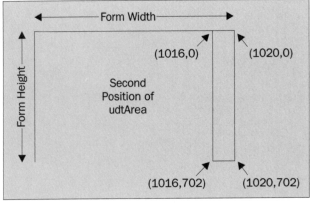

When `FillRect` is called this time, the color value has changed slightly due to following lines of code in the loop:

```
dblCurrentRed = dblCurrentRed + dblRedInc
lngCurrentRed = IIf(dblCurrentRed > 255, 255, _
    IIf(dblCurrentRed < 0, 0, CLng(dblCurrentRed)))
dblCurrentGreen = dblCurrentGreen + dblGreenInc
lngCurrentGreen = IIf(dblCurrentGreen > 255, 255, _
    IIf(dblCurrentGreen < 0, 0, CLng(dblCurrentGreen)))
dblCurrentBlue = dblCurrentBlue + dblBlueInc
lngCurrentBlue = IIf(dblCurrentBlue > 255, 255, _
    IIf(dblCurrentBlue < 0, 0, CLng(dblCurrentBlue)))
```

We keep on shifting the rectangle and changing the color until the entire form has been touched. Just in case we missed any part of the form due to round-off errors, we do one more `FillRect` call at the end:

```
udtAreaLng.Top = 0
udtAreaLng.Left = 0
lngBrushHandle = CreateSolidBrush(RGB _
(lngCurrentRed, lngCurrentGreen, lngCurrentBlue))
lngRet = FillRect(RefForm.hDC, udtAreaLng, lngBrushHandle)
lngRet = DeleteObject(lngBrushHandle)
CreateGradient = True
```

Adding the Gradient to the Main Form

Again, I had to make some modifications so we could add a gradient to our main form. Here's what the form looks like now:

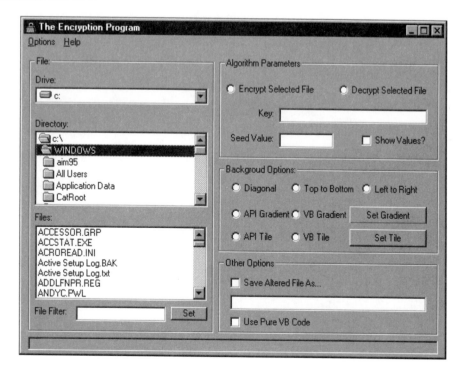

To make sure we're on the same page, here's a list of all the new control names:

Object	Contained In	Property	Value
Frame	frmMain	Name	fraMain
		Index	3
		Caption	Background Options:
Frame	fraMain(3)	Name	fraMain
		Index	6
		Caption	(leave blank)
		BorderStyle	0 - None
Option Button	fraMain(6)	Name	optStyle
		Index	0
		Caption	Diagonal
Option Button	fraMain(6)	Name	optStyle
		Index	1
		Caption	Top to Bottom
Option Button	fraMain(6)	Name	optStyle
		Index	2
		Caption	Left to Right
Frame	fraMain(3)	Name	fraMain
		Index	4
		Caption	(leave blank)
		BorderStyle	0 - None
Option Button	fraMain(4)	Name	optGradient
		Index	0
		Caption	API Gradient
Option Button	fraMain(4)	Name	optGradient
		Index	1
		Caption	VB Gradient
Command Button	fraMain(4)	Name	cmdSetGradient
		Caption	Set Gradient
Frame	fraMain(3)	Name	fraMain

Object	Contained In	Property	Value
		Index	5
		Caption	(leave blank)
		BorderStyle	0 - None
Option Button	`fraMain(5)`	Name	`optTile`
		Index	0
		Caption	API Tile
Option Button	`fraMain(5)`	Name	`optTile`
		Index	1
		Caption	API Tile
Command Button	`fraMain(5)`	Name	`cmdSetTile`
		Caption	Set Tile

We've used a little trick here with the seven option buttons in the **Background Options:** frame. Each set of option buttons is contained within another frame that has its `BorderStyle` equal to zero (or **None**). This allows a group of option buttons to work within a container; if we didn't do this, we'd only be able to select one out of the seven. Also, notice that we've added the form's maximize button to the form, which is done by setting the form's `BorderStyle` property equal to **2 - Sizeable**. This is to let us see the gradient in all of its glory, since the frames will take up most of the initial real estate.

Place the following code in the `Click` event of `cmdSetGradient`.

```
Private Sub cmdSetGradient_Click()

    SetGradient

End Sub
```

Here's what `SetGradient` itself looks like (you should also place this code in the `frmMain`):

```
Private Sub SetGradient()

  On Error GoTo error_SetGradient

  Dim blnRet As Boolean
  Dim lngGradient As Long

  Screen.MousePointer = vbHourglass

  If optStyle(0).Value = True Then
      lngGradient = 0
  ElseIf optStyle(1).Value = True Then
      lngGradient = 1
  Else
```

```
        lngGradient = 2
    End If

    If optGradient(0).Value = True Then
        blnRet = CreateGradient(Me, lngGradient, _
            RGB(0, 0, 0), RGB(0, 0, 255))
    Else
        '  VB Code
    End If

    Screen.MousePointer = vbDefault

    Exit Sub

error_SetGradient:

    Screen.MousePointer = vbDefault

End Sub
```

As you can see, we're already anticipating a VB implementation, which we'll go over in the next section. The color values are hard-coded right now, but in the next chapter we'll see an API call that we can use to allow a user to pick a color very easily.

That's it for the API implementation. Run the code, select the **API Gradient** option button and click on the **Set Gradient** button. Here's what a blue-to-black gradient looks like in dazzling black and white:

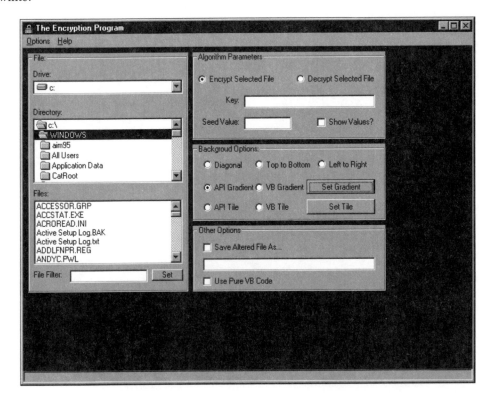

Revisiting the MessageBox Call

If you recall from Chapter 4, I said that I would address an issue with using `MsgBox` over
`MessageBox`. Well, here's the perfect time to do this. The first thing we'll do is add two calls in the
`cmdSetGradient`'s `Click` event like this:

```
Private Sub cmdSetGradient_Click()

    SetGradient
    MsgBox "Gradient is complete."
    MessageBox Me.hwnd, "Gradient is complete.", "Gradient", _
            MB_OK + MB_ICONASTERISK

End Sub
```

Also, make sure the `AutoRedraw` property is set to `False` on `frmMain`, and add a call to
`SetGradient` to the form's `Paint` event like this:

```
Private Sub Form_Paint()

    SetGradient

End Sub
```

This will add a gradient every time you resize the form, but that's the kind of behavior we want for
this example.

Now comment out the `MessageBox` call like this:

```
Private Sub cmdSetGradient_Click()

    SetGradient
    MsgBox "Gradient is complete."
'    MessageBox Me.hwnd, "Gradient is complete.", "Gradient", _
'            MB_OK + MB_ICONASTERISK

End Sub
```

Now push the **Set Gradient** button. Before you hit the **OK** button, move the message box around a
bit. Does your screen end up looking like this?

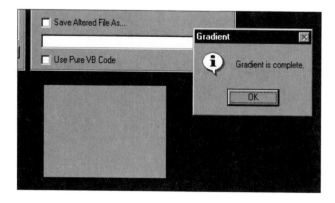

Now do the same thing as before, only this time use the `MessageBox` call by commenting out the `MsgBox` call.

```
Private Sub cmdSetGradient_Click()

    SetGradient
'   MsgBox "Gradient is complete."
    MessageBox Me.hwnd, "Gradient is complete.", "Gradient", _
            MB_OK + MB_ICONASTERISK

End Sub
```

Now when we move the message box around, we don't get any holes! The reason we got holes in the first place is that, by using the `MsgBox` command, any `Paint` messages sent to the form are queued up, waiting to be processed. Once you get rid of the message box, the events fire. By using the `MessageBox` call, the `Paint` events do not get queued up, and you don't get a bunch of ugly holes. I know, this isn't earth-shattering news, but if your applications start to get color-crazy, you'll know who to thank. (No, I don't mean me, I mean the good folks in Redmond.)

> Note that, depending upon your setup of Windows, you might actually get a "trail" instead of a "hole". If your windows always repaint whenever you move the form, then you'll get the trail effect.

VB Implementation

To create a gradient on a form using pure VB code, we're going to use the `Line` method, which has the following syntax:

```
Form.Line [Step] (x1, y1) [Step] (x2, y2), [color], [B][F]
```

The funny thing with this method is that the only required arguments are the `(x1, y1)` and `(x2, y2)` points to designate the starting and ending points of the line. If you don't set anything else (including the form name) the `Line` method assumes that the line should start at the point `(CurrentX, CurrentY)` on the form that currently has the focus (note that `CurrentX` and `CurrentY` have nothing to do with the control focus per se). The last two values, B and F, are weird ones as well. If you use B, you're telling VB that you really want to draw a box using the specified coordinates, and if you use the F character along with B (note that you can't use F without B), VB will fill the box with the color specified by the color argument. If you don't specify F with B, VB fills the box with the form's `FillColor` and sets the style of the box equal to the form's `FillStyle` property. It's an oddball, that's for sure, but you'll see in the implementation that the function is pretty straightforward once you use it for a while.

We'll begin by adding some code to our `SetGradient` procedure to call our VB implementation. Add the highlighted code to your procedure.

```
Private Sub SetGradient()

  On Error GoTo error_SetGradient

  Dim blnRet As Boolean
  Dim lngGradient As Long

  Screen.MousePointer = vbHourglass

  If optStyle(0).Value = True Then
      lngGradient = 0
  ElseIf optStyle(1).Value = True Then
      lngGradient = 1
  Else
      lngGradient = 2
  End If

  If optGradient(0).Value = True Then
      blnRet = CreateGradient(Me, lngGradient, _
          RGB(0, 0, 0), RGB(0, 0, 255))
  ElseIf optGradient(1).Value = True Then
      blnRet = VBCreateGradient(Me, lngGradient, _
          RGB(0, 0, 0), RGB(0, 0, 255))
  End If

  Screen.MousePointer = vbDefault

  Exit Sub

error_SetGradient:

  Screen.MousePointer = vbDefault

End Sub
```

Now onto the gradient function! Let's create a procedure called `VBCreateGradient`, which has the same arguments and return value that `CreateGradient` has. `RefForm` is the form to add the gradient to, `Direction` determines which way the gradient should flow (0 for diagonal, 1 for vertical and 2 for horizontal), and `StartingColor` and `EndingColor` speak for themselves. The return value is a `Boolean` which returns `True` on success and `False` on error. Here's what the code looks like (as before, please add it to the `GradientLib` module):

```
Public Function VBCreateGradient(RefForm As Form, _
    Direction As Long, StartingColor As Long, _
    EndingColor As Long) As Boolean

On Error GoTo error_VBCreateGradient

Dim dblDiff As Double
Dim dblMax As Double
Dim dblProp As Double
Dim intLoop As Integer
Dim lngColor As Long
Dim lngBlueChange As Long
Dim lngBlueEnd As Long
Dim lngBlueInc As Long
Dim lngBlueStart As Long
Dim lngGreenChange As Long
```

```
Dim lngGreenEnd As Long
Dim lngGreenInc As Long
Dim lngGreenStart As Long
Dim lngPrevScale As Long
Dim lngRedChange As Long
Dim lngRedEnd As Long
Dim lngRedInc As Long
Dim lngRedStart As Long

If Not RefForm Is Nothing Then

    With RefForm

        lngPrevScale = .ScaleMode
        .DrawStyle = vbInsideSolid
        .DrawMode = vbCopyPen
        .ScaleMode = vbPixels
        .DrawWidth = 2

        If Direction = 0 Then
            ' Figure out the diagonal length.
            dblMax = Sqr((.ScaleHeight ^ 2) + (.ScaleWidth ^ 2))
        ElseIf Direction = 1 Then
            dblMax = CDbl(.ScaleHeight)
        Else
            dblMax = CDbl(.ScaleWidth)
        End If

        lngBlueStart = Int(StartingColor / BLUE_COLOR)
        lngGreenStart = Int((StartingColor - _
           (lngBlueStart * BLUE_COLOR)) / GREEN_COLOR)
        lngRedStart = Int(StartingColor - _
           (lngBlueStart * BLUE_COLOR) - CLng(lngGreenStart * GREEN_COLOR))
        lngBlueEnd = Int(EndingColor / BLUE_COLOR)
        lngGreenEnd = Int((EndingColor - _
           (lngBlueEnd * BLUE_COLOR)) / GREEN_COLOR)
        lngRedEnd = Int(EndingColor - _
           (lngBlueEnd * BLUE_COLOR) - CLng(lngGreenEnd * GREEN_COLOR))
        lngBlueInc = lngBlueEnd - lngBlueStart
        lngRedInc = lngRedEnd - lngRedStart
        lngGreenInc = lngGreenInc - lngGreenStart

        .Enabled = False

        For intLoop = 0 To CLng(dblMax)
            dblDiff = (CDbl(intLoop) / dblMax)
            lngBlueChange = lngBlueInc * dblDiff
            lngRedChange = lngRedInc * dblDiff
            lngGreenChange = lngGreenInc * dblDiff
            lngColor = RGB(lngRedStart + lngRedChange, _
              lngGreenStart + lngGreenChange, lngBlueStart + lngBlueChange)

            If Direction = 0 Then

                ' Draw the horizontal line first.
                RefForm.Line (.ScaleWidth * dblDiff, _
                    .ScaleHeight * dblDiff)- _
                    (.Width, .ScaleHeight * dblDiff), lngColor
```

```
'  Now the vertical.
       RefForm.Line (.ScaleWidth * dblDiff, _
           .ScaleHeight * dblDiff)- _
           (.ScaleWidth * dblDiff, .Height), lngColor

    ElseIf Direction = 1 Then

        '  Top to bottom, so draw a horizontal line.
       RefForm.Line (0, intLoop)-(.Width, intLoop), lngColor

    ElseIf Direction = 2 Then

        '  Left to right, so draw a vertical line.
       RefForm.Line (intLoop, 0)-(intLoop, .Height), lngColor

    Else

    End If

  Next intLoop

  .Enabled = True
  .ScaleMode = lngPrevScale

End With

VBCreateGradient = True

Else

  VBCreateGradient = False

End If

Exit Function

error_VBCreateGradient:

VBCreateGradient = False

  If RefForm.Enabled = False Then
    RefForm.Enabled = True
  End If

End Function
```

Run the application once more, but this time, select the **VB Gradient** option button before clicking on the **Set Gradient** command button.

This time the blue-black gradient is in the opposite direction. Remember that unlike the API implementation we have not reversed our starting and ending colors.

Again, let's dissect it step by step. As we did in the API implementation, we change the `ScaleMode` to work with pixels (we restore the previous setting at the end of the function by extracting it from `lngPrevScale`):

```
.ScaleMode = vbPixels
```

We make sure that the `DrawStyle` is set to `vbInsideSolid`, which will completely fill the lines we will make:

```
.DrawStyle = vbInsideSolid
```

We also set the `DrawMode` equal to `vbCopyPen`, which will ensure that the lines are colored the way we want them to be:

```
.DrawMode = vbCopyPen
```

The `DrawWidth` is set to 2, thereby guaranteeing that all of our lines will be at least 2 pixels thick. I tried setting this to 1, but the gradient didn't look as smooth as the API version.

```
.DrawWidth = 2
```

The next thing we do is determine how many lines we'll have to draw. If we want a horizontal or vertical gradient, we simply set `dblMax` equal to `ScaleWidth` or `ScaleHeight`. However, if we're going to make a diagonal gradient, things get interesting. We figure out what the length of the diagonal is across the form, and set `dblMax` equal to that value. This may not make sense right now, but hang on - I'll explain why we do this in a moment.

```
If Direction = 0 Then
    ' Figure out the diagonal length.
    dblMax = Sqr((.ScaleHeight ^ 2) + (.ScaleWidth ^ 2))
ElseIf Direction = 1 Then
    dblMax = CDbl(.ScaleHeight)
Else
    dblMax = CDbl(.ScaleWidth)
End If
```

Next, we break the `StartingColor` and `EndingColor` values into their red, green and blue components, and figure out the difference between the two values:

```
lngBlueStart = Int(StartingColor / BLUE_COLOR)
lngGreenStart = Int((StartingColor - _
   (lngBlueStart * BLUE_COLOR)) / GREEN_COLOR)
lngRedStart = Int(StartingColor - _
   (lngBlueStart * BLUE_COLOR) - CLng(lngGreenStart * GREEN_COLOR))
lngBlueEnd = Int(EndingColor / BLUE_COLOR)
lngGreenEnd = Int((EndingColor - _
   (lngBlueEnd * BLUE_COLOR)) / GREEN_COLOR)
lngRedEnd = Int(EndingColor - _
   (lngBlueEnd * BLUE_COLOR) - CLng(lngGreenEnd * GREEN_COLOR))
lngBlueInc = lngBlueEnd - lngBlueStart
lngRedInc = lngRedEnd - lngRedStart
lngGreenInc = lngGreenInc - lngGreenStart
```

This is different from the API implementation, where we simply incremented the entire color value on each `FillRect` operation. However, when coloring the lines, I couldn't get the lines to look right using a similar technique. By breaking each primary color out of the RGB value and differentiating them separately, I was able to achieve the correct gradient. The BLUE_COLOR (65536, or 2^{16}) and GREEN_COLOR (256, or 2^8) are used to shift the bits around in the color values.

Now we get to the fun part. We enter a `For...Next` loop that is based on the maximum length of the form. We increment the color values appropriately, and create a RGB color based on these new values:

```
For intLoop = 0 To CLng(dblMax)
        dblDiff = (CDbl(intLoop) / dblMax)
        lngBlueChange = lngBlueInc * dblDiff
        lngRedChange = lngRedInc * dblDiff
        lngGreenChange = lngGreenInc * dblDiff
        lngColor = RGB(lngRedStart + lngRedChange, _
           lngGreenStart + lngGreenChange, lngBlueStart + lngBlueChange)
```

Then we have three options for the gradient. I'll go over the horizontal gradient code first, and then we'll look at the diagonal option:

```
    ElseIf Direction = 2 Then

        ' Left to right, so draw a vertical line.
        RefForm.Line (intLoop, 0)-(intLoop, .Height), lngColor

    Else
```

Let's say that the `ScaleHeight` was 400, and we're at the 200th pixel. Therefore, if we replace the variables in the `Line` method with actual values (except for the color value), here's what we'd get:

```
    RefForm.Line (200, 0)-(200, 400), lngColor
```

Basically, all we're doing is drawing a vertical line 1 pixel thick with a specified color. Now the next time we run into this code, we get:

```
    RefForm.Line (201, 0)-(201, 400), lngColor
```

We've moved the line over 1 pixel, and depending on the starting and ending color values, we may have changed the color as well.

The code to create horizontal lines is very similar to that above. However, the diagonal option is somewhat odd. Recall that we set `dblMax` equal to the diagonal length of the form. Therefore, when we're in the `For...Next` loop for a diagonal gradient, we're really "walking down the diagonal". Let's use some actual values to clear this up. Say the `ScaleWidth` was 350, and the `ScaleHeight` was 600. Recall from those old geometry classes that the length of a right triangle's hypotenuse is:

$$c^2 = a^2 + b^2$$

In our case, that gives us:

$$350^2 + 600^2 = 482500$$

The square root of this is approximately 694.62, which is what we use as the ending value of the `For...Next` loop.

Let's assume that we're at the 420th pixel of the diagonal. We need to draw two lines, one in the horizontal direction and one in the vertical direction. The code for these lines looks like this:

```
' Draw the horizontal line first.
RefForm.Line (.ScaleWidth * dblDiff, _
    .ScaleHeight * dblDiff)- _
    (.Width, .ScaleHeight * dblDiff), lngColor

' Now the vertical.
RefForm.Line (.ScaleWidth * dblDiff, _
    .ScaleHeight * dblDiff)- _
    (.ScaleWidth * dblDiff, .Height), lngColor
```

Substituting the values in for the horizontal line, we get:

```
RefForm.Line (212, 363)- (.Width, 363), lngColor
```

Conversely, for the vertical line, we get:

```
RefForm.Line (212, 363)- (212, .Height), lngColor
```

We've effectively drawn two lines from the 420th pixel in the diagonal. Here's what that looks like in the coordinate system:

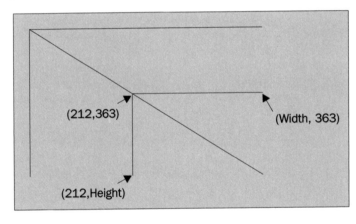

Eventually, we get to the bottom of the diagonal, and the algorithm ends.

Comparing the Implementations

Let's use the Stopwatch class again to see which implementation is faster. Add the following highlighted code to your SetGradient procedure:

```
Private Sub SetGradient()

  On Error GoTo error_SetGradient

  Dim blnRet As Boolean
  Dim lngGradient As Long
  Dim objWatch As Stopwatch

  Screen.MousePointer = vbHourglass
```

```
    If optStyle(0).Value = True Then
        lngGradient = 0
    ElseIf optStyle(1).Value = True Then
        lngGradient = 1
    Else
        lngGradient = 2
    End If

    Set objWatch = New Stopwatch

    If optGradient(0).Value = True Then
        objWatch.StartClock
        blnRet = CreateGradient(Me, lngGradient, _
            RGB(0, 0, 0), RGB(0, 0, 255))
        objWatch.StopClock
    ElseIf optGradient(1).Value = True Then
        objWatch.StartClock
        blnRet = VBCreateGradient(Me, lngGradient, _
            RGB(0, 0, 0), RGB(0, 0, 255))
        objWatch.StopClock
    End If

    MessageBox Me.hwnd, "Time is " & objWatch.View & " seconds.", _
        "Gradient", MB_OK + MB_ICONASTERISK
    Set objWatch = Nothing

    Screen.MousePointer = vbDefault

    Exit Sub

error_SetGradient:

    Screen.MousePointer = vbDefault

    If Not objWatch Is Nothing Then
        Set objWatch = Nothing
    End If

End Sub
```

I ran 10 trials of each gradient type for both implementations using a red to green gradient. I also maximized the main form on all test runs - my monitor was set up for 16 bit colors at a 1024*768 resolution. Here's what I got:

Gradient Style	API	VB	Conclusion
Diagonal	0.048	2.45	API (51 times faster)
Left to Right	0.041	2.87	API (70 times faster)
Top to Bottom	0.028	0.32	API (11 times faster)

As you can see, there's no doubt as to which method we should use. The API implementation clearly beats out the VB implementation, creating the gradient anywhere from 11 to 70 times faster than the VB code.

However, as with any analysis, we must make sure that we don't jump to hasty conclusions. Maybe there's a way that we can vastly improve the pure VB solution to speed things up a bit. Or maybe the API calls are the way to go with gradients. We can, however, say with confidence that the API solution is the right one for now.

Tiling Images Across a Form

Now that we're starting to get comfortable with the graphical world of windows, let's give the users another choice. Gradients are nice, but let's allow the users to take an image and tile it across the form. To tile an image across the form, we'll need to take image data from one location and copy it across the form's background. The `BitBlt` API call works nicely to solve this problem. We'll take a detailed look at this call, since you can use it to do a lot of image processing rather quickly.

The API Implementation

Let's take a look at the four API calls that we need to tile an image:

BitBlt

```
Declare Function BitBlt Lib "gdi32" Alias "BitBlt" _
    (ByVal hDestDC As Long, ByVal x As Long, _
    ByVal y As Long, ByVal nWidth As Long, _
    ByVal nHeight As Long, ByVal hSrcDC As Long, _
    ByVal xSrc As Long, ByVal ySrc As Long, _
    ByVal dwRop As Long) As Long
```

This API call really does a lot of the work. It can be used for different kinds of image processing, but we'll use it to copy image information from one source to another. The first argument, `hDestDC`, specifies the target device context of the bitmap information. This can be any DC that contains bitmap information. The `x` and `y` arguments are used to specify the upper-left hand corner that the image will be copied to. The `nWidth` and `nHeight` are the width and height of the bitmap image. The `hSrcDC` is the DC where we will get the image from. The `xSrc` and `ySrc` specify the upper-left hand corner of the bitmap in the source DC. The last argument, `dwRop`, is used to define the kind of operation we'd like to do with the bitmap. As we'll see, we'll use the `SRCCOPY` constant to specify a simple copy operation. However, we can do 14 other operations, like merging the bitmap with a pattern. The `BitBlt` function is nice to use to copy bitmaps, but remember that it can do a lot more than that - check the SDK on this function for more information.

CreateCompatibleDC

```
Declare Function CreateCompatibleDC Lib "gdi32" _
    (ByVal hdc As Long) As Long
```

This function simply creates a memory DC that's compatible with the device context specified by `hdc` (hence the function name). When you use `BitBlt` to copy an image into a DC, the DC has to be a memory DC. For example, the form in VB is currently using the screen as its image area. Therefore, you can't directly use this image area to copy bitmaps to. You have to create a memory DC to allow a bitmap to have an area to draw to.

SelectObject

```
Declare Function SelectObject Lib "gdi32" _
    (ByVal hdc As Long, ByVal hObject As Long) As Long
```

This function takes the handle specified by hObject and replaces the object of the same type located within hdc. For example, if you had a handle to a brush, and you wanted to use that brush within a DC, you can use this function to replace the current brush used by the DC. If you don't get a return value of zero, you have the handle of the object you just replaced. Hang onto this value, because you'll have to call SelectObject again and set hObject to this return value, thereby restoring the old object handle. If we didn't do this, the DC would be stuck using the object that we gave it (like our own brush handle) and this may lead to some unexpected results.

DeleteDC

```
Declare Function DeleteDC Lib "gdi32" _
    (ByVal hdc As Long) As Long
```

If you ever created a DC, you'll have to delete it to prevent memory leaks. DeleteDC does just that, taking a DC as its only argument. Note that this should never be done on VB's hdc property values. Although these are valid DCs, we didn't create then, so we shouldn't try to delete them. Also, don't use DeleteObject to delete DCs you've created. DeleteObject is only used for handles; using this API call to delete DCs can lead to unexpected results.

The TileImage Function

Now let's take a look at the TileImage function. This function takes the image in the picture box and tiles it across the form. It returns a True on success and a False on failure. Add the TileImage function and the four API calls we have just looked at to the GradientLib module.

```
Public Function TileImage(RefForm As Form, _
    ImageToTile As PictureBox) As Boolean

On Error GoTo error_TileImage

Dim lngBitmapHandle As Long
Dim lngFormHeight As Long
Dim lngFormWidth As Long
Dim lngPictureHeight As Long
Dim lngPictureWidth As Long
Dim lngPrevScale As Long
Dim lngRet As Long
Dim lngSourceDC As Long
Dim lngX As Long
Dim lngY As Long

If Not RefForm Is Nothing And Not ImageToTile Is Nothing Then

    With ImageToTile
        lngPrevScale = .ScaleMode
        .ScaleMode = vbPixels
        lngPictureHeight = .ScaleHeight
        lngPictureWidth = .ScaleWidth
        .ScaleMode = lngPrevScale
```

```
        End With

        With RefForm
            lngPrevScale = .ScaleMode
            .ScaleMode = vbPixels
            lngFormHeight = .ScaleHeight
            lngFormWidth = .ScaleWidth
            .ScaleMode = lngPrevScale
        End With

        lngSourceDC = CreateCompatibleDC(RefForm.hdc)
        lngBitmapHandle = SelectObject(lngSourceDC, _
            ImageToTile.Picture.Handle)

        For lngX = 0 To lngFormWidth Step lngPictureWidth

            For lngY = 0 To lngFormHeight Step lngPictureHeight
                lngRet = BitBlt(RefForm.hdc, lngX, lngY, _
                    lngPictureWidth, lngPictureHeight, _
                    lngSourceDC, 0, 0, SRCCOPY)
            Next lngY

        Next lngX

        lngRet = SelectObject(lngSourceDC, lngBitmapHandle)
        lngRet = DeleteDC(lngSourceDC)

        TileImage = True

    Else

        TileImage = False

    End If

    Exit Function

error_TileImage:

    If Not RefForm Is Nothing Then
        RefForm.Tag = Err.Number & "   " & Err.Description
    End If

    TileImage = False

End Function
```

As we did in `CreateGradient`, we check to see that the arguments are valid.

```
If Not RefForm Is Nothing And Not ImageToTile Is Nothing Then
```

If they are, we get their measurements in pixels and restore their `ScaleMode` properties.

```
    With ImageToTile
        lngPrevScale = .ScaleMode
        .ScaleMode = vbPixels
        lngPictureHeight = .ScaleHeight
        lngPictureWidth = .ScaleWidth
        .ScaleMode = lngPrevScale
    End With
```

```
With RefForm
    lngPrevScale = .ScaleMode
    .ScaleMode = vbPixels
    lngFormHeight = .ScaleHeight
    lngFormWidth = .ScaleWidth
    .ScaleMode = lngPrevScale
End With
```

Then, we create a compatible memory DC for the form's DC using the `CreateCompatibleDC` call.

```
lngSourceDC = CreateCompatibleDC(RefForm.hdc)
```

After that's done, we select the picture box's image into this memory DC using the `SelectObject` call.

```
lngBitmapHandle = SelectObject(lngSourceDC, _
        ImageToTile.Picture.Handle)
```

The rest is actually pretty simple. We enter two `For...Next` loops that move through the form's window area in step sizes equal to the width and the height of the image. We copy the image to the form using the `BitBlt` function.

```
For lngX = 0 To lngFormWidth Step lngPictureWidth

    For lngY = 0 To lngFormHeight Step lngPictureHeight
        lngRet = BitBlt(RefForm.hdc, lngX, lngY, _
            lngPictureWidth, lngPictureHeight, _
            lngSourceDC, 0, 0, SRCCOPY)
    Next lngY

Next lngX
```

Note that the source DC is not the picture box's `hdc` value, but the memory DC, `lngSourceDC`, we just created. After the tiling is complete, we reselect the image handle, `lngBitmapHandle`, into the memory DC using `SelectObject`, and then we finish the function by deleting the memory DC.

```
lngRet = SelectObject(lngSourceDC, lngBitmapHandle)
lngRet = DeleteDC(lngSourceDC)
```

To me, this doesn't seem as involved as the gradient code. The memory DC may be the one confusing part about `TileImage` - why do we have to do it? Simply because we can't draw directly to the form's DC; we have to have a compatible DC in memory to draw to. I realize that it may seem inefficient to do this, but, for better or for worse, this is the way Windows works. Just remember that if you're doing any other kind of image processing and the code isn't working, you may have forgotten to create a memory DC.

Calling the TileImage Function

To make sure that our tiling code is correct, add a picture box to `frmMain` called `picTile` as shown here:

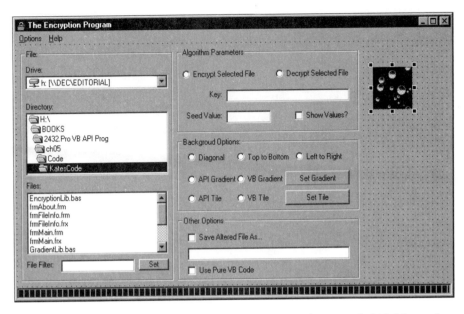

Now set the `Autosize` property to `True` so that our image isn't cropped if it's bigger than `picTile`. We also need to set the `BorderStyle` property to `0 - None`.

For the `Picture` property, browse to any image that you have on your computer. I've used a bitmap from my `C:\Windows` directory.

Now resize `frmMain` so that `picTile` is hidden and the form looks like this once more:

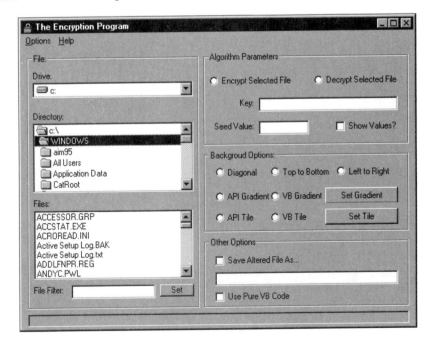

Now enter the following code into the Click event of cmdSetTile:

```
Private Sub cmdSetTile_Click()

    SetTile

End Sub
```

Add the SetTile method to the code in frmMain:

```
Private Sub SetTile()

  On Error GoTo error_SetTile

  Dim blnRet As Boolean

  Screen.MousePointer = vbHourglass

  If optTile(0).Value = True Then
      blnRet = TileImage(Me, picTile)
  Else
      '   VB method
  End If

  Screen.MousePointer = vbDefault

  Exit Sub

error_SetTile:

  Screen.MousePointer = vbDefault

End Sub
```

This code is very straightforward. If the API Tile option button has been selected we call TileItem passing in frmMain and picTile as the arguments.

```
If optTile(0).Value = True Then
    blnRet = TileImage(Me, picTile)
Else
    '   VB method
End If
```

If everything works, you should see something like this (of course what you actually see depends upon which image you use):

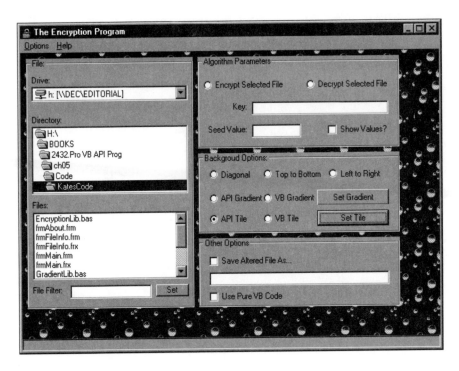

VB Implementation

To call the VB implementation code we need to add to our `SetTile` method. Make the following amendments to your code:

```
Private Sub SetTile()

  On Error GoTo error_SetTile

  Dim blnRet As Boolean

  Screen.MousePointer = vbHourglass

  If optTile(0).Value = True Then
      blnRet = TileImage(Me, picTile)
  ElseIf optTile(1).Value = True Then
      blnRet = VBTileImage(Me, picTile)
  End If

  Screen.MousePointer = vbDefault

  Exit Sub

error_SetTile:

  Screen.MousePointer = vbDefault

End Sub
```

Now type the following function into the `frmMain` code window:

```
Public Function VBTileImage(RefForm As Form, _
    ImageToTile As PictureBox) As Boolean

  On Error GoTo error_VBTileImage

  Dim lngX As Long
  Dim lngY As Long

  If Not RefForm Is Nothing And Not ImageToTile Is Nothing Then

    For lngX = 0 To RefForm.Width Step ImageToTile.Width
        For lngY = 0 To RefForm.Height Step ImageToTile.Height
            RefForm.PaintPicture ImageToTile.Picture, lngX, lngY
        Next lngY
    Next lngX

    VBTileImage = True

  Else

    VBTileImage = False

  End If

Exit Function

error_VBTileImage:

  If Not RefForm Is Nothing Then
    RefForm.Tag = Err.Number & "  " & Err.Description
  End If

  VBTileImage = False

End Function
```

We're really doing the same kind of operation here in `VBTileImage`. After checking that there is a form to tile and an image to tile with, we move through the form's window space in increments determined by the image's size.

```
If Not RefForm Is Nothing And Not ImageToTile Is Nothing Then

    For lngX = 0 To RefForm.Width Step ImageToTile.Width
        For lngY = 0 To RefForm.Height Step ImageToTile.Height
```

Then, we use the `PaintPicture` method on the form to copy an image to a specified location.

```
RefForm.PaintPicture ImageToTile.Picture, lngX, lngY
```

That's it! Now run the Encryption application again, this time selecting **VB Tile**. Once more, the image will be tiled over frmMain.

In terms of code size, this implementation is much easier to follow. But how does compare to the API code?

Comparing the Implementations

As we did with the gradient functions, let's compare the performance of the API implementation with that of VB. Add the following highlighted code to your `SetTile` method:

```
Private Sub SetTile()

  On Error GoTo error_SetTile

  Dim blnRet As Boolean
  Dim objTimer As Stopwatch

  Screen.MousePointer = vbHourglass

  Set objTimer = New Stopwatch

  If optTile(0).Value = True Then
      objTimer.StartClock
      blnRet = TileImage(Me, picTile)
      objTimer.StopClock
  Else
      objTimer.StartClock
      blnRet = VBTileImage(Me, picTile)
      objTimer.StopClock
  End If

  MessageBox Me.hWnd, "Time is " & CStr(objTimer.View) & _
          " seconds.", "Tile Time", MB_ICONHAND And MB_OK

  Screen.MousePointer = vbDefault

  Exit Sub

error_SetTile:

  Screen.MousePointer = vbDefault

End Sub
```

I ran the `TileImage` and `VBTileImage` functions ten times each (the screen resolution was the same). Here's what the averages were:

API	VB	Conclusion
0.058	0.079	API (1.36 times faster)

The difference isn't as big this time around, but the API implementation is a bit faster.

If you want to have the form tile whenever the form is resized, simply call `SetTile` *from the form's* `Paint` *event.*

Rotating Text

We are going to move away from the main form for now, and concentrate on the About form. The first thing that we'll do is rotate some randomized text on the form. After we've done with that, we'll actually change the form's geometry from a rectangle to an ellipse.

The AlterLabels Method

If you bring up `frmAbout` in VB, you'll notice that there are three labels on the form. We also have a timer on the form along with a Close command button. `frmAbout` looks something like this:

The space between the second label and the command button is another label that has its `Caption` property set when the form is loading. The `Interval` property of the timer is initially set to 5 seconds. Whenever the timer fires, it calls the `AlterLabels` method, which looks like this:

```
Private Sub tmrAbout_Timer()

    AlterLabels

End Sub
```

The `AlterLabels` method simply scrambles the text around. You should enter the following code into the **General** section of `frmAbout`:

```
Private Sub AlterLabels()

  On Error GoTo error_AlterLabels

  Dim lngCharValue As Long
  Dim lngLabel As Long
  Dim lngLength As Long
  Dim lngPosition As Long

  If tmrAbout.Interval = 5000 Then
    tmrAbout.Interval = 1000
  End If
```

```
    lngLabel = Int((3 * Rnd) + 1)

    Select Case lngLabel
      Case 1
          lngLength = Len(lblTitle.Caption)
      Case 2
          lngLength = Len(lblCreatedBy.Caption)
      Case 3
          lngLength = Len(lblVersion.Caption)
    End Select

    lngPosition = Int((lngLength * Rnd) + 1)

    lngCharValue = Int((126 * Rnd) + 1)

    If lngCharValue < 33 Then
        lngCharValue = lngCharValue + 33
    End If

    Select Case lngLabel
      Case 1
          lblTitle.Caption = Left$(lblTitle.Caption, lngPosition - 1) & _
              Chr$(lngCharValue) & Right$(lblTitle.Caption, _
              lngLength - lngPosition)
      Case 2
          lblCreatedBy.Caption = Left$(lblCreatedBy.Caption, _
              lngPosition - 1) & Chr$(lngCharValue) & _
              Right$(lblCreatedBy.Caption, lngLength - lngPosition)
      Case 3
          lblVersion.Caption = Left$(lblVersion.Caption, _
              lngPosition - 1) & Chr$(lngCharValue) & _
              Right$(lblVersion.Caption, lngLength - lngPosition)
    End Select

Exit Sub

error_AlterLabels:

End Sub
```

Let's take a quick tour of this procedure. We first change the timer's interval rate to 1 second if it's currently set at 5 seconds.

```
If tmrAbout.Interval = 5000 Then
  tmrAbout.Interval = 1000
End If
```

This is done to show the form in a normal state for 5 seconds before we start to play with its appearance.

Then, we randomly pick a label on the form, and get the length of that label's `Caption` property.

```
lngLabel = Int((3 * Rnd) + 1)

Select Case lngLabel
  Case 1
      lngLength = Len(lblTitle.Caption)
  Case 2
      lngLength = Len(lblCreatedBy.Caption)
  Case 3
      lngLength = Len(lblVersion.Caption)
End Select
```

Next, we randomly pick a position in the label:

```
lngPosition = Int((lngLength * Rnd) + 1)
```

Then we generate a character that will replace the current character.

```
lngCharValue = Int((126 * Rnd) + 1)
```

Note that we alter the random character if necessary to make it a printable character.

```
If lngCharValue < 33 Then
    lngCharValue = lngCharValue + 33
End If
```

Finally, we replace the character with the new one.

```
Select Case lngLabel
  Case 1
      lblTitle.Caption = Left$(lblTitle.Caption, lngPosition - 1) & _
        Chr$(lngCharValue) & Right$(lblTitle.Caption, _
        lngLength - lngPosition)
  Case 2
      lblCreatedBy.Caption = Left$(lblCreatedBy.Caption, _
        lngPosition - 1) & Chr$(lngCharValue) & _
        Right$(lblCreatedBy.Caption, lngLength - lngPosition)
  Case 3
      lblVersion.Caption = Left$(lblVersion.Caption, _
        lngPosition - 1) & Chr$(lngCharValue) & Right$(lblVersion.Caption, _
        lngLength - lngPosition)
End Select
```

Lastly, let's add some code to the `cmdClose_Click` event of `frmAbout`:

```
Private Sub cmdClose_Click

  Unload Me
  Set frmAbout = Nothing

End Sub
```

To see the `AlterLabels` method in action, run the Encryption application again and select Help | About. If you keep `frmAbout` on the screen for a while, it will look something like this:

Now let's stretch the scrambling idea even more. To rotate the text, we will have to replace our labels with picture boxes and keep track of the text information in string variables. That's OK, though - we're all used to changing the original design to meet the user's needs, right?

Fonts and Windows

A discussion on fonts could take up an entire chapter at the very least, so I'll cover the absolute basics for our purposes. As most of us have seen when using a word processing tool like MS Word, we can choose from a large selection of fonts like Courier and Times New Roman. Each of these fonts have properties that can be altered to be underlined, italicized, bolded and so on. However, when you send your document that uses the Absolutely Bizzare font to a friend that doesn't have that font loaded on their PC, there's a problem. The document has to resolve how this font is to be displayed on the screen. There are a couple of ways to solve this problem. You could embed the font information directly into the document, but that would increase the size of the file. You could just ship the font file to the user, but that may violate some copyright restrictions.

Fortunately, Windows handles the resolution for you. Whenever you specify a font in a program, you're specifying a logical font and not an actual physical font. Therefore, when the logical font needs to be rendered onto a printer or screen, Windows will map the logical font information to a physical font. If an exact match exists, Windows uses that font; otherwise, a font that has the "best" match is used. Although the output on your friend's monitor may not look the same as yours, it allows the document to be viewed without shipping the exact font information. Of course, if your friend wants to see the font directly, they would need to get that physical font information.

Logical Fonts

To create a logical font in Windows, we use the LOGFONT UDT:

```
Public Type LOGFONT
    lfHeight As Long
    lfWidth As Long
    lfEscapement As Long
    lfOrientation As Long
    lfWeight As Long
    lfItalic As Byte
    lfUnderline As Byte
    lfStrikeOut As Byte
    lfCharSet As Byte
    lfOutPrecision As Byte
```

```
      lfClipPrecision As Byte
      lfQuality As Byte
      lfPitchAndFamily As Byte
      lfFaceName As String * 32
    End Type
```

lfHeight and lfWidth

These parameters are used to specify the height and width of the logical font in pixels. If these are set to zero, the driver will determine reasonable default values. Otherwise, you can specify the values yourself, although for `lfHeight`, you must make the value negative. This forces Windows to match a font that has a character height equal to the positive value of `lfHeight`.

lfEscapement

This specifies the angle that the text should be displayed at in tenths of a degree counterclockwise from the x-axis. For example, if we set `lfEscapement` equal to 186, the font angle would be at 18.6° from the x-axis.

lfOrientation

This specifies an angle in tenths of a degree counterclockwise from the x-axis for the baseline of the characters.

lfWeight

This determines the weight of the font. You can specify any value from 1 to 1000, but here are the standard values that we will use:

```
    Public Enum FontWeights
       FW_DONTCARE = 0
       FW_THIN = 100
       FW_EXTRALIGHT = 200
       FW_LIGHT = 300
       FW_NORMAL = 400
       FW_MEDIUM = 500
       FW_SEMIBOLD = 600
       FW_BOLD = 700
       FW_EXTRABOLD = 800
       FW_HEAVY = 900
    End Enum
```

If you really don't care, you can use the `FW_DONTCARE` value, which tells Windows to figure it out for you. As we'll see with the rest of the parameters, most of them have default values that force Windows to determine what the best value is.

lfItalic

If this is set to zero, the font won't be italic; otherwise, set it equal to 1 to make the font italic.

lfUnderline

Set this equal to 1 to underline the characters or zero for no underlining.

lfStrikeOut

Same as `lfUnderline`: 1 to strikeout, 0 for no striking.

lfCharSet

This specifies the character set to use. You can choose from one of the following values:

```
Public Enum FontCharSets
    ANSI_CHARSET = 0
    DEFAULT_CHARSET = 1
    SYMBOL_CHARSET = 2
    MAC_CHARSET = 77
    SHIFTJIS_CHARSET = 128
    HANGEUL_CHARSET = 129
    CHINESEGIG5_CHARSET = 136
    OEM_CHARSET = 255
End Enum
```

lfOutPrecision

This determines the output precision for the font. This is used to determine how detailed you want the font to be. You can choose from one of the following values:

```
Public Enum FontOutPrecisions
    OUT_DEFAULT_PRECIS = 0
    OUT_STRING_PRECIS = 1
    OUT_CHARACTER_PRECIS = 2
    OUT_STROKE_PRECIS = 3
    OUT_TT_PRECIS = 4
    OUT_DEVICE_PRECIS = 5
    OUT_RASTER_PRECIS = 6
    OUT_TT_ONLY_PRECIS = 7
    OUT_OUTLINE_PRECIS = 8
End Enum
```

lfClipPrecision

If a font needs to be clipped for any reason, this value determines the precision of the clipping. Valid values are:

```
Public Enum FontClipPrecisions
    CLIP_DEFAULT_PRECIS = 0
    CLIP_CHARACTER_PRECIS = 1
    CLIP_STROKE_PRECIS = 2
    CLIP_LH_ANGLES = 16
    CLIP_TT_ALWAYS = 32
    CLIP_EMBEDDED = 128
    CLIP_TO_PATH = 4097
End Enum
```

lfQuality

You can specify the quality of the font from the following values:

```
Public Enum FontQuality
    DEFAULT_QUALITY = 0
    DRAFT_QUALITY = 1
    PROOF_QUALITY = 2
End Enum
```

lfPitchAndFamily

This parameter actually specifies two attributes: the pitch and family of the font, like Roman or Swiss. You can choose one value from each of the following enumerations:

```
Public Enum FontPitch
    DEFAULT_PITCH = 0
    FIXED_PITCH = 1
    VARIABLE_PITCH = 2
End Enum

Public Enum FontFamily
    FF_DONTCARE = 0
    FF_ROMAN = 16
    FF_SWISS = 32
    FF_MODERN = 48
    FF_SCRIPT = 64
    FF_DECORATIVE = 80
End Enum
```

lfFaceName

This parameter specifies the name of the font that you want to use. You can set this equal to vbNullString if you want Windows to determine what font to use based on the other values in LOGFONT. Note that the entire length of the string cannot exceed 32 character.

Quick Summary of LOGFONT

There's a lot of information that I just gave you, most of which wasn't explained in any great detail (like what is the font pitch anyway?). For our purposes, we don't need to define any of these parameters, so we'll use the default values. However, please remember that you have a lot of flexibility with this UDT if you want to do more font manipulation than what we're going to do in this chapter.

Before we continue, please add all of these enumerations and the LOGFONT UDT to a new module called FontLib. We'll be using them in the next section.

Modifying the frmAbout Screen

The first thing we have to do is get rid of the labels and add one picture box called picAbout. We don't want to replace each label with a picture box because we're going to draw all of the text to one location, but we'll still keep each line of information separate by using form-level string variables. Then resize the form so that it looks something like this:

Now let's add four variable declarations to the **Declarations** section of `frmAbout`:

```
Private m_lngAngle As Long
Private m_strCreatedBy As String
Private m_strTitle As String
Private m_strVersion As String
```

The `m_lngAngle` variable will be used to keep track of the current font angle.

Now we must return to the `AlterLabels` method and make the following changes:

```
Private Sub AlterLabels()

  On Error GoTo error_AlterLabels

  Dim lngCharValue As Long
  Dim lngLabel As Long
  Dim lngLength As Long
  Dim lngPosition As Long

  If tmrAbout.Interval = 5000 Then
    tmrAbout.Interval = 1000
  End If

  lngLabel = Int((3 * Rnd) + 1)

  Select Case lngLabel
    Case 1
        lngLength = Len(m_strTitle)
    Case 2
        lngLength = Len(m_strCreatedBy)
```

```
    Case 3
        lngLength = Len(m_strVersion)
    End Select

    lngPosition = Int((lngLength * Rnd) + 1)

    lngCharValue = Int((126 * Rnd) + 1)

    If lngCharValue < 33 Then
        lngCharValue = lngCharValue + 33
    End If

    Select Case lngLabel
      Case 1
          m_strTitle = Left$(m_strTitle, lngPosition - 1) & _
              Chr$(lngCharValue) & Right$(m_strTitle, _
              lngLength - lngPosition)
      Case 2
          m_strCreatedBy = Left$(m_strCreatedBy, lngPosition - 1) & _
              Chr$(lngCharValue) & Right$(m_strCreatedBy, _
              lngLength - lngPosition)
      Case 3
          m_strVersion = Left$(m_strVersion, lngPosition - 1) & _
              Chr$(lngCharValue) & Right$(m_strVersion, _
              lngLength - lngPosition)
    End Select

Exit Sub

error_AlterLabels:

End Sub
```

We have to initialize these variables ourselves, so modify the `InitializeForm` method like so:

```
Private Sub InitializeForm()

   Screen.MousePointer = vbHourglass
   m_strCreatedBy = "Created by Victor!"
   m_strTitle = "The Encryption Program"
   m_strVersion = "Version " & CStr(App.Major) & "." _
         & CStr(App.Minor) & "." & CStr(App.Revision)
   ShowAboutInfo
   Randomize
   Screen.MousePointer = vbDefault

End Sub
```

Notice a new method called `ShowAboutInfo`. This procedure takes the information that's stored in our three form-level string variables and displays them in the `picAbout` picture box. Now add this method to `frmAbout`:

```
Private Sub ShowAboutInfo()

  On Error Resume Next

  Dim lngHandleFont As Long
  Dim lngOldFont As Long
```

```
    Dim lngRet As Long
    Dim udtFont As LOGFONT

    With udtFont
        .lfEscapement = m_lngAngle Mod 360
        m_lngAngle = (m_lngAngle + 5) Mod 360
        .lfFaceName = "Times New Roman" & Chr$(0)
        .lfHeight = (16 * -20) / Screen.TwipsPerPixelY
    End With

    lngHandleFont = CreateFontIndirect(udtFont)

    lngOldFont = SelectObject(picAbout.hdc, lngHandleFont)

    picAbout.Cls
    picAbout.CurrentX = picAbout.Width / 4
    picAbout.CurrentY = picAbout.Height / 4
    picAbout.Print m_strTitle & vbCrLf
    picAbout.CurrentX = picAbout.Width / 4
    picAbout.Print m_strCreatedBy & vbCrLf
    picAbout.CurrentX = picAbout.Width / 4
    picAbout.Print m_strVersion & vbCrLf

    lngRet = SelectObject(picAbout.hdc, lngOldFont)

    lngRet = DeleteObject(lngHandleFont)

End Sub
```

First, we take the `udtFont` UDT and set three properties:

```
With udtFont
    .lfEscapement = m_lngAngle Mod 360
    m_lngAngle = (m_lngAngle + 5) Mod 360
    .lfFaceName = "Times New Roman" & Chr$(0)
    .lfHeight = (16 * -20) / Screen.TwipsPerPixelY
End With
```

The angle is determined by the `m_lngAngle` variable, which we increment by 0.5 degrees every time this method is called. Note that we're also using the `Mod` function to make sure that the angle value stays between 0 and 359. Next, we set the font name to `Times New Roman`. You can play with this value depending upon the fonts currently installed on your PC, but be warned that some fonts won't rotate. Finally, we set the height of the font. The -20 value may be confusing at first, but remember that a twip is 1/20 the size of a point on the screen. You might think that we could just set `lfHeight` equal to 16, but this may not work, since the form's resolution may be in twips. Therefore, we have to scale this value by using the `TwipsPerPixelY` property of the `Screen` object. Of course, if there **are** 20 twips to a pixel, we will end up with a height value of 16. In addition, we must set `lfHeight` equal to a negative value to ensure that Windows will set the font size equal to what we want it to be.

Next, we create an indirect (logical) font using `CreateFontIndirect`:

```
lngHandleFont = CreateFontIndirect(udtFont)
```

What's that function? I'm glad you asked (and yes, you should add this to the FontLib module as well):

```
Declare Function CreateFontIndirect Lib "gdi32" _
    Alias "CreateFontIndirectA" (lpLogFont As LOGFONT) As Long
```

This API call takes a LOGFONT UDT as its only argument, and it returns a handle to a logical font (a zero return value signifies failure). Basically, what CreateFontIndirect does is create a font that matches what we have specified in the UDT. However, as the procedure name applies, this font is indirect, or logical; it isn't physical. For example, the font specified by lfFaceName may not exist on the PC that is currently running your code. When you take this font handle and select into a DC using SelectObject (as in the code below) the OS will try and map all of your parameters to a font that is currently installed on the computer.

```
lngOldFont = SelectObject(picAbout.hdc, lngHandleFont)
```

As I mentioned before, your values may not match what the machine has, so remember that there is no guarantee that what you see on your PC will match up with another user's PC.

Once we have selected our logical font into the picture's DC, we can add text to the picture box, and it will be drawn according to the angle specified by lfEscapement:

```
picAbout.Cls
picAbout.CurrentX = picAbout.Width / 4
picAbout.CurrentY = picAbout.Height / 4
picAbout.Print m_strTitle & vbCrLf
picAbout.CurrentX = picAbout.Width / 4
picAbout.Print m_strCreatedBy & vbCrLf
picAbout.CurrentX = picAbout.Width / 4
picAbout.Print m_strVersion & vbCrLf
```

After we're done drawing the text, we select the original font back into the picture's DC:

```
lngRet = SelectObject(picAbout.hdc, lngOldFont)
```

Finally, we delete our logical font:

```
lngRet = DeleteObject(lngHandleFont)
```

Now let's add two more calls to ShowAboutInfo. Enter the following line of code to the AlterLabels method:

```
Select Case lngLabel
    Case 1
        m_strTitle = Left$(m_strTitle, lngPosition - 1) & _
            Chr$(lngCharValue) & Right$(m_strTitle, _
            lngLength - lngPosition)
    Case 2
        m_strCreatedBy = Left$(m_strCreatedBy, lngPosition - 1) & _
            Chr$(lngCharValue) & Right$(m_strCreatedBy, _
```

```
            lngLength - lngPosition)
    Case 3
        m_strVersion = Left$(m_strVersion, lngPosition - 1) & _
            Chr$(lngCharValue) & Right$(m_strVersion, _
            lngLength - lngPosition)
  End Select

ShowAboutInfo

Exit Sub

error_AlterLabels:

End Sub
```

Now add the same line to the Form_Paint event:

```
Private Sub Form_Paint()

   ShowAboutInfo

End Sub
```

Well that's the theory out of the way, let's see what happens in practice. Now display frmAbout once more; here's what you should see:

VB Implementation

As far as I can tell, this can't be done in VB. It's interesting to note, though, that the Font object that some controls expose (like the text box) has some of the properties that the LOGFONT UDT has, like CharSet and Bold. However, the real flexibility comes from the API calls and, in this case, it's the only way to achieve what we want to do.

Modifying the Geometry of a Form

Before we get into the guts of this example, I want to mention two things. The first one is that you can't do this in VB, period, end of story. The second thing is that we won't spend too much time on this example. But I want to stress that this example has a lot of possibilities, especially with ActiveX control design. This example is given more as an introduction to an idea that you may or may not find useful in your development career.

Window Regions

Normally, every window that is created in Windows has an implied geometrical region that is shaped like a rectangle. Most of us are used to seeing windows in this fashion. However, you may have seen some programs that use window shapes that do not use this region. So how can you change your forms to circles? Simple, just use these two calls:

CreateEllipticRgn

```
Declare Function CreateEllipticRgn Lib "gdi32" _
    (ByVal X1 As Long, ByVal Y1 As Long, ByVal X2 As Long, _
    ByVal Y2 As Long) As Long
```

This function simply creates an elliptic region using four arguments. The X1 and Y1 arguments specify the upper-left hand corner of the region, and the X2 and Y2 arguments specify the lower-right hand corner of the region. For example, the following diagram shows how one can draw an ellipse:

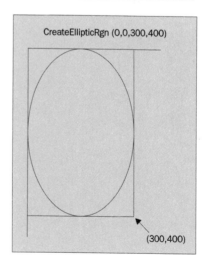

Note that if you want to create a circular region, you would set X2 equal to Y2. If the function is successful, the return value is nonzero - it's also a handle to the region. Also, note that if you look up the documentation on this function, it'll warn you to delete this region after you're done with it. However, as we'll quickly see, the next function contradicts this statement.

SetWindowRgn

```
Declare Function SetWindowRgn Lib "user32" _
    (ByVal hWnd As Long, ByVal hRgn As Long, _
    ByVal bRedraw As Boolean) As Long
```

This function allows you to define the region for the window specified by the hWnd handle. The hRgn function is a handle to a region. bRedraw should be set to True if you want the window to redraw itself immediately after the function call is made.

> **Note that if you reset the region of a window, DO NOT delete the region handle using the DeleteObject function.**

After you have created a window region with CreateEllipticRgn and SetWindowRgn, the OS owns the region defined by hRgn. The OS does not make a copy of this region and you should not make any more function calls with the region handle, particularly not the DeleteObject function. Deleting it would delete the window region, and this could lead to a lot of problems.

Changing the frmAbout's Region

Let's add a function to frmAbout that will create an elliptical region similar to the one shown in the diagram above. Begin by adding the two API functions CreateEllipticRgn and SetWindowRgn to another module called WindowLib.bas. We'll call this function AlterRegion; it's implementation looks something like this:

```
Private Sub AlterRegion()

   On Error Resume Next

   Dim lngRegionHandle As Long
   Dim lngRet As Long
   lngRegionHandle = CreateEllipticRgn(0, 0, 315, 365)

   If lngRegionHandle <> 0 Then
       lngRet = SetWindowRgn(Me.hWnd, lngRegionHandle, True)
   End If

End Sub
```

It's pretty simple. We create an elliptic region using the CreateEllipticRgn function:

```
lngRegionHandle = CreateEllipticRgn(0, 0, 315, 365)
```

If we get a region handle back, we modify the frmAbout's region using the SetWindowRgn function:

```
If lngRegionHandle <> 0 Then
    lngRet = SetWindowRgn(Me.hWnd, lngRegionHandle, True)
End If
```

Now just add a call to our new `AlterRegion` function as follows:

```
Private Sub Form_Load()

    InitializeForm
    AlterRegion

End Sub
```

Provided everything works, we get an **About** form that looks something like this:

I admit, it's pretty ugly. There's a lot more work to be done to make it visually appealing, but when I first found about these calls I was pretty excited. Some people like applications that don't have the gray, rectangular windows with the gray, rectangular buttons. By spending some more time with window regions, you may be able to create some visually unique application.

Summary

In this chapter we briefly examined some of the graphical functionality that `gdi32.dll` provides. As you can imagine there's a lot more you can do with this little DLL so I encourage you to explore some more.

In this chapter we learnt how to:

- ❑ Create gradients
- ❑ Tile images
- ❑ Rotate text
- ❑ Alter window regions

Whenever possible we also tried to implement the above using VB so that we could compare its performance with the API code. We found that in these matters the API code was almost always significantly faster that pure VB.

In the next chapter, we'll back away from the main OS DLLs and use some calls from other DLLs to play sounds and display the common dialog windows.

6

API Calls Outside of Win32

In the last three chapters, we've taken a look at some of the calls that you can make from the three main Windows OS DLLs: `kernel32`, `user32`, and `gdi32`. In this chapter, we're going to step away from the OS world and move into some other DLLs that you may find on your PC.

Therefore in this chapter we'll cover:

- ❑ Multimedia functions
- ❑ The common dialog windows
- ❑ File information functions

We're also going to take a break from the Encryption program for a while and just work on some separate "mini" applications. These applications are strictly to show how a few particular calls work; in no way am I expecting that you would model your applications after the GUI interfaces you'll see. However, I think we all write the one-form-one-button applications just to see if we can get some kind of technology to work the way we think it should before we run amok in our real applications. We're also not going to do any comparisons between VB and the API calls either, so kick back and relax with this chapter!

Playing Wave And MIDI Files

Most of us are familiar with wave files (they end with the `WAV` file extension). It's a binary file that contains information about sound. If you're a musician that works with a synthesizer, the term MIDI shouldn't be foreign either. Virtually all modern keyboards allow you to control other keyboards using MIDI, and some will even write your programmed songs to a MIDI file on a disk. In this section, we'll take a look at these file types in more detail. Then, we'll discuss the API calls that we can use to play these files. Finally, we'll create a small application in VB to test out these calls. (Note: If you don't have a sound card on your PC, you may not be able to make some of these calls, or, if you can, you won't hear anything. Sorry about that.)

Before we get into the WAV and MIDI file formats, I'd like to direct your attention to the following web site: www.wotsit.org. *It has a lot of information on file formats, so if you're ever curious about the specification of a particular binary file format, I'd start here.*

The WAV File

The **Waveform Audio File Format**, or WAV file, is a binary file that describes sound information. Wave information is also found in RIFF files, which describes more general characteristics like playlists and other multimedia formats, but we're concerned about the WAV characteristics in particular. As we'll see when we start to play WAV files in VB, we don't have to know what this format is, but it's good to know what's inside these files.

A WAVEFORMAT UDT defines the kind of sound information that follows it in the file. The UDT looks like this:

```
Type WAVEFORMAT
    wFormatTag As Integer
    nChannels As Integer
    nSamplesPerSec As Long
    nAvgBytesPerSec As Long
    nBlockAlign As Integer
End Type
```

Let's take a look at each parameter in more detail. The wFormatTag parameter is used to define the format category of the WAV data. There are a number of different values that this parameter can be set to, like WAVE_FORMAT_PCM. This specifies that the WAV data is in the **pulse code modulation** format, or PCM. The nChannels parameter specifies the number of channels that are represented in the data. For example, setting this parameter equal to 2 states that we have stereo sound (a left and right channel).

The next parameter, nSamplesPerSec, could take up an entire college course in digital signal processing if we really wanted to explain the digital recording of sound, so I'll simply define it by saying that it's the number of sample points of sound data per second. Believe me, there's a lot more to it than this, but just remember that the more samples you take per second, the "clearer" the sound will be. Of course, by taking more samples, your file size will increase as well.

Just like it says, the nAveBytesPerSec specifies the average number of bytes per second of sampled sound. Note that this is an average, but it allows software to pre-allocate buffer space in memory for the sampled sound. Finally, the nBlockAlign parameter specifies the block alignment of the data.

The MIDI File

Generally speaking, a `WAV` file contains information about a recorded sound. A `MIDI` file also contains information about sound, but not the sound itself per se. A `MIDI` file tells a computer to play a certain sound with certain attributes (like pitch, decay, sustain, etc.). Therefore, you can think of a `MIDI` file as a kind of controller file. The nice thing about `MIDI` files is that you can take them and play them on a bunch of different processing units, like a PC or a synthesizer, and they usually sound the same. However, the file format is quite complex, as it not only contains information about how to play the sound, but when and for how long as well. The whole purpose of the `MIDI` file was to allow musicians to record songs on a synthesizer without having to record the sound itself. Therefore, they could exchange song information with a portable, or cross-platform. (Kind of analogous to the Java of the music world.) There are a bunch of UDTs that can describe this data but since this is a book on API not synthesized music, I'll leave it up to the interested reader to look at the specifics of the file structure.

The Winmm.DLL

If you're interested in producing your own software program to create `MIDI` files, then by all means read up on the `MIDI` file format specifications. But most of us just want to play an alarm sound when the database connection goes down in our program; we simply don't care about the byte structure of the `WAV` file. Fortunately, the `winmm.DLL` has a nice set of APIs that allow us to play `WAV` and `MIDI` files. Let's go over the `WAV` file calls first, and then we'll discuss the `MIDI` file calls.

The PlaySound Call

The `PlaySound` gives you a lot of options if you want to play a `WAV` file. Here's the definition:

```
Declare Function PlaySound Lib "winmm.dll" _
    Alias "PlaySoundA" (ByVal lpszName As String, _
    ByVal hModule As Long, ByVal dwFlags As Long) As Long
```

lpszName

This argument specifies the sound to play. It can be either a specific `WAV` file, an event defined in the `WIN.INI` file that plays a sound, or an alias to a file, event, or resource. As we'll see in a moment with the `dwFlags` parameter, we can specify how the call should interpret this data.

hModule

This should be set to zero unless we're specifying a resource for the sound data. In which case this parameter must be equal to the file handle for the executable file where the resource is contained.

dwFlags

This parameter can take a combination of the following values:

```
Enum SoundCommands
    SND_ALIAS = &H10000
    SND_ALIAS_ID = &H110000
    SND_ALIAS_START = 0
```

```
    SND_APPLICATION = &H80
    SND_ASYNC = &H1
    SND_FILENAME = &H20000
    SND_LOOP = &H8
    SND_MEMORY = &H4
    SND_NODEFAULT = &H2
    SND_NOSTOP = &H10
    SND_NOWAIT = &H2000
    SND_PURGE = &H40
    SND_RESOURCE = &H40004
    SND_SYNC = &H0
  End Enum
```

I'll leave an explanation of some of the values for later when we start our developing the sound application.

The SoundDemo Application

Now that we have the function definition to play a sound, let's create a standard EXE application called SoundDemo in VB to test out some of the command options. Add a module and call it SoundLib, then add the PlaySound API call and SoundCommands enumeration to this file (both with Public scope). Here's a screen shot of the one and only form in the application:

Here's a brief listing of all the controls on the form:

Object	Property	Setting
Form	Name	frmMain
TextBox	Name	txtFile
Option Button	Name	optSynch

Object	Property	Setting
	Index	0
	Caption	Synchronous
Option Button	Name	optSynch
	Index	1
	Caption	Asynchronous
Option Button	Name	optSynch
	Index	2
	Caption	Be Quiet!
CheckBox	Name	chkLoopSound
Option Button	Name	optMIDI
	Index	0
	Caption	Start MIDI File
Option Button	Name	optMIDI
	Index	1
	Caption	Pause MIDI File
Option Button	Name	optMIDI
	Index	2
	Caption	Resume MIDI File
Option Button	Name	optMIDI
	Index	3
	Caption	Stop MIDI File
	Enabled	False
Command Button	Name	cmdWavPerform
Command Button	Name	cmdMIDIPerform

We'll cover the MIDI stuff in a moment; for now, let's concentrate on WAV files. As you can see, there's only two ways to play the WAV file: synchronous or asynchronous. Let's take a look at the code that's called from the **WAV Perform** command button:

```
Private Sub cmdWAVPerform_Click()

    PlayTheSound
End Sub
```

```
Private Sub PlayTheSound()

    Dim lngCommand As Long
    Dim lngRet As Long

    On Error GoTo error_PlayTheSound

    Screen.MousePointer = vbHourglass

'   Stop any current sound from playing
    lngRet = PlaySound(vbNullString, 0, SoundCommands.SND_PURGE)

'   Now play the sound determined by the options selected.
    If optSynch(2).Value = True Then
     ' We don't do anything else

    Else
        If optSynch(0).Value = True Then
            lngCommand = SoundCommands.SND_SYNC
        Else

            If chkLoopSound.Value = vbChecked Then
                lngCommand = SoundCommands.SND_ASYNC Or _
                             SoundCommands.SND_LOOP
            Else
                lngCommand = SoundCommands.SND_ASYNC
            End If

        End If

        lngRet = PlaySound(txtFile.Text, 0, lngCommand)

        If lngRet = 0 Then
         ' Report the error.
        End If

    End If

    Screen.MousePointer = vbDefault

    Exit Sub

error_PlayTheSound:

    Screen.MousePointer = vbDefault

    MsgBox Err.Number & "  " & Err.Description, _
        vbOKOnly + vbExclamation, "Sound Error"

End Sub
```

First, we stop any sound that's currently playing by making a call to PlaySound, with pszSound equal to vbNullString, and fdwSound equal to SND_PURGE:

```
lngRet = PlaySound(vbNullString, 0, SoundCommands.SND_PURGE)
```

Next, we determine what kind of behavior the user wants by looking at the option button values. If the user selected the Be Quiet button, then we're done, because we've already stopped any current sound from playing. If the 0th one is selected, then we use the SND_SYNC value. Otherwise, we use the SND_ASYNC value. By having an asynchronous playing option, we can have the application start up a recorded conversation in the background and immediately return the control back to the application:

```
If optSynch(0).Value = True Then
    lngCommand = SoundCommands.SND_SYNC
Else

    If chkLoopSound.Value = vbChecked Then
        lngCommand = SoundCommands.SND_ASYNC Or _
                        SoundCommands.SND_LOOP
    Else
        lngCommand = SoundCommands.SND_ASYNC
    End If

End If

lngRet = PlaySound(txtFile.Text, 0, lngCommand)
```

Note that we can also loop a WAV file, however, we can only do this with an asynchronous sound event; if we could loop a synchronous sound, our program would be caught in an endless loop. Also, we could use the FileExists function that we created in the Encryption project to make sure that the file path given is correct, but since the PlaySound won't work if the path is invalid, I simply didn't bother to make the check.

Note that if you type in a filename that is technically correct but doesn't exist on your PC, the default beep will be played

That's all the code needed for playing a sound. I've included a couple of WAV files in the Test Files directory. You have your choice of a doorbell (doorbl.wav), a car driving by (driveby.wav), or a brief flute noise (musica.wav). Personally, I like playing the doorbell file asynchronously with the loop effect on. It reminds me of a really pushy neighbor. There should also be some WAV files installed with Windows that you could use: try the Windows/Media directory.

The mciSendString Call

Now that we have the ability to play WAV files, let's look at another call that will let us play MIDI files. It's name is mciSendString, and its declaration looks like this (you should also add it to SoundLib):

```
Declare Function mciSendString _
    Lib "winmm.dll" Alias "mciSendStringA" _
    (ByVal lpstrCommand As String, _
    ByVal lpstrReturnString As String, _
    ByVal uReturnLength As Long, ByVal hwndCallback As Long) _
    As Long
```

This call is one of the most interesting API calls I've ever seen. There's only one argument called `lpstrCommand` that we're really concerned about for our purposes; the others will be set to zero or `vbNullString`. What makes that argument interesting to me is that you can put together a set of valid commands that the function understands, and it will process them for you. Some of the valid commands that I'm aware of are: `Capability`, `Close`, `Info`, `Open`, `Pause`, `Play`, `Record`, `Resume`, `Set`, `Save`, `Seek`, `Status`, and `Stop`. Following is a brief description of what these commands can do:

Command Name	Description
Capability	Returns information about what a MIDI sequencer can and cannot do.
Close	Closes a MIDI device if it's open.
Info	Retrieves information depending upon other commands given with this one.
Open	Opens the MIDI device.
Pause	Pauses a MIDI device if it's currently playing a MIDI sequence.
Play	Starts a MIDI sequence.
Record	Starts the recording of a MIDI sequence.
Resume	Resumes a MIDI sequence if paused.
Set	Used to set channels on and off, specifies the MIDI port to use, etc.
Save	Saves MIDI sequence data.
Seek	Moves to a specific position in the MIDI sequence.
Status	Used to retrieve information about the device.
Stop	Stops the MIDI sequence currently being played.

Some of these commands also take arguments, like the `Capability` command. For example, if you made the following call:

```
Dim lngRet as Long
Dim strCommand as String

strCommand = "Capability can record"
lngRet = mciSendString(strCommand, vbNullString, 0, 0)
```

`lngRet` would equal a non-zero if the computer could not record MIDI data. Therefore, the return value's meaning will vary depending upon the commands being sent, but no matter what the command is, a non-zero value indicates some kind of error. A zero return value indicates success.

This is reversed from what we've seen from the Win32 calls, which serves as a good example to read up on any documentation you can find about the call. Never assume that all API calls act in the same way, even if they come from the same corporation.

This brings up an interesting problem. How do we report errors? We've been using the `GetLastError` and `FormatMessage` APIs to get extended error information, but when we use any calls from `winmm.dll`, there's no guarantee that this will work. Therefore, I recommend you use the `mciGetErrorString` function (you guessed it, please add it to `SoundLib`), which is declared like this:

```
Declare Function mciGetErrorString _
    Lib "winmm.dll" Alias "mciGetErrorStringA" _
    (ByVal dwError As Long, ByVal lpstrBuffer As String, _
    ByVal uLength As Long) As Long
```

The first argument, `dwError`, should be set to the error code returned by `mciSendString`. The second argument, `lpstrBuffer`, is a `String` variable pre-allocated to a length equal to `uLength`. If we get a value of 1 as the return value, we have the error message in `lpstrBuffer` (we'll have to find the null-termination character in the string ourselves - I'll demonstrate this in a moment). Otherwise, there's no error message for the error code given.

Let's expand the `SoundDemo` project to explore some of the possibilities of the `mciSendString` call.

It should be noted that you use this call to play WAV files as well. Frankly, you can use it to play CDs, animation files, VCRs, etc. This little function has a lot of power, so I encourage you to look into this function in more detail after this chapter is done.

Extending the SoundDemo Project

Before we look at the code underneath the `cmdMIDIPerform` button, let's add a progress bar, called `ProgressBar`, and a timer, called originally `Timer`, to the form. Disable the timer and set its Interval property to 500. These will give us a chance to see some of the return arguments of `mciSendString` in action. The form should now look like this:

The MIDI Perform command button calls the `MIDITheFile` method on its `Click` event like We'll call the `MIDITheFile` routine from the `Click` event of `cmdMIDIPerform`:

```
Private Sub cmdMIDIPerform_Click()

    MIDITheFile

End Sub
```

Here's the `MIDITheFile` routine:

```
Private Sub MIDITheFile()

    Dim lngRet As Long
    Dim strCommand As String

    On Error GoTo error_MIDITheFile

    Screen.MousePointer = vbHourglass

    If optMIDI(0).Value = True Then
    '   Open the file and create an alias.
        strCommand = "Open " & """" & Trim$(txtFile.Text) & """" & _
                    " Alias MIDIfile"
        lngRet = mciSendString(strCommand, vbNullString, 0, 0)

        If lngRet <> 0 Then
            ShowMCIError lngRet
        Else
            ProgressBar.Value = 0
            ProgressBar.Max = GetStatus("Length")
            Timer.Enabled = True
    '       Start the music.
            strCommand = "Play MIDIfile"
            lngRet = mciSendString(strCommand, vbNullString, 0, 0)

            If lngRet <> 0 Then
                ShowMCIError lngRet
            Else
            '   Enable/disable where appropriate
                optMIDI(0).Enabled = False
                optMIDI(1).Enabled = True
                optMIDI(2).Enabled = False
                optMIDI(3).Enabled = True
            End If
```

```
        End If

    ElseIf optMIDI(1).Value = True Then
    '  Pause the sound.
        strCommand = "Pause MIDIfile"
        lngRet = mciSendString(strCommand, vbNullString, 0, 0)

        If lngRet <> 0 Then
            ShowMCIError lngRet
        Else
        '  Enable/disable where appropriate
            optMIDI(0).Enabled = False
            optMIDI(1).Enabled = False
            optMIDI(2).Enabled = True
            optMIDI(3).Enabled = True
        End If

    ElseIf optMIDI(2).Value = True Then
    '  Resume the sound.
        strCommand = "Resume MIDIfile"
        lngRet = mciSendString(strCommand, vbNullString, 0, 0)

        If lngRet <> 0 Then
            ShowMCIError lngRet
        Else
        '  Enable/disable where appropriate
            optMIDI(0).Enabled = False
            optMIDI(1).Enabled = True
            optMIDI(2).Enabled = False
            optMIDI(3).Enabled = True
        End If

    ElseIf optMIDI(3).Value = True Then
    '  Stop the sound.
        strCommand = "Close MIDIfile"
        lngRet = mciSendString(strCommand, vbNullString, 0, 0)
        Timer.Enabled = False
        If lngRet <> 0 Then
            ShowMCIError lngRet
        Else
        '  Enable/disable where appropriate
            optMIDI(0).Enabled = True
            optMIDI(1).Enabled = False
            optMIDI(2).Enabled = False
            optMIDI(3).Enabled = False
        End If

Else
'  Do nothing
End If

Screen.MousePointer = vbDefault
```

```
    Exit Sub

error_MIDITheFile:

    Screen.MousePointer = vbDefault

    MsgBox Err.Number & "  " & Err.Description, _
        vbOKOnly + vbExclamation, "MIDI Error"

End Sub
```

A fair amount of the code deals with UI maintenance (for example, we want to disable the Start MIDI File and Pause MIDI File option buttons if we've successfully paused a MIDI playback), so we won't deal with that logic in this explanation. Let's take a look at the commands we used to manipulate the MIDI file.

The first command that we use is for starting up the file by using the `Open` command with the `Alias` argument:

```
strCommand = "Open " & """" & Trim$(txtFile.Text) & """" &
                    " Alias MIDIfile"
lngRet = mciSendString(strCommand, vbNullString, 0, 0)
```

We don't just use the `Play` command to start the MIDI playback because it doesn't understand long file names, so we have to open it first, give it an alias, and then start the playback using the alias. If your MIDI files exists in the 8.3 file format naming convention under directories that don't have more than 8 characters in the name, then you're set. But there's no guarantee that this will always be the case, so the `Open`/`Play` mechanism is more stable.

Before we `Play` the file we need to set up the progress bar and enable the timer. We reset the bar back to 0, then we set the `Max` property according to the length of the file. To do this I have created a function called `GetStatus`, which will be useful later, that returns the length of the alias file:

```
ProgressBar.Value = 0
ProgressBar.Max = GetStatus("Length")
```

The `GetStatus` function uses the `Status` command for the `lpstrCommand` argument of `mciSendString`. We also pass in a parameter (in this case `"Length"`) as the `Status` command, like the `Capability` command, can accept several parameters:

```
Private Function GetStatus(Command As String) As Integer

    Dim lngRet As Long
    Dim strReturn As String * 255
    Dim intLength As Integer
    Dim strCommand as String

    strCommand = "Status MIDIfile " & Command
    lngRet = mciSendString(strCommand, strReturn, 255, 0)

    If lngRet <> 0 Then
```

```
        ShowMCIError lngRet
        Exit Function
    End IF

    intLength = InStr(strReturn, Chr$(0))
    GetStatus = Val(Left$(strReturn, intLength - 1))

End Function
```

Unlike the previous instances of mciSendString in this project we are using the lpstrReturnString and uReturnLength arguments:

```
lngRet = mciSendString(strCommand, strLength, 255, 0)
```

The Status command, unlike Play, Stop, Pause or Resume, returns a string value, which is stored in the lpstrReturnString argumen (in this case, strReturn). However, the API calls needs to know how much data in can place in the string variable so we need to declare strReturn as a fixed length string:

```
Dim strReturn As String * 255
```

We also need to pass the length of the string in the uReturnLength argument.

In this instance we specify Length as a parameter for the Status command. In a moment we'll also specify Position. As the call returns these values as a string we need to manipulate this value to return an integer which we can use with the progress bar:

```
intLength = InStr(strReturn, Chr$(0))
GetStatus = Val(Left$(strReturn, intLength - 1))
```

Once we have setup the progress bar for this file we can finally begin to Play it:

```
strCommand = "Play MIDIfile"
lngRet = mciSendString(strCommand, vbNullString, 0, 0)
```

The other three commands only work if we've successfully started a MIDI playback. If we want to stop the playback completely, we use the Close command:

```
strCommand = "Close MIDIfile"
lngRet = mciSendString(strCommand, vbNullString, 0, 0)
```

If we simply want to suspend the playback, we use the Pause command:

```
strCommand = "Pause MIDIfile"
lngRet = mciSendString(strCommand, vbNullString, 0, 0)
```

The Resume command will restart a playback from the last pause point:

```
strCommand = "Resume MIDIfile"
lngRet = mciSendString(strCommand, vbNullString, 0, 0)
```

Note that if we ever run into an error, we call the ShowMCIError procedure:

```
If lngRet <> 0 Then
    ShowMCIError lngRet
```

Here's the code for this error routine:

```
Private Sub ShowMCIError(ErrorCode As Long)

    Dim lngError As Long
    Dim strError As String
    Dim lngRet As Long

    On Error Resume Next

'   Report the error.
    strError = String$(129, " ")
    lngError = mciGetErrorString(ErrorCode, strError, 128)
    If lngError = 1 Then
        strError = Left$(strError, InStr(strError, Chr$(0)))
    Else
        strError = "Unknown MIDI Error"
    End If

    Screen.MousePointer = vbDefault

    MsgBox strError, vbOKOnly + vbExclamation, _
        "MIDI Error"

    lngRet = mciSendString("Close MIDIfile", vbNullString, 0, 0)

End Sub
```

It simply uses the mciGetErrorString call we saw earlier. One final thing that you'll notice is that we close the file. This is simply to avoid an error next time we try to assign MIDIfile as an alias because VB thinks the alias is already in use.

Finally we need to code the timer's Timer event so that the progress bar gets updated as the file plays:

```
Private Sub Timer_Timer()

    Dim lngRet As Long

    ProgressBar.Value = GetStatus("Position")

    If ProgressBar.Value = ProgressBar.Max Then
        lngRet = mciSendString("Close MIDIfile", vbNullString, 0, 0)
        If lngRet <> 0 Then ShowMCIError lngRet
        Timer.Enabled = False
    End If

End Sub
```

In this case we are using the Position parameter of the Status command to track the progress of the file.

Note that we also Close *the file upon completion. This may not be so obvious in this case but if we had been playing an* AVI *file then the window would have been left open if we did not close it.*

That's all the code required to play MIDI files. Again I have included a few sample .mid files in the Test Files directory or alternatively you should find some in the Windows/Media directory.

A Quick, Final Word on Multimedia

While most business applications don't rely heavily on sound, the calls you've seen have a fair amount of power associated with them, especially the mciSendString command. However, there are other options that are available for advanced multimedia development, like **OpenGL** and **DirectX**. I've never had a need to investigate these technologies myself, but keep those names in the back of your mind - you never know when you'll have to add a lot of multimedia capabilities to your application.

The Common Dialog Windows

In many Windows applications, like Notepad and Write, you may have noticed that they always have the same dialog windows for application functions like opening and saving a file, choosing the fonts for the text in a window, or changing the color of some geometrical object. This can be done by any Windows application, since Windows allows any application to open these standard dialog windows. The calls needed to use these dialog windows can be found in the comdlg32.dll file. In this section, we'll take a look at the file and color dialog windows to see how they work.

The Common Dialog Control

Before we look at these calls, I want to make a brief point about this control. All of the dialog windows that Windows has can be controlled using this control in VB. However, I have one big problem with this approach. By using a control approach rather than a component approach, you're forced to have a form to "host" or contain the control. This may not be a big deal in most projects, but why a control in the first place? There are other controls like this in VB, like the MAPI and timer ActiveX controls, that really should be non-visual DLL or EXE components. OK, I'll get off the soapbox for now and move on to the dialog details.

Wait...one more point. This "feature" of VB (forcing form loads to host non-visual controls) annoyed me so much with the timer control that I just created my own non-visual component in VB using API calls (which I'll go over in detail in Chapter 8). Therefore, I didn't need a form anymore to use a timer. Personally, I hope that VB starts introducing more and more components that replace the non-visual controls. It may seem like a nit, but I don't want to have a dummy form to host a MAPI control in a middleware business component that I wrote.

The Color Dialog

The color dialog screen is used to allow the user to pick a specific color from a palette. The user may also select from custom palettes as well. Depending on the properties the application set to display the dialog window, it may look like this:

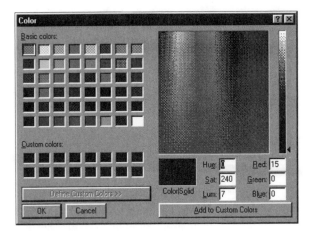

As you can see, the user has a fair amount of choices as to what they can do. They can simply pick a color from the boxes on the left, or they can move the cross-hair cursor on the right to pick a color from the palette. The palette will change depending upon the screen color settings on the PC. Let's take a look at the API call needed to show this dialog.

The ChooseColor Call

The ChooseColor call is the only call you'll need to show the color dialog box:

```
Declare Function ChooseColor Lib "comdlg32.dll" Alias _
    "ChooseColorA" (pChoosecolor As ChooseColor) As Long
```

The only argument to this function, pChoosecolor, is defined as a UDT called CHOOSECOLOR. When I first saw this, I thought that there would be a naming conflict between the function name and the UDT, so I renamed the function to VBChooseColor. As it turns out, it's not a naming conflict - VB can tell the difference between a function call and the usage of a UDT even if they're named the same. I changed it back to ChooseColor, simply to illustrate the fact that you can do it, but you may want to rename it to avoid some needless confusion and to make your code easier to read.

> *One side effect of keeping the function and UDT named the same is that VB only keeps one capitalization style. Most UDTs used by APIs that we've seen are in upper-case letters, but in this case, it will have the same format as the function name.*

The ChooseColor UDT allows us to customize the dialog window to some extent. Here's its definition:

```
Type ChooseColor
    lStructSize As Long
    hwndOwner As Long
    hInstance As Long
    rgbResult As Long
    lpCustColors As Long
    flags As Long
    lCustData As Long
    lpfnHook As Long
    lpTemplateName As String
End Type
```

Let's walk through the parameters of this UDT. The `lStructSize` contains the size of the UDT in bytes. Usually this parameter is set just before the call to `ChooseColor` is made. The `hwndOwner` parameter specifies a window that owns the dialog box. `hInstance` can be used to specify a handle to a dialog box template, but we won't cover that in this book. The `rgbResult` parameter is used to identify the color that the user picked. This parameter can also be set to a RGB color value to set a default color value in the dialog box.

`lpCustColors` allows you to specify up to 16 custom colors on the dialog window. To do this, you have to create an array of a `Long` data type, and fill in each value with a RGB value. This is a nice feature to have, especially if the user created some custom colors from a previous usage of the color dialog window.

The `flags` parameter can take 1 or more of the following enumerated values:

```
Enum ColorCommands
    CC_ANYCOLOR = &H100
    CC_ENABLEHOOK = &H10
    CC_ENABLETEMPLATE = &H20
    CC_ENABLETEMPLATEHANDLE = &H40
    CC_FULLOPEN = &H2
    CC_PREVENTFULLOPEN = &H4
    CC_RGBINIT = &H1
    CC_SHOWHELP = &H8
    CC_SOLIDCOLOR = &H80
End Enum
```

The "`ENABLE`" values deal with templates and callback functions and since I'll cover these later in the book and we aren't going to be using them here, I won't bother discussing them here. Let's stick with the basics. The `CC_ANYCOLOR` forces the dialog box to display all available colors in the Basic colors section. The `CC_FULLOPEN` and `CC_PREVENTFULLOPEN` tell the dialog box whether or not to show the full palette on the right-hand side of the box.

Note that the user will still be able to show this section even if it's not initially shown; preventing the section from initially displaying does not disable the Define Custom Colors>> button.

If you've specified a color in `rgbDisplay`, then make sure to include `CC_RGBINIT` in `flags` - then the color defined in `rgbDisplay` will be selected as the default. The `CC_SHOWHELP` value displays the Help button on the dialog box (you have to have a window handle specified in `hwndOwner` to receive the help message, but this gets into callback territories and subclassing, which we'll address in the next two chapters with different examples). Finally, specifying `CC_SOLIDCOLOR` forces the dialog box to display only solid colors in the Basic colors section.

Back to the rest of the UDT parameters. The `lCustData` and `lpfnHook` allow you to process messages sent from the dialog box as you see fit; we'll pass on this feature. Finally, the `lpTemplateName` allow you to name the template defined by `hInstance`.

The return value of `ChooseColor` lets us know if the user actually selected a color or not. If a non-zero value is returned, the `rgbDisplay` value will contain the RGB color value chosen by the user. Otherwise, either the user simply canceled the dialog box, or an error occurred. Now that we have all that we need to show this dialog box, let's create a sample application to play with the call.

There is a function called `CommDlgExtendedError` *that you can use to see if an error occurred when a zero value is returned by* `ChooseColor`. *In fact,* `CommDlgExtendedError` *can be used for any of the APIs that display dialog boxes from* `commdlg.dll`. *For our purposes, we'll simply treat a zero value as a canceled dialog box. Also, note that the SDK says that you should use this function to return error information. Therefore, don't use the* `GetWin32ErrorDescription` *function that we have been using to get error messages from common dialog errors.*

The CommonDialogDemo Project

As we did in the previous section, we'll create another project in VB to work with the dialog calls. Call the project `CommonDialogDemo`, then add a module and call it `ComDlgLib`. Into this module copy the `ChooseColor` API function and UDT plus the `ColorCommands` enum defined above making sure they all have `Public` scope. Then construct the main screen to look like this:

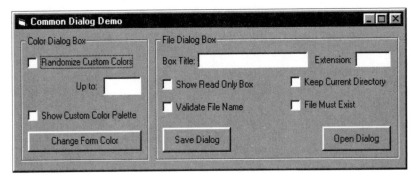

Here's a list of all the controls:

Object	Property	Setting
Form	Name	frmMain
CheckBox	Name	chkRandomColors
CheckBox	Name	chkShowFullBox
TextBox	Name	txtColors
Command Button	Name	cmdChangeFormColor
TextBox	Name	txtBoxTitle
TextBox	Name	txtDefaultExtension
CheckBox	Name	chkShowReadOnly
CheckBox	Name	chkValidateFileName
CheckBox	Name	chkKeepCurDir
CheckBox	Name	chkFileMustExist
Command Button	Name	cmdSave
Command Button	Name	cmdOpen

Don't worry about the **File Dialog** frame for now - we'll get to those in the next section. The **Change Form Color** button will change the background color of the form using the color dialog box. Let's take a look at the ChangeFormColor method, which is called on the Click event of the cmdChangeFormColor command button like this:

```
Private Sub cmdChangeFormColor_Click()

    ChangeFormColor

End Sub
```

The ChangeFormColor routine uses the ChooseColor API call to change the background color of the form:

```
Private Sub ChangeFormColor()

    Dim lngC As Long
    Dim lngColors(1 To 16) As Long
    Dim lngNumColors As Long
    Dim lngRet As Long
    Dim udtColor As ChooseColor

    On Error GoTo error_ChangeFormColor

    Screen.MousePointer = vbHourglass

    With udtColor
    '   Set the structure size.
        .lStructSize = Len(udtColor)
    '   Set the default value equal to the current color.
        .rgbResult = Me.BackColor
        .hwndOwner = Me.hWnd
        .hInstance = 0

        If chkRandomColors.Value = vbChecked Then
        '   Make sure a long value was entered!
            lngNumColors = CLng(txtColors.Text)

            If lngNumColors > 16 Then
                lngNumColors = 16
            ElseIf lngNumColors < 0 Then
                lngNumColors = 1
            End If

            For lngC = 1 To (lngNumColors)
            '   Generate a random color.
                lngColors(lngC) = Int((16777216 * Rnd) + 1)
            Next lngC

        End If

        .lpCustColors = VarPtr(lngColors(1))

    '   Make sure that our initial color is used.
        .flags = ColorCommands.CC_RGBINIT

        If chkShowFullBox.Value = vbChecked Then
        '   Show the full palette.
            .flags = .flags Or ColorCommands.CC_FULLOPEN
```

```
                    End If
                    Screen.MousePointer = vbDefault

              '    Now let the user select the color.
                    lngRet = ChooseColor(udtColor)

                    If lngRet <> 0 Then
                    '    Reset the background color.
                        Me.BackColor = .rgbResult
        End If

            End With

            Screen.MousePointer = vbDefault

            Exit Sub

        error_ChangeFormColor:

            Screen.MousePointer = vbDefault

            MsgBox Err.Number & "   " & Err.Description

        End Sub
```

This code has a subtle, interesting code trick, so let's walk through its implementation to make sure we understand it. We first set up some of the udtColor's parameters, like the hwnd and hInstance values:

```
'    Set the structure size.
     .lStructSize = Len(udtColor)
'    Set the default value equal to the current color.
     .rgbResult = Me.BackColor
     .hwndOwner = Me.hWnd
     .hInstance = 0
```

Nothing unusual so far. However, the next If statement is where the magic is introduced. I decided to allow the user to have the program generate up to 16 random custom colors (not something I would recommend for the professional business program, mind you). To do this, I use the lngColors array that has 16 elements. If the user checked the chkRandomColors check box, I create up to 16 random custom colors.

```
If chkRandomColors.Value = vbChecked Then
'    Make sure a long value was entered!
     lngNumColors = CLng(txtColors.Text)

     If lngNumColors > 16 Then
         lngNumColors = 16
     ElseIf lngNumColors < 0 Then
         lngNumColors = 1
     End If

     For lngC = 1 To (lngNumColors)
     '    Generate a random color.
         lngColors(lngC) = Int((16777216 * Rnd) + 1)
     Next lngC

End If
```

The magical number 16777216 is the largest RGB color value (each color is defined using 8 bits. There are three colors: red, green, and blue. Therefore, $2^8*2^8*2^8 = 16777216$.) The number of random colors generated depends upon the value entered into txtColors (note than an error will be caught if the user doesn't enter in a correct numerical value).

So what's the trick that I mentioned before? It's the one line of code that lets the structure know what these custom colors should be:

```
.lpCustColors = VarPtr(lngColors(1))
```

VarPtr is one of those undocumented functions that we briefly talked about in Chapter 2. In this case, it comes in extremely handy. If you look at Microsoft's documentation on ChooseColor, it explicitly states that lpCustColors is a pointer to an array of COLORREF, or RGB, values (which is why we declared the array as a Long). However, this isn't like the case where we pass in the first element of the array to have an API call get a pointer to the array. For example, if we tried to do this:

```
.lpCustColors = lngColors(1)
```

lpCustColors would now have the actual value of lngColors(1). Whatever that value translate to a memory pointer, we're virtually guaranteed to throw a memory exception. For example, on a test run of the program on my machine, lngColors(1) was equal to 12997983, but VarPtr(lngColors(1)) was equal to 6333784.

> *Note that if you wanted to retrieve the custom colors generated by a user, you'd have to use the* CopyMemory *API call to retrieve the color values pointed at by* lpCustColors.

Finally, we set the flags parameter to show the entire color dialog box (CC_FULLOPEN) along with using our default color (CC_RGBINIT) if the user checked the chkShowFullBox check box:

```
' Make sure that our initial color is used.
  .flags = ColorCommands.CC_RGBINIT

If chkShowFullBox.Value = vbChecked Then
' Show the full palette.
  .flags = .flags Or ColorCommands.CC_FULLOPEN
End If
```

Here's what I got one time when I asked for 13 random colors:

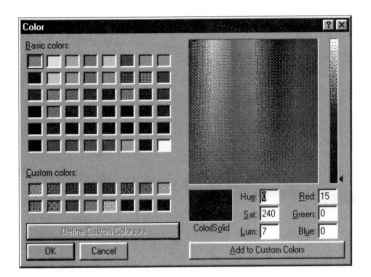

Although it may be hard to see the difference in the randomly generated colors, notice that the last three boxes in the Custom colors: section are not set.

The File Dialog

The file dialog screen is used to retrieve information from the user to determine what files should be opened or saved. It does **NOT** actually perform the open and save operations; it only lets you know the file(s) that the user selected. Therefore, your program still has to open and/or save the file selected. However, having a standard file dialog screen available will save you a lot of time trying to come up with one yourself. Here's a screen shot of what the file dialog box looks like:

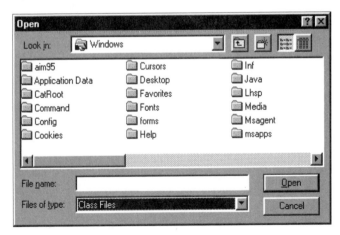

Let's take a look at the two API calls needed to open and save the chosen files, along with the one UDT that is used by both of the calls.

GetOpenFileInfo and GetSaveFileInfo

These two functions are very similar to the `ChooseColor` API that we just used:

```
Declare Function GetOpenFileName Lib "comdlg32.dll" Alias _
    "GetOpenFileNameA" (pOpenfilename As OPENFILENAME) As Long

Declare Function GetSaveFileName Lib "comdlg32.dll" Alias _
    "GetSaveFileNameA" (pOpenfilename As OPENFILENAME) As Long
```

They both have only one argument, pOpenfilename, which is defined as an OPENFILENAME UDT (we'll get to its definition shortly). In both cases, if the return value is non-zero, the user did not cancel the dialog box and either selected or entered in the file name. You can check one of the lpstrFile parameter of pOpenfilename to see what the file path is. As with the color dialog box, we'll assume a return value of zero signifies a cancellation on the user's behalf.

The OPENFILENAME UDT

This is by far one of the biggest UDTs I've seen in a while:

```
Type OPENFILENAME
    lStructSize As Long
    hwndOwner As Long
    hInstance As Long
    lpstrFilter As String
    lpstrCustomFilter As String
    nMaxCustFilter As Long
    nFilterIndex As Long
    lpstrFile As String
    nMaxFile As Long
    lpstrFileTitle As String
    nMaxFileTitle As Long
    lpstrInitialDir As String
    lpstrTitle As String
    flags As Long
    nFileOffset As Integer
    nFileExtension As Integer
    lpstrDefExt As String
    lCustData As Long
    lpfnHook As Long
    lpTemplateName As String
End Type
```

We won't go over the ones we've already discussed in the ChooseColor UDT (like lStructSize and hwndOwner) – they have the same meaning here as they did in the other one – so let's start with lpstrFilter. It allows you to define the file filters that show up in the Files of type: combo box. The filter is defined in pairs – the first value is the filter description, and the second value is the filter patterns. You can define multiple filter patterns if you wish, but a semicolon must separate each pattern. Each pair is separated by the null character (chr$(0)). Also, the lpstrFilter string must be terminated by at least two null characters. Here's a code snippet to show you how all of this is set up:

```
udtFile.lpstrFilter = "Class Files" & Chr$(0) & "*.cls" & _
                    Chr$(0) & "Other VB Files" & Chr$(0) & _
                    "*.vbp;*.cls;*.bas;*.frm" & Chr$(0)
```

This code would create two file types, one that would select class files, and the other that would select other kinds of VB files. Notice that we didn't end the string with two null characters, since VB already ends the string with a null character for us.

If you want, you can use custom filters similar to the `lpCustColors` *parameter in the* `ChooseColor` *UDT. You would set the* `lpstrCustomFilter` *equal to a memory buffer that would be used to retrieve and set filter information. We won't cover this here, but it may be useful if a user wants to set up some predefined filters than they want to reuse.*

`nMaxCustFilter` defines the maximum size for the filter. Also, you can pre-select which filter item will be used by setting `nFilterIndex` equal to the pair you want selected (note that this value is 1-based). If you don't set this parameter yourself, the first pattern will be used by default.
The `lpstrFile` parameter is used to set and/or retrieve the filename in the dialog box. You can set it equal to a null string if you like, but we have to use this parameter to figure out what the user chose, so we should set it equal to a pre-initialized string. You also set `nMaxFile` equal to the buffer size.

> **Note that the MS documentation specifies that this should be at least 256 characters long. If you don't make the buffer big enough, the dialog box will return a zero and** `CommDlgExtendedError` **would report a** "buffer size too small" **error.**

The `lpstrFileTitle` and `nMaxFileTitle` parameters are very similar to these parameters, but they only contain the filename and extension without the fully qualified path of the file.

If you want the dialog box to start in a specific path, you can set this using the `lpstrInitialDir` parameter. If you don't care about this, the dialog box will use the current directory. The `lpstrTitle` parameter allows you to customize the title bar of the dialog box; the box will use the **Save As** or **Open** titles if you don't specify one.

But wait, there's more! The `flags` parameter has a lot of values that we can use to initialize the dialog box. Here are all of the valid values:

```
Enum FileCommands
    OFN_ALLOWMULTISELECT = &H200
    OFN_CREATEPROMPT = &H2000
    OFN_ENABLEHOOK = &H20
    OFN_ENABLETEMPLATE = &H40
    OFN_ENABLETEMPLATEHANDLE = &H80
    OFN_EXPLORER = &H80000
    OFN_EXTENSIONDIFFERENT = &H400
    OFN_FILEMUSTEXIST = &H1000
    OFN_HIDEREADONLY = &H4
    OFN_LONGNAMES = &H200000
    OFN_NOCHANGEDIR = &H8
    OFN_NODEREFERENCELINKS = &H100000
    OFN_NOLONGNAMES = &H40000
    OFN_NONETWORKBUTTON = &H20000
    OFN_NOREADONLYRETURN = &H8000
    OFN_NOTESTFILECREATE = &H10000
```

```
    OFN_NOVALIDATE = &H100
OFN_OVERWRITEPROMPT = &H2
    OFN_PATHMUSTEXIST = &H800
    OFN_READONLY = &H1
    OFN_SHAREAWARE = &H4000
    OFN_SHAREFALLTHROUGH = 2
    OFN_SHARENOWARN = 1
    OFN_SHAREWARN = 0
    OFN_SHOWHELP = &H10
    OFS_MAXPATHNAME = 128
End Enum
```

We'll only touch on those that are useful for our purposes. The OFN_ALLOWMULTISELECT value allows the user to select multiple files from the dialog box. If you do this, the lpstrFile parameter will separate the files with null characters (now that buffer size becomes really important!).

The OFN_CREATEPROMPT will display a message box if the file entered doesn't exist yet. Again, this does not create the file; it only warns the user of the non-existence of the file.

OFN_EXPLORER specifies that the box uses the Explorer-like style. You only need to specify this flag if you're allowing multiple file selects, custom templates or hook procedures (although we will address callback functions in the next chapter, this does lead to window message processing and other complex issues, something that we won't address here).

The OFN_FILEMUSTEXIST and OFN_PATHMUSTEXIST can be used to force the user to specify files that already exist.

Note that these two values have to be specified together using the Or *operator.*

If you use OFN_HIDEREADONLY, the **Read Only** check box will **NOT** show up (as is the situation in the screen shot earlier). If you don't specify the parameter, then the check box will be displayed underneath the **Files of type:** combo box. This can be useful if you want to assure a user that you will not alter the contents of a file. You can also specify that the box is checked when the dialog box opens by specifying the OFN_READONLY.

OFN_NOCHANGEDIR will reset the current directory to what it was before the box was opened. This means that if the current directory was c:\mydir and the user selected a file from D:\Thisdir, the current directory will remain C:\Mydir if OFN_NOCHANGEDIR is used. One of the more interesting values is OFN_NODEREFERENCELINKS. If the user selects a LNK file and this value is not given, you will actually have the name of the referenced file in lpstrFile. If you want to use the shortcut file, you have to specify this value.

Having said all that, we're still not done with the parameter list for OPENFILENAME! However, I only want to cover two more parameters. The first one is nFileOffset, which lets you know how long the path is in lpstrFile. For example, if lpstrFile was equal to D:\Thisdir\Thatdir\Theother.txt, nFileOffset would equal 19 (the path is the first 19 characters, or D:\Thisdir\Thatdir\). The other parameter is lpstrDefExt, which allows you to specify a default file extension. You can set this to anything you want, but Windows will only use the first three characters (note that this only applies for the GetSaveFileName). The API calls will append this extension to the file name if the user did not specify an extension.

This isn't one of the more trivial APIs you'll find. Its complexity comes from its only argument, which has 20 parameters. You'll probably never use all of the parameters in one call, but let's take a look at the `CommonDialogDemo` to see how these two calls can be used.

The CommonDialogDemo Project Revisited

Let's take a look at the two API calls in action. You'll note that our UI options in `frmMain` do not support all of the combinations possible in the `OPENFILENAME` UDT - we're more concerned about the differences between the two. If you'll notice, each command button calls the `FileDialogAPI`. The routine accepts a parameter `APIType` which it uses to differentiate between the command buttons. The **Open Dialog** button passes in `0` and **Save Dialog** passes in `1`:

```vb
Private Sub cmdOpen_Click()

    FileDialogAPI 0

End Sub
```

```vb
Private Sub cmdSave_Click()

    FileDialogAPI 1

End Sub
```

```vb
Private Sub FileDialogAPI(APIType As Long)

    Dim lngRet As Long
    Dim udtFile As OPENFILENAME

    On Error GoTo error_FileDialogAPI

    Screen.MousePointer = vbHourglass

    With udtFile
        .lStructSize = Len(udtFile)
        .hwndOwner = Me.hWnd
        .hInstance = App.hInstance
        .lpstrFilter = "Class Files" & Chr$(0) & "*.cls" & Chr$(0) & _
                       "Other VB Files" & Chr$(0) & _
                       "*.bas;*.frm;*.vbp" & Chr$(0) & _
                       "My Files" & Chr$(0) & "my*.*" & Chr$(0)
        .nFilterIndex = 1
        .lpstrFile = String$(1025, " ")

    ' Just to be safe...
        .nMaxFile = Len(.lpstrFile) - 1

    ' Add the title.
        .lpstrTitle = Trim$(txtBoxTitle.Text)

    ' Add the default extension.
        .lpstrDefExt = Trim$(txtDefaultExtension.Text)

    ' Now add the flags.
        If chkFileMustExist.Value = vbChecked Then
            .flags = .flags Or FileCommands.OFN_FILEMUSTEXIST
```

```
            End If

            If chkKeepCurDir.Value = vbChecked Then
                .flags = .flags Or FileCommands.OFN_NOCHANGEDIR
            End If

            If chkShowReadOnly.Value = vbUnchecked Then
                .flags = .flags Or FileCommands.OFN_HIDEREADONLY
            End If

            If chkValidateFileName.Value = vbUnchecked Then
                .flags = .flags Or FileCommands.OFN_NOVALIDATE
            End If

            If APIType = 1 Then
                lngRet = GetSaveFileName(udtFile)
            Else
                lngRet = GetOpenFileName(udtFile)
            End If

            If lngRet <> 0 Then
                Screen.MousePointer = vbDefault
                MsgBox "Returned file: " & vbCrLf & _
                        Trim$(.lpstrFile), _
                        vbOKOnly + vbInformation, _
                        "File Return"
            End If

        End With
        Screen.MousePointer = vbDefault

        Exit Sub

error_FileDialogAPI:

        Screen.MousePointer = vbDefault

        MsgBox Err.Number & " " & Err.Description

End Sub
```

We start by setting up the udtFile UDT. The filter is set up similar to the code snippet I gave before, but this time the filter has a pattern that looks for files that start with the characters "my". Note the use of the wildcard character "*" which basically says, "it doesn't matter what character or characters go here":

```
With udtFile
    .lStructSize = Len(udtFile)
    .hwndOwner = Me.hWnd
    .hInstance = App.hInstance
    .lpstrFilter = "Class Files" & Chr$(0) & "*.cls" & Chr$(0) & _
                "Other VB Files" & Chr$(0) & _
                "*.bas;*.frm;*.vbp" & Chr$(0) & _
                "My Files" & Chr$(0) & "my*.*" & Chr$(0)
    .nFilterIndex = 1
```

lpstrFile is equal to a string with 1025 spaces, and, for safety's sake, we only allow a maximum of 1024 characters on a return value. The title bar and default extension are set as well according to the text boxes; if the user didn't enter anything, they'll just have their default values anyway:

```
.lpstrFile = String$(1025, " ")

' Just to be safe...
.nMaxFile = Len(.lpstrFile) - 1

' Add the title.
.lpstrTitle = Trim$(txtBoxTitle.Text)

' Add the default extension.
.lpstrDefExt = Trim$(txtDefaultExtension.Text)
```

Now we set the flags parameter. The user can specify if the **Read Only** box should be displayed, the current directory can change, the file must exist, and the file name must be valid:

```
' Now add the flags.
If chkFileMustExist.Value = vbChecked Then
   .flags = .flags Or FileCommands.OFN_FILEMUSTEXIST
End If

If chkKeepCurDir.Value = vbChecked Then
   .flags = .flags Or FileCommands.OFN_NOCHANGEDIR
End If
If chkShowReadOnly.Value = vbUnchecked Then
   .flags = .flags Or FileCommands.OFN_HIDEREADONLY
End If

If chkValidateFileName.Value = vbUnchecked Then
   .flags = .flags Or FileCommands.OFN_NOVALIDATE
End If
```

Finally, we display either the **Open** or **Save** dialog box according to the value that was passed in:

```
If APIType = 1 Then
   lngRet = GetSaveFileName(udtFile)
Else
   lngRet = GetOpenFileName(udtFile)
End If
```

After the API function returns, we check the return value and display the result if the function was successful.

A Quick, Final Word on Dialog Boxes

We didn't cover all of the dialog boxes that you can call from comdlg32.dll, like the printer and font boxes, but with the information given in this section, you'll have no problems working with those. I can't recommend whether or not you should use the control in VB or go straight to the API calls. The VB control is a bit easier to work with, and encapsulates the API calls well. However, by using the APIs, you go right to the source. There's a trade-off here in either case, and I'll let you decide what's best for your purposes.

Extending Windows Functionality

We're familiar with copying files from Chapter 2, but we didn't show the status of the copying operation itself. In this section, we'll create a small project that will display the file operations window that most of us have seen in Windows Explorer. The really cool thing about these functions is that we get the ability to perform copy or delete functions with a "Cancel" option, something that wouldn't be trivial to pull off in VB.

The SHFileOperation Call

If you've ever copied, moved, or deleted files in Windows Explorer, you've probably seen a screen that looks something like this:

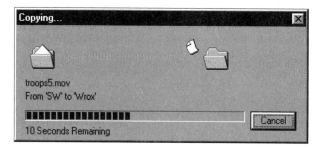

To have this window pop-up out of your own application, use the SHFileOperation call:

```
Declare Function SHFileOperation Lib "shell32.dll" _
    Alias "SHFileOperationA" (lpFileOp As SHFILEOPSTRUCT) As Long
```

Just like every other call we've seen in this chapter, the arguments are simple - it's the parameters that kill you! The lpFileOp argument is a SHFILEOPSTUCT UDT, which looks like this:

```
Type SHFILEOPSTRUCT
    hwnd As Long
    wFunc As Long
    pFrom As String
    pTo As String
    fFlags As Integer
    fAnyOperationsAborted As Long
    hNameMappings As Long
    lpszProgressTitle As String
End Type
```

Let's walk through the parameters. Yup, hwnd is the handle of the calling window (no surprises there). The wFunc parameter can take any one of the following enumerated values:

```
Enum FileFunctions
    FO_COPY = &H2
    FO_DELETE = &H3
    FO_MOVE = &H1
    FO_RENAME = &H4
End Enum
```

The names speak for themselves - we've got all the power we need for file operations. The pFrom and pTo parameters are exactly like the lpstrFilter parameter in OPENFILENAME. You separate multiple file names (wildcard characters are allowed) using a null character, and the list must end with two null characters. Note that you don't have to specify what pTo is on a delete operation. The fFlags parameter can take a combination of one or more of the following enumerated values:

```
Enum FileFlags
    FOF_ALLOWUNDO = &H40
    FOF_CONFIRMMOUSE = &H2
    FOF_FILESONLY = &H80
    FOF_MULTIDESTFILES = &H1
    FOF_NOCONFIRMATION = &H10
    FOF_NOCONFIRMMKDIR = &H200
    FOF_RENAMEONCOLLISION = &H8
    FOF_SILENT = &H4
    FOF_SIMPLEPROGRESS = &H100
    FOF_WANTMAPPINGHANDLE = &H20
End Enum
```

Let's go over most of these values. FOF_ALLOWUNDO specifies that you want Windows to undo the operation if the user cancels it. FOF_FILESONLY should be used when your operation will be performed with filenames containing wildcard characters. FOF_MULTIDESTFILES is tricky. You can specify a destination file for each source file, but there must be a one-to-one correspondence with this relationship. For example, if I did this:

```
udtShell.pFrom = "C:\File1.txt" & chr$(0) & "C:\File2.txt"
```

I could either dump all the files into one directory by not using the FOF_MULTIDESTFILES options and setting pTo like this:

```
udtShell.pTo = "C:\"
```

Or, I could use the FOF_MULTIDESTFILES option and set pTo up like this:

```
udtShell.pTo = "D:\Newfile1.txt" & chr$(0) & "C:\Newdir\Newfile2.txt"
```

FOF_NOCONFIRMATION will always respond with the **Yes for All** option whenever a dialog box is displayed. If you don't want a confirmation of a new directory being made for whatever reason, specify FOF_NOCONFIRMMKDIR. FOF_NOERRORUI will prevent a dialog box from being displayed if an error occurs.

FOF_RENAMEONCOLLISION will tell the OS to rename destination files if there is a name collision in the destination location. This may be nice if you want to make sure that the file will get saved on a name collision, but you'll have to use another flag (defined at the end of this section) to get what the new name is.

If you don't want to display the names of the files that are being manipulated by the current shell operation, specify FOF_SIMPLEPROGRESS (note that the progress bar which displays the status of the operation will still be shown in the window). You may not want to specify this flag for some business applications, because the progress window gives users an idea as to what the program is doing.

However, for applications that can't display windows (like NT services), this flag is definitely needed. If you don't want the status window to show up at all, you can use the `FOF_SILENT` flag.

`FOF_WANTMAPPINGHANDLE` must be used along with `FOF_RENAMEONCOLLISION` to grab some extra information about the renamed files. (I'll explain how this works ina moment).

The `fAnyOperationAborted` will be a non-zero value if the user canceled the operation. Even if some files were copied before the users canceled the operation `fAnyOperationAborted` would still be equal to a non-zero value.

`hNameMappings` will contain a handle to an array of `SHNAMEMAPPING` UDTs if any files were renamed during the operation (note that this only occurs if the `FOF_WANTMAPPINGHANDLE` is specified in `fFlags`). This UDT looks like this:

```
Type SHNAMEMAPPING
    pszOldPath As String
    pszNewPath As String
    cchOldPath As Long
    cchNewPath As Long
End Type
```

The first two members of this UDT, `pszOldPath` and `pszNewPath`, are used to store the old and new names of the file path, respectively. `cchOldpath` and `cchNewPath` are used to let you know how many characters are in each buffer.

Finally, if you want your own title in the progress dialog box, you can set `lpszProgressTitle` equal to that title, but you must use the `FOF_SIMPLEPROGRESS` value to show the title.

The SHDemo Project

I've created one final test project that we can use to play with the `SHFileOperation` function. Before we continue, please add the `SHFileOperation` API call along with the UDTs and the enumerations defined in this section to a module called `ShellLib` with `Public` scope. Set up the form to look like this:

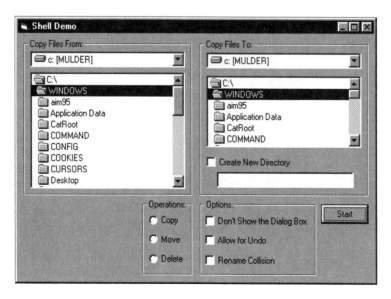

Object	Property	Setting
Form	Name	frmShellDemo
DriveListBox	Name	drvFrom
DirListBox	Name	dirFrom
DriveListBox	Name	drvTo
DirListBox	Name	dirTo
CheckBox	Name	chkNewDir
TextBox	Name	txtNewDir
Option Button	Name	optOp
	Index	0
	Caption	**Copy**
Option Button	Name	optOp
	Index	1
	Caption	**Move**
Option Button	Name	optOp
	Index	2
	Caption	**Delete**
CheckBox	Name	chkDontShow
CheckBox	Name	chkAllowUndo
CheckBox	Name	chkRenameCollision
Command Button	Name	cmdStart

The form allows you to choose the source and destination directories to either move, copy, or delete files. You can also create a new destination directory. Let's take a look at the RunFileOperation method, which is called from the Click event of cmdStart:

```
Private Sub cmdStart_Click()

    RunFileOperation

End Sub


Private Sub RunFileOperation()

    Dim lngRet As Long
    Dim strRet As String
    Dim udtFileOp As SHFILEOPSTRUCT
```

```
On Error GoTo error_RunFileOperation

Screen.MousePointer = vbHourglass

strRet = ValidateInterface

If strRet <> "" Then
'   Let the user know of the problems.
    MsgBox strRet, vbOKOnly + vbExclamation, "Data Error"
Else

    With udtFileOp
        .hwnd = Me.hwnd
        If optOp(0).Value = True Then
            '   Copy
            .wFunc = FileFunctions.FO_COPY
        ElseIf optOp(1).Value = True Then
            '   Move
            .wFunc = FileFunctions.FO_MOVE
        Else
            '   Delete
            .wFunc = FileFunctions.FO_DELETE
        End If

    '   Set the from and to paths correctly.
        .pFrom = dirFrom.Path & "\*.*" & Chr$(0)

        If chkNewDir.Value = vbChecked Then

            If InStr(dirTo.Path, "\") > 0 Then
                .pTo = dirTo.Path & txtNewDir.Text
            Else
                .pTo = dirTo.Path & "\" & txtNewDir.Text
            End If

        Else
            .pTo = dirTo.Path
        End If

        .pTo = .pTo & "\" & Chr$(0)

    '   Now set up all the flags.
        .fFlags = .fFlags Or FileFlags.FOF Or FileFlags.FOF_FILESONLY

        If chkAllowUndo.Value = vbChecked Then
            .fFlags = .fFlags Or FileFlags.FOF_ALLOWUNDO
        End If

        If chkDontShow.Value = vbChecked Then
            .fFlags = .fFlags Or FileFlags.FOF_SILENT
        End If

        If Me.chkRenameCollision.Value = vbChecked Then
            .fFlags = .fFlags Or FileFlags.FOF_RENAMEONCOLLISION
        End If

    '   Now run the function.
        lngRet = SHFileOperation(udtFileOp)

        If lngRet <> 0 Then
```

```
                    MsgBox "SHFileOperation Failed."

            Else
                If .fAnyOperationsAborted <> 0 Then
                    MsgBox "Aborted Operation"
                End If

            End If

        End With

    End If
    Screen.MousePointer = vbDefault

    Exit Sub
error_RunFileOperation:

    Screen.MousePointer = vbDefault

    MsgBox Err.Number & "  " & Err.Description, _
        vbOKOnly + vbExclamation, "Program Error"

End Sub
```

It's pretty simple. The ValidateInterface checks to see if the source and destination directories have been specified. It returns " " on success and error information on failure - its implementation looks like this:

```
Private Function ValidateInterface() As String

    On Error GoTo error_ValidateInterface

'   Check the source directory.
    If dirFrom.Path = "" Then
        ValidateInterface = "Please select a source directory."
        Exit Function
    End If

'   Check the destination directory.
    If dirTo.Path = "" Then
        If chkNewDir.Value = vbChecked And _
        txtNewDir.Text = "" Then
        ValidateInterface = "Please select a " & _
                                "destination directory."
        Exit Function
    End If
    End If

    Exit Function

error_ValidateInterface:

    ValidateInterface = Err.Description

End Function
```

Assuming that `ValidateInterface` verifies the directories we then specify the correct file operation according to the user's selections in the option buttons, drive list boxes and directory list boxes:

```
If optOp(0).Value = True Then
'   Copy
    .wFunc = FileFunctions.FO_COPY
ElseIf optOp(1).Value = True Then
'   Move
    .wFunc = FileFunctions.FO_MOVE
Else
'   Delete
.wFunc = FileFunctions.FO_DELETE
End If

'   Set the from and to paths correctly.
.pFrom = dirFrom.Path & "\*.*" & Chr$(0)

If chkNewDir.Value = vbChecked Then

    If InStr(dirTo.Path, "\") > 0 Then
        .pTo = dirTo.Path & txtNewDir.Text
    Else
        .pTo = dirTo.Path & "\" & txtNewDir.Text
    End If

Else
    .pTo = dirTo.Path
End If

.pTo = .pTo & "\" & Chr$(0)
```

If they are, we then set these directories, and. We also set `fFlags` equal to the correct number of values to do what the user requests with the check boxes:

```
'   Now set up all the flags.
    .fFlags = .fFlags Or FileFlags.FOF Or FileFlags.FOF_FILESONLY

    If chkAllowUndo.Value = vbChecked Then
        .fFlags = .fFlags Or FileFlags.FOF_ALLOWUNDO
    End If

    If chkDontShow.Value = vbChecked Then
        .fFlags = .fFlags Or FileFlags.FOF_SILENT
    End If

    If Me.chkRenameCollision.Value = vbChecked Then
        .fFlags = .fFlags Or FileFlags.FOF_RENAMEONCOLLISION
    End If
```

Finally, we call `SHFileOperation` to do everything for us:

```
lngRet = SHFileOperation(udtFileOp)
```

A Quick, Final Word on File Operations

I really like this function. It's very similar to the common dialog boxes, where you're calling functions that create standard dialog boxes or perform operations in a standard, Windows-like fashion. This was the first time I ever used this function, but now that I have, I think I'm going to start using it whenever I need to do file operations.

Summary

In this chapter, we saw how we can extend our applications further by using API calls from DLLs other than the core DLLs that we've been investigating.

We now should be able to:

❑ Add sound and other multimedia functions to our apps
❑ Use the common dialog boxes using only API calls
❑ Display the status of file operations

In the next chapter, we'll start to take a look at one of the biggest changes to the VB environment: the ability to support callback procedures through the use of the `AddressOf` operator.

7

Callbacks and the AddressOf Operator

Throughout this book, we've been looking at API calls that have opened up a lot of doors to the lower levels of the Windows OS. File manipulation, graphics, multimedia...we've covered the basics, and I'm sure you've seen some interesting possibilities to extend the examples I've given. The funny thing is, we haven't even touched upon the good stuff yet!

In this chapter, we'll cover:

- ❑ Windows callbacks
- ❑ Function pointers
- ❑ The AddressOf operator

In my opinion, callbacks and the AddressOf operator have been key in making VB a serious Windows development tool and by the end of this chapter I hope that you can begin to see their potential.

What is a Callback?

When I first saw the AddressOf keyword in a VBPJ article, I didn't quite understand just what it was doing. It excited me because it has something to do with an address to a function, something that I remember reading about in a C++ book from ages past, but when I tried to run their example code, I crashed VB something fierce. Mind you, it wasn't VBPJ's fault; I was just playing around with a new feature. But because I don't like it when someone else experiences the same programming pain that I went through, I decided to give a "real-world" experience that demonstrates what a callback is. Hopefully, once we move back into the VB world, you'll be able to see the power and the dangers that the AddressOf operator has.

OK, the real reason I'm doing this is because I've always wanted to write a fictional short story, and this may be my only chance to do it. Sorry if it's not up there with Shakespeare. I should also note that any resemblance to my friends, family, or work situations (both past and present) are purely coincidental. Where necessary, names have been changed to protect the guilty.

Callbacks in the Real World

The world of dissatisfied end-users. They who want a 2 billion record, 6 table join query in Access 97 to run in 1 nanosecond on an 8 Meg 486 box with only a 250 Meg hard drive. (Never mind the physical impossibility of this scenario; the requirement happened somehow). And of course, if it's not ready by 5:00, the CEO won't get his report, and the search for the innocent will begin.

So I'm slaving away at my desk, trying every trick that I know to produce a miracle of biblical proportions. Just as I start to see a way out, (it involved selling stolen merchandise on the black market and using the money to buy a quad-processor machine with 2 Gig of memory, but that's another story), the phone rings.
Disgruntled, I answer, "What?"

A meek voice responds on the other end, "Um...Jason? It's Bob...um, down in the Data Entry area."

My heart sank. Bob doesn't like to bother people, even if his PC is on fire. He was one of the more reasonable end-users I knew, but since he didn't say anything until the server blew up, I knew the request was going to be serious.

"Yes, Bob, what's up?" I asked wearily.

"Well...um, I was...um, wondering, um...we need a...um...small calculator program. Could you...uh, do this for us?"

We all dream of calls like this.

"Actually, you already have something like that..."

"Oh, sorry, " Bob interrupts, "but...uh, I have to go. Could you call me back at 4535 in 30 minutes?"

"I guess so, I'll talk to you later." I wondered if Moses ever had interruptions like this.

After I spent the next half-hour convincing my boss that we needed a more robust PC to pull off the query (and I would **NOT** be the one to sell the merchandise), I dialed 4535. However, I was shocked to hear another man's voice on the other end saying, "Marketing Department, Jeff speaking."

Whoops, did I call the wrong number? No, my phone display showed that I called the extension Bob gave me, so I answered, "Um...I'm sorry, is Bob there?"

"Nope, you must have the wrong number."

Sure enough, when I got off the phone and looked up Bob's extension, it was 4534 and not 4535. Oh well, we all make mistakes. So I dialed the right number this time, but now a woman's voice responds, "Janet speaking."

Janet! Who is Janet? "I'm sorry, but I'm looking for Bob in Data Entry..."

"Sorry," Janet interrupts rather rudely, "but he was terminated after he made a request for a programmer to create an application that we already have on our PC. I have taken over his responsibilities, his desk, and his phone. By the way, are you that programmer?"

"Um...yes."

"Good. Could you create an online adhoc reporting application for us that goes against our invoice data? And it needs to be done by today."

A More Formal Definition of a Callback

All pathetic attempts at humor aside, we all run into callback situations every day. Somebody asks us to perform some task that we can't fulfill at the present moment, so we call them back at a later time. Depending upon the characteristics of the given task, we may have to call them back multiple times to let them know what's going on.

In the Windows world, the same situation occurs. A client may request some information from the OS. Rather than sending a huge chunk of information right back, the server takes the address (or phone number if you will) of a function, and calls this function periodically to return the requested information in smaller pieces. Here's a diagram to illustrate the callback logic:

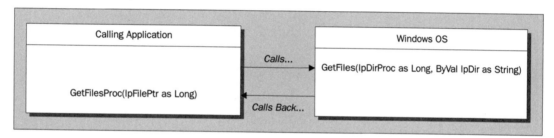

However, just as we've all experienced in the real world, sometimes we get the "wrong number", or function address. The calling function will then try to call that function, but will probably get an angry response in turn. (Of course, it's a very complex problem to have an OS figure out how to "look up" the correct function and call it instead.) Or, once you have called the correct function, you really don't know what's going to go on after that. A program can implement the callback function in an entirely different manner than all the others. That's perfectly acceptable, and in fact, highly desirable. The function that's making the callback should not be responsible for what the receiver will do with any of the information it will send.

Callbacks are used for a wide variety of situations in Windows. Some of them are:

❑ Creating Threads
❑ Enumerating System Information
❑ Subclassing
❑ Timers

As the list implies (and by no means is it complete), the OS uses callback functions in a number of its calls. If you can't pass the address of your function to these calls, you can't use them. Period. Once you see what's possible if you can do callbacks, you realize how limited you are.

The AddressOf Operator

Unfortunately, this limitation existed in VB for its first 4 versions. Callbacks were possible in VB 4.0, but you had to use a third-party ActiveX control to handle the callback for you. Most of the VB programmers (like me) didn't even know that this limitation existed, but those C++ Windows programmers who started to learn VB saw this shortcoming (along with a bunch of other ones) and didn't like it. They were used to callbacks, and using a control to handle this for them wasn't very appealing.

To be fair, this situation is understandable; since VB is rumored never to directly support pointers of any kind in any way, shape, or form. As I stated before, pointers lead to a lot of power; just make sure you handle the live wires very carefully, lest you receive a rude shock. VB is meant to be a friendly environment where you can quickly create front-end Windows applications. However, the gurus are always asking for more of the lower-level features, and in version 5, Microsoft gave them the `AddressOf` operator.

The `AddressOf` operator does nothing more than return the address of a procedure in VB. For example, if you had a procedure called `MyCallback` declared in a module within your project like this:

```
Public Function MyCallback()

End Function
```

and you wanted to retrieve the address of this function, all you'd have to do is:

```
...
ShowAddressOfFunction AddressOf MyCallback
...
```

where `ShowAddressOfFunction` is defined like this:

```
Private Sub ShowAddressOfFunction(lngAddr As Long)

   MsgBox "Address is: " & CStr(lngAddr)

End Sub
```

Pretty slick! You now have the address, or phone number if you will, of the function. Any Win32 API calls that need an address to a function are now open to any VB developer. No third-party controls needed. Freedom to invoke virtually any API call known to the Windows development world. Talk about being drunk with power!

Well, not exactly...

AddressOf Limitations

Before we start using our new found freedom with reckless abandon, let's go over some of the limitations and dangers that the `AddressOf` operator has:

Callback Functions Must be Declared Within Modules

With Win32 API calls, you can only declare a callback function within a module, and they must be declared with `Public` scope. These are the only procedures that `AddressOf` will work with. So what about procedures defined within class modules?

Class Modules Functions are Off-Limits

The reason for this gets into the depths of COM (some of which we'll cover in the next chapter), but the end result is that you can't do it. For example, if you had a method in your class `IVendor` called `ReceiveInfo`, you couldn't use the `AddressOf` operator to get the address of `ReceiveInfo`. Basically, every function, method, and property of an object in VB is stored in a virtual table, or **vtable**, which contains addresses to the real set of functions. Therefore, trying to get an address to these functions doesn't make a lot of sense (although it would be nice to callback on these procedures, wouldn't it?)

VB Cannot Use the Function Address

There's nothing in VB that allows you to use the value returned by `AddressOf` to invoke that function. The `AddressOf` operator was introduced to let developers use more of the OS API calls that required a function address, and that's all. (Of course, there is a way to use that value in a sneaky sort of way using another API call – I'll demonstrate this interesting technique later on in the chapter.)

AddressOf Only Works with Your Functions

You can't use the `AddressOf` operator on API functions like `CreateFile` and `CopyMemory`. VB's IDE will scream and holler if you try to do this.

Don't Let Errors Back-Propagate

What happens if you don't have any error handling in your callback procedure? Usually, if the procedure doesn't take responsibility to handle the error, the caller of the procedure becomes responsible to handle the error. But with a callback procedure, the caller is not within your program, so who knows what horrors you will bring upon your users for doing this? The easiest way to get around this is to use the catch-all error phrase `On Error Resume Next`.

Make Sure the Callback Procedure is Correct

If you declared `MyCallback` with three arguments, and the callback procedure's signature requires four arguments, more horrors await those who invoke your application. Double-check the documentation for the callback procedure.

There may be others that I've missed, but these rules should steer you clear of a fair amount of problems usually associated with using the `AddressOf` operator for the first time.

By the way, I should mention that the rule-of-thumb to save your code often should become a commandment (if it hasn't already) when you use the `AddressOf` operator. Because it deals with memory addresses, a topic not covered very frequently in VB in a direct sense, the chance of causing a memory exception is higher. Remember to save your work!

Callbacks with the AddressOf Operator

Let's take a look at four examples of using the callback procedure in VB. One involves the `EnumThreadWindows` function that will list all of the window handles that we created on the current thread. This project is a good one to demonstrate the `AddressOf` operator, but it also has the additional effect of showing the difference between running your project in VB's IDE and as a standalone application. The second example uses the `EnumTimeFormats` function to list all of the Windows time formats. This one is interesting because it revisits the `CopyMemory` function that we saw in Chapter 2 due to a callback return value. The third example uses the `EnumObjects` function to retrieve information about pens and brushes for a given device context. This one will demonstrate the necessity to read the documentation on the functions, because the callback function uses one of its UDT return values in two different ways. Finally, we'll revisit the `CommonDialogDemo` application from the previous chapter where we displayed file dialog boxes. There was a parameter in a UDT that takes a function address as its value. Now that we've reached the callback chapter, we'll be able to cover this UDT parameter in more detail.

The EnumThreadWindows Call

Before we discuss this call, let's back up for a second and briefly go over a Windows **process**. VB programmers, and most Windows users in general, are used to calling this a program or executable. However, the correct technical term is a process. Each process must have at least one main thread, which can in turn create more threads.

Alas, VB isn't the most wonderful tool to create a multithreaded executa...er, process. VB's IDE is not free threaded, which means that it forces each application to run on one thread, and one thread only. This shows up if you try to create an ActiveX EXE with multiple threads per object; every object runs in the same thread until you compile the application and let it run outside of the IDE. If you try to use the `CreateThread` API call within VB, the IDE won't be as nice as the previous example. More often than not, it will say "bye-bye" and die a grotesque death (a compiled VB application that uses `CreateThread` will work, providing other multithreading issues like starvation and deadlocks are addressed in the design).

In any event, there's an API call named `EnumThreadWindows` that will show all of the windows that were created by the current thread. Here is its declaration:

```
Declare Function EnumThreadWindows Lib "user32" (ByVal dwThreadId _
    As Long, ByVal lpfn As Long, ByVal lParam As Long) As Long
```

The first argument, `dwThreadId`, is the thread that you want to find window handles from. In VB, this is pretty easy, since we know that there's only one running thread, and its value is exposed by the `App` object via the `ThreadID` property. The `lpfn` argument needs a pointer to a function – this is where the `AddressOf` operator will come into play - which is called for each handle found in the thread. The last argument, `lParam`, can be anything you want it to be. Windows won't do anything with this value, other than pass it on to the callback function. Therefore, it's up to you whether you want to use this value to inform the callback function of a specific task that you want it to do.

The `lpfn` argument requires that the function it's pointing at have the following signature:

```
Public Function EnumThreadWindowsProc(ByVal hwnd As Long, ByVal lParam _
    As Long) As Long
```

Well, something like this. It has to have two arguments, both of which have to be of a Long data type. It also has to return a Long data type value. If the return value is non-zero, then EnumThreadWindows will keep calling the function as long as there are hwnds to find. If the return value is 0 (or FALSE), then EnumThreadWindows will stop and cause EnumThreadWindows to return an error code of zero. The names of the functions and arguments are irrelevant to Windows. I'll hold off on giving a precise definition of what the information the arguments contain for now; we'll address that in the next section.

Now that we have the two main functions to find all of the window handles created by a thread, let's create a sample program to demonstrate EnumThreadWindows.

You could also use EnumChildWindows *to pull off the same functionality, but having the word "thread" appeals to me more. Not that I don't like kids; in actuality, I don't like to sew. But in the hopes that some version of VB will finally have a free-threaded IDE, I'll stick with* EnumThreadWindows.

The ThreadWindowDemo Application

This application has only one command button, which, when clicked, will list all of the handles currently available in the application. Here's a screenshot of the form:

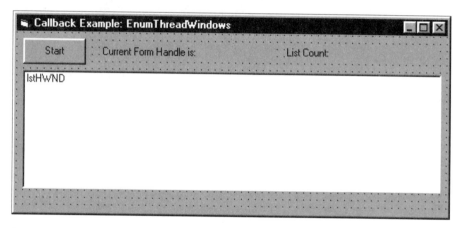

Here's a list of control information for this project:

Object	Property	Setting
Form	Name	frmMain
Command Button	Name	cmdStart
Label	Name	lblFormHWND
Label	Name	lblCount
ListBox	Name	lstHWND
	IntegralHeight	False

You should also add the EnumThreadWindows API call to a module called ThreadWindowLib. When the cmdStart command button is clicked, the StartThreadEnum method is called like this:

```
Private Sub cmdStart_Click()

    StartThreadEnum

End Sub
```

Here's StartThreadEnum:

```
Private Sub StartThreadEnum()

    Dim lngRet As Long

    On Error GoTo error_StartThreadEnum

    Screen.MousePointer = vbHourglass

'   Reset all the UI results.
    lstHWND.Clear
    lblCount.Caption = ""
    lblFormHWND.Caption = "Current Form HWND is " & Me.hwnd

'   Call the enum function, which contains a callback procedure.
    lngRet = EnumThreadWindows(App.ThreadID, _
                    AddressOf EnumThreadWindowsProc, 0)

    Screen.MousePointer = vbDefault

    If lngRet = 0 Then
'   Error occurred.
        MsgBox "Enum Error:  " & Err.LastDllError
    Else
'   The function successfully enumerated all the window handles.
        lblCount.Caption = "List Count = " & lstHWND.ListCount
    End If

    Exit Sub

error_StartThreadEnum:

    Screen.MousePointer = vbDefault

    MsgBox Err.Number & "  " & Err.Description

End Sub
```

First, we clear out the list box as well as the labels that show the form's hwnd value and the total number of items in the list:

```
lstHWND.Clear
lblCount.Caption = ""
lblFormHWND.Caption = "Current Form HWND is " & Me.hwnd
```

Then we call EnumThreadWindows, using the ThreadID value from the App object and the AddressOf operator to pass the address of EnumThreadWindowsProc to EnumThreadWindows:

```
lngRet = EnumThreadWindows(App.ThreadID, _
                    AddressOf EnumThreadWindowsProc, 0)
```

Finally, we check the return value – if it's non-zero, we display the number of items in the list in
lblCount.

```
If lngRet = 0 Then
' Error occurred.
    MsgBox "Enum Error:  " & Err.LastDllError
Else
' The function successfully enumerated all the window handles.
    lblCount.Caption = "List Count = " & lstHWND.ListCount
End If
```

One thing to note about functions that perform callbacks on other functions. Depending upon the function you call, that procedure may return immediately after you make the call (asynchronous) or you may have to wait until the function is done (synchronous), as is the case with EnumThreadWindows. *Make sure you read the SDK on the API function to determine what the callback behavior is, because it will affect the overall behavior of your program.*

So what happens when EnumThreadWindows is called? Well, it calls EnumThreadWindowsProc each time it finds a window created by the specified thread. Here's what it looks like (remember this needs to be in the code module):

```
Public Function EnumThreadWindowsProc(ByVal hwnd As Long, ByVal _
    lParam As Long) As Long

    Dim lngRet As Long
    Dim strClassName As String
    Dim strWindowText As String

' Get that error handling in there!
    On Error GoTo error_EnumThread

' Allocate space.
    strClassName = String$(512, " ")
    strWindowText = String$(512, " ")

' Get the class names and window text.
    lngRet = GetClassName(hwnd, strClassName, Len(strClassName) - 1)
    lngRet = GetWindowText(hwnd, strWindowText, Len(strWindowText) - 1)

' Chop the strings off before the null characters, if any exist.
    strClassName = Left$(strClassName, _
                    InStr(1, strClassName, Chr$(0)) - 1)
    strWindowText = Left$(strWindowText, _
                    InStr(1, strWindowText, Chr$(0)) - 1)

' Fill the list box.
    frmMain.lstHWND.AddItem hwnd & ", ClassName = " & strClassName _
        & ", WindowText = " & strWindowText

' Return a 1 for success, so  Windows can continue.
    EnumThreadWindowsProc = 1
```

```
Exit Function

error_EnumThread:

'  Return a 0 for failure, so Windows can stop.
   EnumThreadWindowsProc = 0

End Function
```

First, we set up the error handling, which is critical in a callback procedure:

```
'  Get that error handling in there!
   On Error GoTo error_EnumThread
```

We need to set the length of the two string variables for use with a couple of additional API calls:

```
'  Allocate space.
   strClassName = String$(512, " ")
   strWindowText = String$(512, " ")
```

Then, we use the hwnd value to...hey, what's going on here?

```
lngRet = GetClassName(hwnd, strClassName, Len(strClassName) - 1)
lngRet = GetWindowText(hwnd, strWindowText, Len(strWindowText) - 1)
```

Where did GetClassName and GetWindowText come from? Well, I put them in there to retrieve more information about the window specified by hwnd. Let's spend some time going over what these functions are doing.

First of all, here are the function definitions (which you should add to ThreadWindowLib):

```
Declare Function GetWindowText Lib "user32" Alias "GetWindowTextA" _
    (ByVal hwnd As Long, ByVal lpString As String, ByVal cch As Long) _
    As Long
```

```
Declare Function GetClassName Lib "user32" Alias "GetClassNameA" _
    (ByVal hwnd As Long, ByVal lpClassName As String, ByVal nMaxCount As _
    Long) As Long
```

The GetWindowText is pretty easy - it's the caption text of the window. You set hwnd to the window in question. lpClassName is a buffer used to return the caption text. cch should be set to the length of lpClassName (this is why we set the strings to a specific length). If the return value is non-zero, the call was successful; otherwise, an error occurred.

The GetClassName is a little bit more obscure, but it's not that big of a deal. In essence, every window is based off of a class, which defines attributes of a window. The OS uses this class as a starting point to create a window. Since there are different types of window classes that define different windows (like buttons and combo boxes), the GetClassName gives us that class name. It's similar to the name of a class module and the objects derived from that class. Every object is different, but they all come from that base class. The arguments are similar to GetWindowText, except that lpString is used to get the class name instead of the window caption.

Note that VB uses the base Windows classes, but you're not going to see these names when we run this demo application. VB doesn't expose all of the functionality of these classes, so you'll see some non-Windows class names as a result. In the next chapter, we'll rip through this wall using subclassing.

As we'll see in a moment, these two API calls give us some extra information about the windows along with their respective hwnd values, which we help us determine which window is which. Once we get this additional information, we add it to the list box on the main form:

```
frmMain.lstHWND.AddItem hwnd & ", ClassName = " & strClassName _
    & ", WindowText = " & strWindowText
```

In a professional application, this wouldn't be advised, because it's too restrictive and you may not be able to rely upon one form being in memory all the time. However, in our case, we can get away with it, since frmMain will always be up for the lifetime of the application.

One more thing before we continue. Let's add this code to the Resize event of frmMain:

```
Private Sub Form_Resize()

   On Error Resume Next

   If WindowState <> vbMinimized Then
      With lstHWND
         .Move .Left, .Top, Me.Width - 375, Me.Height - 1260
      End With
   End If

End Sub
```

This allows the list box to grow and shrink relative to the size of the window. Now, if you run the application in VB, you might see something like this:

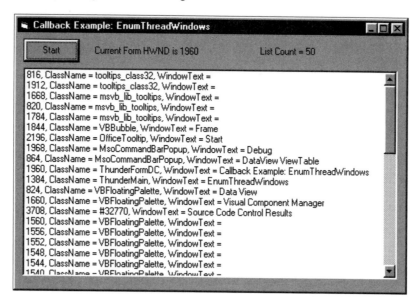

However, if you run a compiled version of the application, you may see something like this:

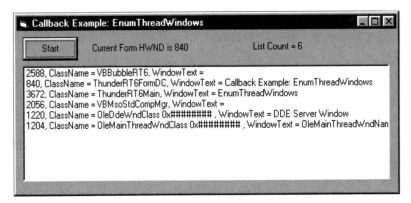

Your results may differ, but you should see the difference. When we run the application in VB, we get all of the window handles of VB itself! This makes sense because VB is "hosting" the application, and since the application's thread is the same as VB's thread, you should see all of those window handles. Once you're outside of the VB world, all of those windows disappear.

> *Look at the class names closely (note that a "class" in this scenario is not the same thing as a VB class). The "thunder" term is a holdover from the early days of VB – it was the code name of the project before the 1.0 version came out. I guess some things just never go away.*

The EnumTimeFormats Call

We're going to move away from the `EnumThreadWindows` call, and move onto our second example that uses the `EnumTimeFormats` call. Just like the name says, this call gives you all of the time formats for your location, or, as we say in the Windows world, your **locale**. Here's the declaration:

```
Declare Function EnumTimeFormats Lib "KERNEL32" Alias _
    "EnumTimeFormatsA" (ByVal lpTimeFmtEnumProc As Long, ByVal Locale As _
    Long, ByVal dwFlags As Long) As Long
```

The first argument, `lpTimeFmtEnumProc`, will contain the function address of a function to call for each time format. The `Locale` argument is used to specify the time formats to return depending on the locale given. Locales are used in a number of different ways, from defining the language used to the calendar type. There are three enumerated values that you can use:

```
Enum Locales
    LOCALE_NEUTRAL = 0
    LOCALE_USER_DEFAULT = &H400
    LOCALE_SYSTEM_DEFAULT = &H800
End Enum
```

Note that the values I got for `LOCALE_USER_DEFAULT` and `LOCALE_SYSTEM_DEFAULT` may vary depending upon the locale settings you have on your machine. Finally, the last argument, `dwFlags`, isn't be used yet and must be set to zero.

Finding the values of these constants isn't easy. They're determined by a C macro in a header file, which is territory that VB programmers usually don't walk on. If you can find the C header file `winnls.h`, *you (or someone you know who knows C) could write a program to get the locale values for you, since they are defined by the* `MAKELCID` *macro. Or, you could use the* `LocaleConstants.Exe` *program that is located within the* `Test Files` *directory if you download the code from Wrox's web site. It's a MFC application written by Bill Daley that displays these values in a window.*

So what does the callback function format look like? Funny you should ask:

```
Public Function TimeFormatsCallback(ByVal TimeFormat As Long) As Long
```

The `TimeFormat` argument is a tricky one. It's a pointer to a character array, or `String` data type, that contains the time format information. This is similar to what we saw with `GetEnvironmentStrings` in Chapter 2. Therefore, we'll have to dredge `CopyMemory` out from the dungeons to do the dirty work for us.

The TimeFormats Project

Let's take a look the `EnumTimeFormats` call within an application called `TimeFormats` to show how it works. Here's a screen shot of the form:

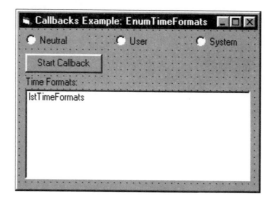

Now here's a list of the control settings needed for this project:

Object	Property	Setting
Form	Name	frmMain
Option Button	Name	optType
	Caption	Neutral
	Index	0
Option Button	Name	optType

Table Continued on Following Page

Object	Property	Setting
	Caption	User
	Index	1
Option Button	Name	optType
	Caption	System
	Index	2
Command Button	Name	cmdStartCallBack
List Box	Name	lstTimeFormats

Also, add the EnumTimeFormats and CopyMemory API call to a module called TimeFormatsLib. Plus the Locales enum as defined for your locale.

When the command button cmdStartCallback is clicked, we call GetTimeFormats:

```
Private Sub cmdStartCallback_Click()

    GetTimeFormats

End Sub
```

GetTimeFormats is a form method that determines which time formats we're looking for from the option buttons:

```
Private Sub GetTimeFormats()

'   This function gets all of the time formats
'   through EnumTimeFormats

    Dim lngRet As Long
    Dim lngFormat As Long

    On Error GoTo error_GetTimeFormats

    Screen.MousePointer = vbHourglass

    lstTimeFormats.Clear

'   Determine the format.
    If optType(0).Value = True Then
        lngFormat = Locales.LOCALE_NEUTRAL

    ElseIf optType(1).Value = True Then
        lngFormat = Locales.LOCALE_USER_DEFAULT

    ElseIf optType(2).Value = True Then
        lngFormat = Locales.LOCALE_SYSTEM_DEFAULT

    Else
    End If
```

```
' Call the API function.
lngRet = EnumTimeFormats(AddressOf TimeFormatsCallback, _
                         lngFormat, 0)

Screen.MousePointer = vbDefault

If lngRet = 0 Then
    MsgBox "EnumTimeFormats Error:  " & Err.LastDllError
End If

Exit Sub

error_GetTimeFormats:

    Screen.MousePointer = vbDefault
    MsgBox Err.Number & "   " & Err.Description

End Sub
```

As you can see, we set `lngFormat` to the kind of the locale the user is interested in looking at as determined by the option buttons:

```
If optType(0).Value = True Then
    lngFormat = Locales.LOCALE_NEUTRAL

ElseIf optType(1).Value = True Then
    lngFormat = Locales.LOCALE_USER_DEFAULT

ElseIf optType(2).Value = True Then
    lngFormat = Locales.LOCALE_SYSTEM_DEFAULT
```

Then, we call `EnumTimeFormats`, passing the address of the `TimeFormatsCallback` function:

```
lngRet = EnumTimeFormats(AddressOf TimeFormatsCallback, _
                         lngFormat, 0)
```

Here's how I implemented `TimeFormatsCallback` (which you should add to the `TimeFormatsLib` module). It takes the time format and adds it to the list box on `frmMain`. We can do this because we know that `frmMain` will always be up.

```
Public Function TimeFormatsCallback(ByVal TimeFormat As Long) As Long

    Dim strInfo As String

'   Add the error handling!
    On Error GoTo error_TimeFormatsCallback

'   Allocate space in the buffer.
    strInfo = String$(1000, " ")

'   Copy the information into strInfo.
    CopyMemory ByVal strInfo, ByVal TimeFormat, Len(strInfo)

    strInfo = Left$(strInfo, InStr(strInfo, vbNullChar) - 1)
    frmMain.lstTimeFormats.AddItem strInfo
```

```
'   We'll return a 1 for success to continue the callbacks.
    TimeFormatsCallback = 1
    Exit Function

error_TimeFormatsCallback:

'   We'll return a 0 for an error
    TimeFormatsCallback = 0

End Function
```

Again, we make sure we have error handling in the callback procedure to prevent back-propagation:

```
'   Add the error handling!
    On Error GoTo error_TimeFormatsCallback
```

Then, we allocate 1K of space to `strInfo` (probably more than is necessary for a time format), and retrieve the information out of `TimeFormat` into this string via `CopyMemory`:

```
strInfo = String$(1000, " ")

CopyMemory ByVal strInfo, ByVal TimeFormat, Len(strInfo)
```

We then trim `strInfo`, and add it to the list box on `frmMain`:

```
strInfo = Left$(strInfo, InStr(strInfo, vbNullChar) - 1)
frmMain.lstTimeFormats.AddItem strInfo
```

Finally, just like the `EnumThreadWindowsProc` call in the previous section, we need to return a non-zero value to get the next time format back, if there is another one:

```
TimeFormatsCallback = 1
```

Here's what I get when I run the program:

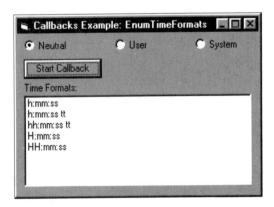

This example was pretty easy because we had already tackled the string pointer problem before, and we were able to transfer that knowledge to this situation. It's nice when you can start to reuse your information base, isn't it?

The EnumObjects Function

The last example uses the `EnumObjects` function to retrieve information about pens and brushes. Its declaration looks like this:

```
Declare Function EnumObjects Lib "gdi32" (ByVal hDC As Long, _
    ByVal n As Long, ByVal lpGOBJEnumProc As Long, lpVoid As Any) As Long
```

The first argument, `hDC`, is the device context that we want get information about. The `n` argument points to a value that determines what UDT will show up in the callback. It can be one of the following enumerated values:

```
Enum ObjectTypes
    OBJ_PEN = 1
    OBJ_BRUSH = 2
End Enum
```

If `n` is equal to `OBJ_PEN`, we'll get a `LOGPEN` UDT in the callback; otherwise, `n` can be set to `OBJ_BRUSH` to have a `LOGBRUSH` on the other end. Since they're very similar, we'll discuss both of them at the same time. Here's how these UDTs are defined:

```
Type LOGBRUSH
    lbStyle As Long
    lbColor As Long
    lbHatch As Long
End Type

Type LOGPEN
    lopnStyle As Long
    lopnWidth As POINTAPI
    lopnColor As Long
End Type
```

As you can see with `LOGPEN`, we'll need the `POINTAPI` UDT we saw in Chapter 5. Both the `lbStyle` and `lopnStyle` parameters are used to determine which kind of style the brush or pen is. Here's a list of enumerated values that can be used to define these styles:

```
Enum BrushTypes
    BS_SOLID = 0
    BS_NULL = 1
    BS_HOLLOW = BS_NULL
    BS_HATCHED = 2
    BS_PATTERN = 3
    BS_DIBPATTERN = 5
    BS_DIBPATTERNPT = 6
    BS_PATTERN8X8 = 7
    BS_DIBPATTERN8X8 = 8
End Enum

Enum LineStyles
    HS_BDIAGONAL = 3
    HS_CROSS = 4
    HS_DIAGCROSS = 5
    HS_FDIAGONAL = 2
```

```
     HS_HORIZONTAL = 0
  HS_VERTICAL = 1
  End Enum

  Enum PenTypes
     PS_SOLID = 0
     PS_DASH = 1
     PS_DOT = 2
     PS_DASHDOT = 3
     PS_DASHDOTDOT = 4
     PS_NULL = 5
     PS_INSIDEFRAME = 6
  End Enum
```

The `lbColor` and `lopnColor` parameters are RGB color values. The remaining parameters are where the similarities between the UDTs break down. The `lbHatch` value in LOGBRUSH UDT is used to define a hatch style for the brush. In the LOGPEN UDT, we get a POINTAPI UDT that defines the width and height of the brush. We'll run into some other rules that govern the meaning of the values within the UDT later in this chapter.

Back to the arguments for `EnumObjects`. The `lpGOBJEnumProc` argument points to our callback function. `lpVoid` is one of those fun `Any` argument that can take whatever you want to put in it, but I'm going to change it to a `Long` data type plus pass it `ByVal` for our purposes. Just remember that the API call won't limit you in this way.

Now let's go over a small application called `EnumObjectsDemo` that demonstrates how we can use `EnumObjects`. Here's a screen shot of the form:

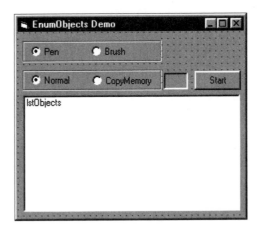

Here's a list of all the object property settings for this application:

Object	Property	Setting
Form	Name	`frmMain`
Option Button	Name	`optObject`
	Caption	Pen

Object	Property	Setting
	Index	0
Option Button	Name	optObject
	Caption	Brush
	Index	1
Option Button	Name	optInvoke
	Caption	Normal
	Index	0
Option Button	Name	optInvoke
	Caption	CopyMemory
	Index	1
Label	Name	lblItems
	BorderStyle	1 - Fixed Single
Command Button	Name	cmdStart
List Box	Name	lstObjects

Also, add the `EnumObjects` API (remember to change the `lpVoid` argument to `ByVal lpVoid As Long`) along with all the enumerations and UDTs defined in this section to a module called `EnumObjectsLib`. (Don't forget the `POINTAPI` UDT.)

Two Callback Object Functions

Now here's the catch. That n argument is a weird one, because it specifies what kind of UDT we receive in the callback function. Therefore, we can approach it in two ways. The first way we'll look at is to define two callback functions, `PenCallback` and `BrushCallback`. Here's what these function declarations look like (please add these to `EnumObjectsLib`):

```
Public Sub BrushCallback(BrushInfo As LOGBRUSH, ByVal ObjData As Long)
```

```
Public Sub PenCallback(PenInfo As LOGPEN, ByVal ObjData As Long)
```

Therefore, we'll force the caller of `EnumObjects` to specify which function to set as the callback. If the caller specifies the wrong function, we'll definitely have memory problems because the byte size of the UDTs differ by 4 bytes (`LOGPEN` is 16 bytes and `LOGBRUSH` is 12 bytes).

These two functions add data to the `lstObjects` list box on `frmMain`, similar to what we've done in the last two examples. I'm not really concerned about the data in the UDTs to any extreme detail, so I won't go over the other enumerated values that show up in the function. Therefore, I'll just show you the code to demonstrate how the functions show data on the pens and brushes of a device context:

```
Public Sub BrushCallback(BrushInfo As LOGBRUSH, ByVal ObjData As Long)

    Dim strStyle As String

'   Error handling!
    On Error Resume Next

    With BrushInfo
        Select Case .lbStyle
            Case BrushTypes.BS_DIBPATTERN
                strStyle = "DIB Pattern (Handle)"
            Case BrushTypes.BS_DIBPATTERN8X8
                strStyle = "DIB Pattern 8*8"
            Case BrushTypes.BS_DIBPATTERNPT
                strStyle = "DIB Pattern (Pointer)"
            Case BrushTypes.BS_HATCHED
                strStyle = "Hatched"
            Case BrushTypes.BS_HOLLOW, _
                BrushTypes.BS_NULL
                strStyle = "Hollow"
            Case BrushTypes.BS_PATTERN
                strStyle = "Pattern"
            Case BrushTypes.BS_PATTERN8X8
                strStyle = "Pattern 8*8"
            Case BrushTypes.BS_SOLID
                strStyle = "Solid"
        End Select

        frmMain.lstObjects.AddItem "Brush Style:  " & strStyle

'       Show color value.
        If .lbColor <> BrushTypes.BS_HOLLOW And _
            .lbColor <> BrushTypes.BS_PATTERN Then
                frmMain.lstObjects.AddItem vbTab & "Color Value:  " _
                    & CStr(.lbColor)
        End If

'       Show hatch style.
        If .lbStyle <> BrushTypes.BS_SOLID And _
            .lbStyle <> BrushTypes.BS_HOLLOW Then
                If .lbStyle = BrushTypes.BS_DIBPATTERN Then
                    frmMain.lstObjects.AddItem vbTab & _
                        "Handle Value:  " & CStr(.lbHatch)
                ElseIf .lbStyle = BrushTypes.BS_DIBPATTERNPT Then
                    frmMain.lstObjects.AddItem vbTab & _
                        "Pointer Value:  " & CStr(.lbHatch)
                ElseIf .lbStyle = BrushTypes.BS_HATCHED Then
                    Select Case .lbHatch
                        Case LineStyles.HS_BDIAGONAL
                            strStyle = "45 Deg. Upward"
                        Case LineStyles.HS_CROSS
                            strStyle = "Cross"
                        Case LineStyles.HS_DIAGCROSS
                            strStyle = "45 Deg. Cross"
```

```
                            Case LineStyles.HS_FDIAGONAL
                                strStyle = "45 Deg. Downward"
                            Case LineStyles.HS_HORIZONTAL
                                strStyle = "Horizontal"
                            Case LineStyles.HS_VERTICAL
                                strStyle = "Vertical"
                    End Select

                    frmMain.lstObjects.AddItem vbTab & _
                            "Hatch Style:  " & strStyle
                ElseIf .lbStyle = BrushTypes.BS_PATTERN Then
                    frmMain.lstObjects.AddItem vbTab & _
                            "Bitmap Handle Value: " & .lbHatch
                End If
            End If
        End With

End Sub


Public Sub PenCallback(PenInfo As LOGPEN, ByVal ObjData As Long)

    Dim strStyle As String

'   Error handling!
    On Error Resume Next

    With PenInfo
    '   Figure out the style.
        Select Case .lopnStyle
            Case PenTypes.PS_DASH
                strStyle = "Dash"
            Case PenTypes.PS_DASHDOT
                strStyle = "Dash Dot"
            Case PenTypes.PS_DASHDOTDOT
                strStyle = "Dash Dot Dot"
            Case PenTypes.PS_DOT
                strStyle = "Dot"
            Case PenTypes.PS_INSIDEFRAME
                strStyle = "Inside Frame"
            Case PenTypes.PS_NULL
                strStyle = "Invisible"
            Case PenTypes.PS_SOLID
                strStyle = "Solid"
        End Select

        frmMain.lstObjects.AddItem "Pen Style:  " & strStyle

    '   Display the pen width.
        frmMain.lstObjects.AddItem vbTab & "Pen Width:  " _
            & .lopnWidth.x

    '   Display the color.
        frmMain.lstObjects.AddItem vbTab & "Pen Color:  " _
            & .lopnColor

    End With

End Sub
```

Now that we have these functions defined, we have to code the UI to invoke them. In the `Click` event of `cmdStart`, we'll call a function called `GetObjects`:

```
Private Sub cmdStart_Click()

   GetObjects

End Sub
```

Here's what `GetObjects` looks like:

```
Private Sub GetObjects()

   Dim lngDC As Long
   Dim lngRet As Long

   On Error GoTo error_GetObjects

   Screen.MousePointer = vbHourglass

'  Get the printer's hDC
   lngDC = Printer.hDC

'  Clear out the UIs.
   lstObjects.Clear
   lblItems.Caption = ""

   If optObject(0).Value = True Then
'     Enumerate the pens.
      lngRet = EnumObjects(lngDC, ObjectTypes.OBJ_PEN, _
                     AddressOf PenCallback, 0&)
   Else
'     Enumerate the brushes.
      lngRet = EnumObjects(lngDC, ObjectTypes.OBJ_BRUSH, _
                     AddressOf BrushCallback, 1&)
   End If

   If lngRet = -1 Then
'     EnumObjects failure.
      Screen.MousePointer = vbDefault
      MsgBox "EnumObjects Failure", vbOKOnly + vbExclamation, _
               "Overload!"
   End If

   lblItems.Caption = CStr(lstObjects.ListCount)

   Screen.MousePointer = vbDefault

   Exit Sub

error_GetObjects:

   Screen.MousePointer = vbDefault

   MsgBox Err.Number & "   " & Err.Description

End Sub
```

`GetObjects` simply uses the `Printer` object's device context and calls the `EnumObjects` API call using the callback routine as specified by the option buttons. Once the list box has been filled by the callback procedures `GetObjects` counts the number of entries and displays that value in the label.

On my PC, which has a black and white desk jet printer, here's what the application shows for the brush callback function:

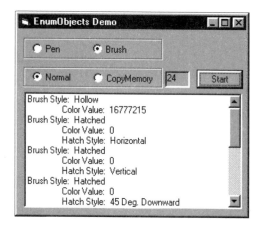

Notice that all of the color values are either 0 or 16777215, or the RGB values for black and white, respectively.

Don't worry about the CopyMemory option button not doing anything. We need to add some more code, which we're just about to do.

One Callback Object Function

Using two functions like this is fine; it's not a "wrong" answer. However, I really like that `CopyMemory` API call, and I wondered if I could use it in this case to use only one callback function. This `GeneralCallback` function would internally resolve which function to call, `PenCallback` or `BrushCallback`. Well, as I found out, `CopyMemory` is one versatile function! Here's what `GeneralCallback` looks like:

```
Public Sub GeneralCallback(ByVal PointerVal As Long, ByVal DataVal _
    As Long)

    Dim udtPStruct As LOGPEN
    Dim udtBStruct As LOGBRUSH

'   Error handling!
    On Error Resume Next

    If DataVal = 0 Then
'     This is a LOGPEN call.
    CopyMemory udtPStruct, ByVal PointerVal, LenB(udtPStruct)
    PenCallback udtPStruct, DataVal

    ElseIf DataVal = 1 Then
'     This is a LOGBRUSH call.
```

```
        CopyMemory udtBStruct, ByVal PointerVal, LenB(udtBStruct)
        BrushCallback udtBStruct, DataVal

        Else
        '  Do nothing.

        End If

   End Sub
```

The first argument is now a `Long` data type, and is passed `ByVal`. This is important; if we passed it in `ByRef`, we wouldn't be able to receive the pointer to the UDT:

```
  Public Sub GeneralCallback(ByVal PointerVal As Long, ByVal DataVal _
      As Long)
```

Next, we look at the value of `DataVal`. If you're wondering where this value has come from then back track to the original `EnumObjects` call. If you remember the original description of the `EnumObjects` syntax there is a `lpVoid` argument which so far we haven't used. (There is a similar argument in the other callbacks we've looked at but so far we've only been setting it to 0.) This argument is used to pass any additional parameters to the callback functions. In this case we need to test which `optInvoke` button has been selected. We therefore set `lpVoid` to either `0&` or `1&` and pass it `ByVal`. This value then gets passes to `GeneralCallback` as the `DataVal` parameter.

If `DataVal` is equal to zero, we dimension a UDT of type `LOGPEN`. Then we use the `CopyMemory` function to copy the data from the information pointed at by `PointerVal` to the UDT. We use the `LenB` function to figure out the size of the UDT in bytes.

```
  CopyMemory udtPStruct, ByVal PointerVal, LenB(udtPStruct)
```

Then we call the `PenCallback` function to process the UDT's data. We do the same thing if `DataVal` is 1; the only difference is now the UDT is a `LOGBRUSH` type and we call `BrushCallback` after the memory is copied. Any other values of `DataVal` are invalid for our purposes. Here's a diagram to show what's going on in `GeneralCallback`:

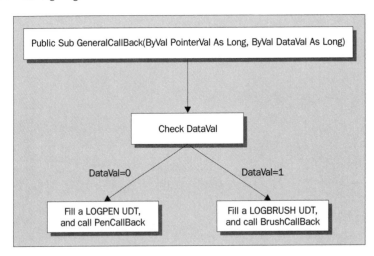

Now we could change our implementation around a bit to make `PenCallback` and `BrushCallback` `Private` functions, and only expose the `GeneralCallback` function to a client. This is nice because it generalizes the interface down to one function.

However, let's leave the two functions `Public` such that we can have the user decide which function to call. That's why there's two option buttons on `frmMain` that allow you to choose which solution you want to experiment with. Now that I've explained the two different implementations of the callback function, let's take a quick look at the revised `GetObjects` function that `frmMain` uses to invoke `EnumObjects` (you'll also need to add `GeneralCallBack` plus `CopyMemory` to the `EnumObjectsLib` module):

```
Private Sub GetObjects()

    Dim lngDC As Long
    Dim lngRet As Long

    On Error GoTo error_GetObjects

    Screen.MousePointer = vbHourglass

'   Get the printer's hDC
    lngDC = Printer.hDC

'   Clear out the UIs.
    lstObjects.Clear
    lblItems.Caption = ""

    If optObject(0).Value = True Then
'       Enumerate the pens.
        If optInvoke(0).Value = True Then
            lngRet = EnumObjects(lngDC, ObjectTypes.OBJ_PEN, _
                        AddressOf PenCallback, 0&)
        Else
            lngRet = EnumObjects(lngDC, ObjectTypes.OBJ_PEN, _
                        AddressOf GeneralCallback, 0&)
        End If

    Else
'       Enumerate the brushes.
        If optInvoke(0).Value = True Then
            lngRet = EnumObjects(lngDC, ObjectTypes.OBJ_BRUSH, _
                        AddressOf BrushCallback, 1&)
        Else
            lngRet = EnumObjects(lngDC, ObjectTypes.OBJ_BRUSH, _
                        AddressOf GeneralCallback, 1&)
        End If

    End If

    If lngRet = -1 Then
'       EnumObjects failure.
        Screen.MousePointer = vbDefault
        MsgBox "EnumObjects Failure", vbOKOnly + vbExclamation, _
                "Overload!"
    End If

    lblItems.Caption = CStr(lstObjects.ListCount)
```

```
        Screen.MousePointer = vbDefault

        Exit Sub

    error_GetObjects:

        Screen.MousePointer = vbDefault
        MsgBox Err.Number & "   " & Err.Description

    End Sub
```

The function has simply been modified to determine whether to use an explicit callback routine or `GeneralCallBack` according to the value of the `optInvoke` option buttons.

Callbacks Without the AddressOf Operator

Even though our discussion of callbacks has primarily centered around the `AddressOf` operator, you can create a callback scenario without the APIs or using `AddressOf`. Let's revisit the Encryption program to show how this is done.

Changing FileCrypt

You may have noticed that there's a progress bar at the bottom of the form. If you have, you're probably wondering why nothing's been done with it. Well, now's the time to use it as an indicator of where the encryption algorithm is in processing the file. To do that, we have to change our `FileCrypt` function around a bit to accept an argument of a `frmMain` type, like this:

```
Public Function FileCrypt(Params As EncryptionParameters, _
    CallbackForm As frmMain) As Boolean
```

There's no reason that `VBFileCrypt` *can't change like this as well, but I wanted to leave one of the functions untouched so we can use it to demonstrate the function address trick I alluded to before.*

Of course, `FileCrypt` calls on `EncryptionAlgorithm` to do the real work, so we'll have to change it as well:

```
Private Sub EncryptionAlgorithm(SourceFileHandle As Long, _
    DestFileHandle As Long, FileParams As EncryptionParameters, _
    CallbackForm As frmMain)
```

We also need to update the calls to `FileCrypt` and `EncryptionAlgorithm` such that they include `frmMain` as a parameter:

```
blnRet = FileCrypt(udtInfo, Me)
```

```
EncryptionAlgorithm lngSourceFile, _
            lngDestFile, Params, frmMain
```

I won't waste the space here displaying the implementation of EncryptionAlgorithm, since we're not changing the algorithm itself. The following code snippet is added just after each buffer is written to the file:

```
lngRet = WriteFile(DestFileHandle, _
                   bytFileInfo(1), _
                   UBound(bytFileInfo), _
                   lngBytesRead, 0)

CallbackForm.UpdateStatus (CDbl(UBound(bytFileInfo) + _
    lngDestPosition - 1) / CDbl(lngFileSize)) * 100#
```

Essentially, we figure out where we are in the writing process, and create a percentage value. However, the keen eye will spot that there's a method that we're calling, namely UpdateStatus. This is the callback to frmMain. Of course, we could call any method on frmMain, but the one we're interested in is UpdateStatus. This is a method that needs to be added to frmMain, and looks like this:

```
Public Sub UpdateStatus(ByVal Val As Double)

    On Error Resume Next

    If Val < 0 Then
        Val = 0
    ElseIf Val > 100 Then
        Val = 100
    End If

    With ProgressBar
        .Value = Val
    End With

End Sub
```

UpdateStatus checks to make sure that Val is between 0 and 100. If it isn't then it sets Val to either 0 or 100 accordingly. Then, the progress bar's Value property is changed to reflect the value given.

> *There is a reason that I declare* CallbackForm *as a specific form,* frmMain. *By doing this, I get the* UpdateStatus *method in the* Quick Info *drop-down box. If I had declared* CallbackForm *as a standard* Form *object, I wouldn't see* UpdateStatus *in* Quick Info. *There's nothing wrong with the latter approach, and it may be advantageous to allow any form to be passed into the function, just as long as it support this function with the correct argument signature.*

Here's a diagram that lays out the callback scenario:

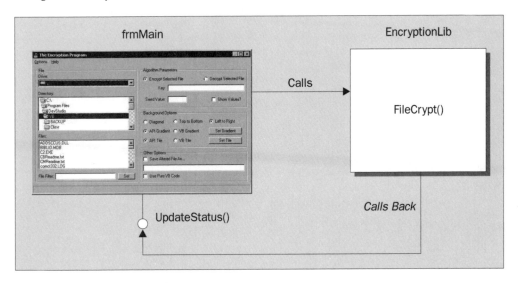

Now, when you run the program, the progress bar gives you an indication as to where the algorithm is in encrypting or decrypting your file:

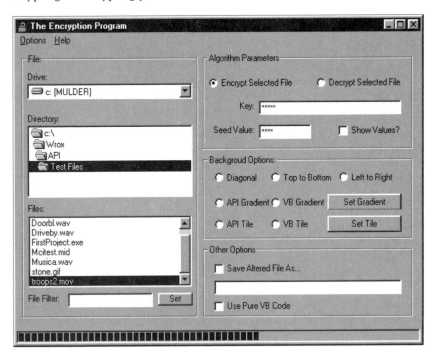

In principle, there isn't much that we're doing that's different from passing around a function address. We give the calling function a location that it can call, just like `AddressOf` does. The difference is that we're using an entire form reference to handle the callback, which exposes a lot more than we probably want the function to know about. With `AddressOf`, we restrict the callback to only one procedure.

Of course, in this project, there's no reason why we couldn't do what we did in the demo projects discussed earlier in the chapter, which is to directly reference `frmMain` in `FileCrypt`. However, if we ever decide to move the encryption logic into a COM component (or a standard DLL compiled using C++ code), we don't have this option (at least not very easily). In the next section, I'll demonstrate how you can call a function in VB having nothing but its address.

A Subtle Trick with Function Pointers in VB

When we looked at the limitations of the `AddressOf` operator, we noticed that we were unable use the function address in VB to call that function. This is a true statement in itself – there's nothing like a `CallFunctionByAddress` operator in VB. But with a little bit of investigation of the APIs, there's a call that can do this for us. It has its own limitations as well, and dangers lurk in its shadowy corners, but if you really want this kind of functionality in VB, then by all means, read on...

The CallWindowProc Procedure

Usually, the `CallWindowProc` API call is used for subclassing windows, where you use it to call functions on specific windows. However, since its main use is to call functions, it can also be used to allow us to call our own module-level functions. Let's take a look at the declaration and arguments in detail (add this to `EncryptionLib`):

```
Declare Function CallWindowProc Lib "user32" Alias "CallWindowProcA" _
    (ByVal lpPrevWndFunc As Long, ByVal hWnd As Long, ByVal Msg As Long, _
    ByVal wParam As Long, ByVal lParam As Long) As Long
```

This first argument, `lpPrevWndFunc`, takes the pointer to a function, or, the value returned by `AddressOf`, if you wish. Normally, you'd pass in the window handle that the function should be called on to the second argument, `hWnd`, (this is for subclassing purposes). In our case, the function exists in a module, which doesn't have a `hWnd` value anyway, so it won't really matter what we specify this value as. Finally, the last three arguments, `Msg`, `wParam`, and `lParam`, can be anything that a `Long` data type can take. We'll see in the next chapter how these arguments work together, but for now we'll control what we do with them.

As you can see, you have some restriction as to what kind of function you can call. The callback function must have the following signature:

```
Public Function WindowProcCallBack(ByVal hWnd As Long, ByVal Msg _
    As Long, ByVal wParam As Long, ByVal lParam As Long) As Long
```

where these four arguments correspond to the last four arguments of `CallWindowProc`. (They will also contain the values of the four arguments in `CallWindowProc`). As we'll see in a moment, this will change how we call the `UpdateStatus` method a bit. Of course, it will have to reside in a module as well (which will force us to call `frmMain` from the module procedure directly and not from an argument reference), but as you'll see, we'll be able to call the function whenever we want.

I would've preferred to do this example using a COM component that contained all of the encryption logic. I think the power of CallWindowProc *would be move evident in this case, but I didn't want to dive deeply into component development in this book; our focus is on the Win32 API layer. We will create components in the next chapter because I didn't want to close the door on COM altogether in this book, but you may want to enhance the encryption program to separate the UI from the algorithm.*

Altering the VBFileCrypt and VBEncryptionAlgorithm Functions

Just like we did with FileCrypt and EncryptionAlgorithm, we have to add an extra argument to these two functions to grab the pointer to the callback function. Here's what they look like now:

```
Public Function VBFileCrypt(Params As EncryptionParameters, CallbackFn _
    As Long) As Boolean
```

```
Private Sub VBEncryptionAlgorithm(SourceFileHandle As Long, _
    DestFileHandle As Long, FileParams As EncryptionParameters, _
    CallbackFn As Long)
```

The CallbackFn takes the result from AddressOf as its value. Since there is no "type" for a function address, you *could* pass in any value that you wanted, but I really wouldn't recommend that.

Therefore, the call to VBFileCrypt from frmMain has to change as well:

```
blnRet = VBFileCrypt(udtInfo, AddressOf WindowProcCallBack)
```

Plus the call to VBEncryptionAlgorithm in VBFileCrypt:

```
VBEncryptionAlgorithm lngSourceFile, _
        lngDestFile, Params, AddressOf WindowProcCallBack
```

What does WindowProcCallBack look like?

```
Public Function WindowProcCallBack(ByVal hWnd As Long, ByVal Msg _
    As Long, ByVal wParam As Long, ByVal lParam As Long) As Long

'   Error handling!
    On Error Resume Next

'   Update the status of the algorithm
    frmMain.UpdateStatus CDbl(Msg)

End Function
```

It's very simple. We take the value of Msg, convert it into a Double, and call UpdateStatus on frmMain (since we have that function available, we might as well use it). This function is called by VBEncryptionAlgorithm as follows:

```
'   Increment the file pointer.
    lngDestPosition = lngDestPosition + lngBytesRead

    dblStatus = (CDbl(UBound(bytFileInfo) + lngDestPosition - 1) _
```

```
                        / CDbl(lngFileSize)) * 100#

    CallWindowProc CallbackFn, 0, CLng(dblStatus), 0, 0
```

The `dblStatus` variable is there simply to contain the status percentage value (you'll need to add a variable declaration for this variable at the top of the procedure). Note that we set `hWnd` to zero, since there is no window handle available to call the function on. Here's a diagram to illustrate the flow of the callback mechanism:

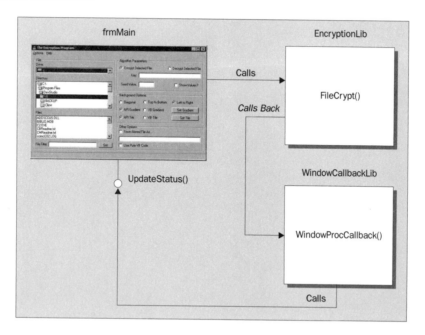

I hope that this example demonstrates the possibilities with `CallWindowProc`. You can also experiment with passing strings through the callback procedure using the undocumented `StrPtr` function to pass even more information in. Try UDTs and objects as well using `VarPtr` and `ObjPtr`. See what breaks, what works, and what makes sense (and, of course, save your work often!).

Revisiting the CommonDialogDemo Project

You should recall that in the previous chapter, we looked at the common dialog API calls in the `CommonDialogDemo` project. If you look back at the definition for the `OPENFILENAME` UDT, you'll see that there was one parameter that we didn't address: `lpfnHook`. It takes an address to a function. Now that we have our callback tool squared away, let's see what we can do with this parameter.

The function definition that `lpfnHook` will perform a callback on should look something like this:

```
    Public Function FileHookProc(ByVal hwnd As Long, ByVal uiMsg As Long, _
        ByVal wParam As Long, ByVal lParam As Long) As Long
```

As you probably can guess, these four parameters are similar to the callback procedure for `CallWindowProc`. Again, we'll see how the last three arguments work together in the next chapter, but to give you a bit of a sneak preview of things to come, let's set up this callback function in our `CommonDialogDemo` application.

First, we need two functions in the `ComDlgLib` module, `FileHookProc` and `AddressOfFn`:

```
Public Function FileHookProc(ByVal hwnd As Long, ByVal uiMsg As Long, _
    ByVal wParam As Long, ByVal lParam As Long) As Long

    Debug.Print hwnd & " " & uiMsg & " " & wParam & " " & lParam

End Function
```

```
Public Function AddressOfFn(ByVal FnAddress As Long) As Long

    AddressOfFn = FnAddress

End Function
```

Neither one of them is really doing much now. The callback procedure will do nothing but add the argument's values to the **Immediate Window**. `AddressOfFn` may seem almost redundant at first. Why do we need a function that returns the argument's value? Well, we can't set a `Long` variable equal to the address of a function using `AddressOf`. However, we need to do this with the UDT's `lpfnHook` parameter. Therefore, we need a function that has one `Long` argument and does nothing but return the argument's value. Here's how we use `AddressOfFn` in our `FileDialogAPI` method:

```
...
.flags = .flags Or FileCommands.OFN_EXPLORER Or _
            FileCommands.OFN_ENABLEHOOK
.lpfnHook = AddressOfFn(AddressOf FileHookProc)
If APIType = 1 Then
    lngRet = GetSaveFileName(udtFile)
Else
    lngRet = GetOpenFileName(udtFile)
End If
...
```

Note that we also need to set the `flags` *such that we can use hook procedures.*

Now, if you run the application and open a file dialog box, you'll notice that the **Immediate Window** is getting a lot of numbers added to it when you move the dialog box, or click on one of its buttons. Here's a screen shot of what my **Immediate Window** looked like when I ran the program:

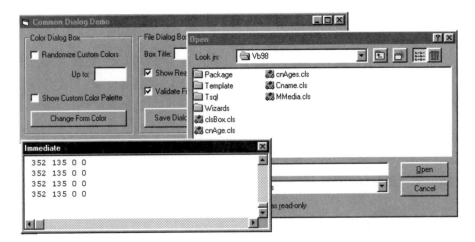

Doesn't look all that interesting does it? Well, let's try to make sense out of one of the callback function's arguments: uiMsg.

uiMsg usually contains a value that relates to a specific Windows event, like losing the focus, or moving across the screen. There's a list of predefined values that every window will process the same way. That doesn't necessarily mean that every window will *respond* to every message the same way; it just means that when a window gets a "move" message, it knows that a program or the OS is requesting that it move somewhere.

I don't like to keep deferring discussions to the next chapter, but I don't want to repeat myself either, so we'll leave the more in-depth investigation of window messages for later. However, let's try to grab one message that the dialog box will receive. Add the following constant to ComDlgLib:

```
Public Const WM_DESTROY = &H2
```

Now update the code to FileHookProc like this:

```
Public Function FileHookProc(ByVal hwnd As Long, ByVal uiMsg As Long, _
    ByVal wParam As Long, ByVal lParam As Long) As Long
    Debug.Print hwnd & " " & uiMsg & " " & wParam & " " & lParam
    If uiMsg = WM_DESTROY Then
        MsgBox "Dialog is being destroyed."
    End If

End Function
```

As the constant's name implies, we're looking for the message that tells the window to destroy itself. Now, when you close the file dialog box, you should see the following message box:

For the most part, I wanted to show you this callback procedure because it illustrated how you can set a UDT's parameter equal to an address of a function. Also, we got a small taste of what is going on with window messaging. I've never used this hook procedure for the file dialog API calls, so I have to be honest in telling you that I really don't know what you'd use it for. But now you know that it's there, in case you do run into a need to have that callback procedure within your application.

Summary

In this chapter, we looked at some real-world examples of callbacks to familiarize ourselves with the concept. We then proceeded to consider how they work within the Windows environment before examining how they are utilized by API calls.

In this chapter we:

- ❑ Covered the AddressOf operator, and how it can be used correctly in VB
- ❑ Investigated two API calls that require a callback function
- ❑ Demonstrated a way in VB to achieve a callback without the AddressOf operator
- ❑ Used the CallWindowProc API call to allow us to call a function within VB

In the next chapter, we'll extend the discussion of the AddressOf operator to component development, which will involve timer calls and subclassing techniques.

COM Components

Introduction

In the previous chapter, we looked at the concept of callbacks and how certain Win32 API calls can be made in VB using the `AddressOf` operator. We also looked at what we can't do with the `AddressOf` operator, such as passing the address of a class module function.

In this chapter, we'll see how these limitations effect component design by creating our own timer component using API calls. Once we understand the API calls and how the callback mechanism comes into play, we'll hide some of the complexity away in a component. Then, we'll go back into the encryption program, and replace VB's Timer control with our new component.

So in this chapter we will cover:

❏ The Component Object Model, COM
❏ In-process and out-of-process components
❏ Subclassing

A (Very) Brief Overview of COM

To sum it up...well, you can't be brief about COM. Many books and articles have been written about Microsoft's venture into the distributed computing realm, and COM is definitely a large part of their vision. What makes it so confusing is the nomenclature surrounding the architecture: Is it ActiveX, or COM, or OLE, or ... what? Once you start investigating some of the details, you'll notice that there's not much difference beneath the covers.

Granted, there's a fine line to draw here between providing a basic explanation of COM and delving into a full-blown discussion on it. I want to give you enough of an understanding such that we can start creating some components later on in the chapter, but I don't want to overwhelm you either. Therefore, what I've decided to do is present to you what I believe is COM's main 'selling point', if you will. As we move though the two projects presented in this chapter, you'll start to pick up more of the COM lingo and how the basics of COM work. I've also included an appendix (C) that describes the inner workings of COM in more detail. Granted, it's not all-inclusive, but it does get into more of the low-level COM workings. Some of the concepts that I'll introduce in this chapter are explained in more detail in Appendix C, so please check it out if you want more information on COM.

> *If you want to learn more about COM in VB, there are several books from Wrox Press that can help you out. The most thorough of which is* Visual Basic 6 COM *by Thomas Lewis (ISBN 1861002130). Less in-depth discussions of COM can also be found in* Beginning Visual Basic 6 Objects *by Peter Wright (ISBN 1-861001-72-X) and* Visual Basic 6 Business Objects *by Rockford Lhotka (ISBN 1-861001-07-X), as well as* Professional MTS & MSMQ Programming with VB and ASP *by Alex Homer and Dave Sussman (ISBN 1-861001-46-0).*

So here it is, the main selling point about COM:

> **COM is interface-driven computing through tightly bound contracts between components.**

Let's break this phrase down a bit more so that we can get more of an idea as to what's going on.

The phrase "interface-driven computing" means that COM allows you to define an interface to your implementations. This is similar to what we've been dealing with in the Win32 realm. You never see the code for `GetTickCount`, but you can use the function call at will. Furthermore, Microsoft can change the inner workings of `GetTickCount` at will, and you'll probably never know the difference. The same holds true in COM, except that now we're moving into the world of components and objects.

We've also run into the contract scenario with the Win32 calls as well. If you use `GetTickCount`, you're assuming that Microsoft won't suddenly change the call from this:

```
Declare Function GetTickCount Lib "kernel32" () As Long
```

to something like this:

```
Declare Function GetTickCount Lib "kernel32" (lpRes as Long) As Long
```

If they did, your old programs would break. That's not your fault, because you're holding up your end of the bargain; Microsoft is the one who changed the contract. Again, the same holds true for COM. If you publish a component within your corporation, for example, you can't change it. As you can imagine, this requires a lot of discipline and effort to make the contract "right" the first time (which means learning object-oriented analysis and design). But by having this strict contract in place, it makes a guarantee to the clients of your component that the published interface will never change.

COM and Win32

Some of the readers out there who picked up this book to try and get a better understanding of the Win32 calls may be wondering why I introduced a whole new world called COM at all. The reasoning behind this is that Microsoft is focusing a lot of energy behind this technology, and it is, in my opinion, critical to start understanding COM to open up new doors in your projects. To be fair, I barely scratched the surface of what COM is all about in the above description. But, by exposing you to what you can do by with COM and the Win32 calls within VB, I hope you'll start seeing that you can use VB for corporate component development.

Creating the APITimer ActiveX DLL Project

As always, the best way to understand the concept of COM is to see an example. We'll start off by creating the framework for our timer component. Once the framework is complete, we'll add the implementation.

Initializing the Project

To create a component, create a new ActiveX DLL project by selecting File I New, then choose ActiveX DLL from the following screen:

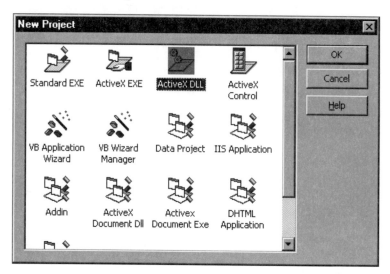

Once VB is done initializing the project, you'll notice that you have one class defined in the project, called Class1.

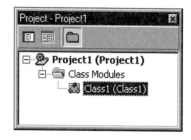

Change that class's Name property to APITimer, and make sure that the Instancing property is set to 5 - MultiUse (the other property values can be left alone). We'll also need a normal module to house our API calls, so add a module and call it TimerLibrary. Once that's done, we need to check some of the project properties. To do this, select P̲roject, then Project1 Prope̲rties..., which will bring up the following screen:

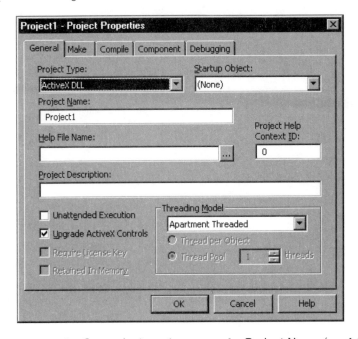

The only properties on the General tab to change are the Project N̲ame (set this to APITimerComponent) and Unatt̲ended Execution (make sure that it's checked). We won't worry about the other tabs in this project.

> *Unattended Execution delves into the subject of COM threading models, which govern if your component is multithreaded or not. Yes, I did say multithreading. It is possible to create objects in VB that run on different threads. Although this is an important topic, it's one that is out of scope for our purposes. Please check the sources I gave at the beginning of this chapter - they can shed more light on this powerful feature.*

Before we save the project, let's add the only public method that the class will have. It's called Enabled, and it looks like this:

```
Public Sub Enabled(Val As Boolean, TimeInterval As Long)

End Sub
```

Once this is added, save the project.

Component Details

Now let's go over some of the framework's attributes in more detail. First, why did we create an ActiveX DLL project and not an ActiveX EXE project? Let's take a look at these different types in more detail.

A component written to a DLL file is an **in-process** component. This means that if another program creates objects from the component, the DLL runs in the same address space that the program does, which can be seen in the following diagram:

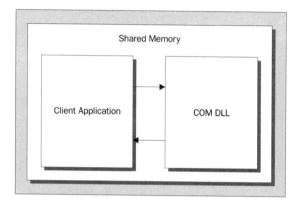

As the diagram shows, the DLL resides in the same process space as the client that is using it. This has the advantage of fast invocation of object properties and methods; the disadvantage of using a DLL is if the component crashes for any reason, it will take the calling program with it.

With an EXE component, it runs **out-of-process**. Therefore, since it runs in its own address space, it won't crash a calling program if it fails. Additionally, an EXE component has the advantage of being able to run on a different system than the client process. However, since it is in its own space, a process called **marshaling** needs to take place to make the method invocations on the object, which is shown in the next diagram:

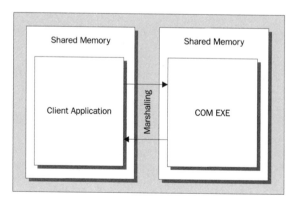

Since the client and the server are in different memory spaces, pointers and addresses to variables are not the same between the two. Marshaling bridges this gap between the two processes to allow communication from one to the other. This is slower than calling a method on a DLL component due to the overhead of cross-process communication. Whenever you design a component, you have to weigh these differences between the two types and determine what best fits your situation.

So what's this `Instancing` property all about? This determines the behavior of your objects, as well as your component. Let's take a brief look at each type:

- ❑ `Private`. This class can only be instantiated within the component itself - no other programs can use this class.
- ❑ `PublicNotCreatable`. Client programs using your component can use objects of this class, but the client cannot create the objects - your component must create them internally and then pass that object's reference to the client. This is useful if you want to have some internal control over when objects can be instantiated.
- ❑ `MultiUse`. This is probably the most common type I've used. The client program can create objects from the class. One instance of the component can be used to produce as many objects as required.
- ❑ `GlobalMultiUse`. This type is similar to `MultiUse` - the difference is that the properties and methods of the class can be invoked just as if they were global functions. You don't need to explicitly create an instance of the class when you use type `GlobalMultiUse`; one will automatically be created for you.
- ❑ `SingleUse` (EXE only). This type allows other applications to create objects from the class, however every object of this class that a client program creates starts a new instance of your component.
- ❑ `GlobalSingleUse` (EXE only). This is similar to `SingleUse`, except that the properties and methods of the class can be invoked as if they were simply global functions.

There are, of course, other aspects of the component project that we haven't touched yet. We'll come back to some of these later, but the primary aspect of the book is Win32, not COM. Therefore, let's move away from the component for now, and see what Windows can give us.

Timer API Calls and Callback Procedure

Now that the component framework is there, we'll take a look at the details of the API calls we need to make in our timer component. But before we delve into these details, let me take a moment to explain why and how I decided to choose timers as an example for callbacks.

Historical Background

During some downtime that I had between projects, I was looking into asynchronous methods within objects and how one could be created in VB. What do I mean by this? Let's say that you have a reporting process that may take a long time depending upon the volume of data needed in the report. You don't want this report job to block the user from doing anything else. Therefore, what would be really nice is to have this job run "in the background" while the user works on some other tasks. This can be seen in the timeline diagram given below:

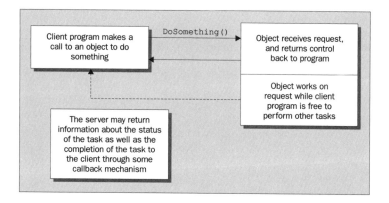

Unfortunately, there is nothing in VB that allows you to run a function or procedure concurrently with another function in the same process. Since I had the time, I decided to find a way to accomplish this feat.

To make a long story short, what I found out is that you should do this by creating a thread to handle the processing via the `CreateThread` API call. As I have mentioned before, in VB, this hurts! However, you can, to a degree, get around this pain by starting up a timer within an object when the report processing is requested, and return the control back to the client. Within the object, the timer's `Timer` event fires, which starts up the actual processing. However, the main problem with all of this is that to use a timer, you have to use the Timer control that comes with VB. This, unfortunately, requires a form to contain the control. In a DLL component, I wasn't thrilled about opening a form just to use a control on that form, especially one that was as simplistic as the Timer control (have I complained about this before?). Therefore, I started to hunt around the Win32 APIs, and I found out how a timer can be made. Since I've already spent time researching and developing this component, I figured that I might as well write on something that I know fairly well and is not as complex to explain as running threads in VB!

> *Be forewarned that, if you use this timer technique within a DLL component, the processing still runs on the same thread as the client's thread. Therefore, once the timer fires and the real processing starts, the client may "lock up" and not allow the user to type in text, press buttons, etc. In an EXE component, the threads are different, so this technique is much more effective in this case; the reason they're on different threads stems from the fact that they're in different processes! That's why creating true threads via API calls, although tricky, is the correct solution.*

SetTimer

The first thing we need to do with our timer is to get it set up. The call to do this is named `SetTimer`, and its declaration looks like this:

```
Declare Function SetTimer Lib "user32" (ByVal hWnd As Long, _
    ByVal nIDEvent As Long, ByVal uElapse As Long, _
    ByVal lpTimerFunc As Long) As Long
```

Let's go through some of the arguments in more detail. The first argument, hWnd, identifies a window with the timer. If this argument is set to 0, the timer isn't associated to a window (this is our situation, since we're creating a non-visual component with no windows). The second argument, nIDEvent, allows you to uniquely identify the created timer. If you set it to 0, the OS will give you an identifier. Personally, if somebody wants to do the work for me, I let them, so I set it to 0. The third argument, uElapse, sets the interval value in milliseconds. For example, if you wanted to mimic a stopwatch, you may set this to 10, which would cause the timer to fire every 1/100 of a second. The final value, lpTimerFunc, is where you pass in the address of a function that the timer will call to signal when another interval has been reached. However, we'll cover that procedure's declaration last. If the function is successful in creating the timer, it returns a non-zero value that uniquely identifies the timer. Otherwise, the function returns a zero if an error occurred.

KillTimer

If you create a timer, you'll have to get rid of it sooner or later. KillTimer does just that - here's the declaration:

```
Declare Function KillTimer Lib "user32" (ByVal hWnd As Long, _
    ByVal nIDEvent As Long) As Long
```

Again, let's go over the arguments. The first argument, hWnd, is a handle to a window with the same properties as SetTimer's hWnd argument. nIDEvent identifies the timer to remove from memory. If the function is successful, a non-zero value is returned; zero is returned on error.

TimerProc

Now we know how to create and destroy a timer. But how do we know when the timer fired? As stated above, the last argument in SetTimer is used to accomplish this feat. It points to the function that will be called when the interval is reached. This function is called TimerProc, and it is declared like this:

```
Function TimerProc(ByVal hWnd As Long, ByVal uMsg As Long, _
    ByVal idEvent As Long, ByVal dwTime As Long) As Long
```

The hWnd argument is the same as before. The second argument, uMsg, specifies the timer message, and isn't important to us for our purposes. The third argument, idEvent, is the timer's identifier - it lets you know which timer just fired. The last argument, dwTime, is rather interesting. It returns the same values as the GetTickCount API call would - the number of milliseconds elapsed since Windows was started. We won't use this argument's value in our component, but it would be nice to use as a sanity check if the object's behavior wasn't acting as expected.

Initial Component Design

Now that we have all of the calls defined, let's determine from a conceptual standpoint how we will internally use these calls.

First, we'll invoke SetTimer with some interval value determined by the user. We'll store the return value in a collection and associate it with an APITimer object reference so we know which Win32 timer object is fired each time TimerProc is called. When TimerProc is called, we'll look up the timer using the identifier in the collection. Then, we'll raise an event in the object, which will notify the client of a passing interval. Finally, if the user wants to shut the timer off, we'll call KillTimer with the appropriate timer identifier.

Now that we know how we want to implement it, we must now determine what's the best way to design the class interfaces effectively. Again, this analysis is beyond the scope of this book, so let's go over this class together to get an idea where I'm going with the design. The following shot of the **Class Builder** window shows the properties, methods and event that we will add to our `APITimer` class over the coming pages:

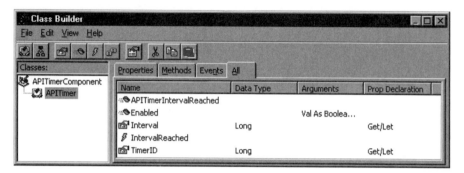

As you can see, the client has only one way to talk to our object, and that's through the `Enabled` method. This method allows the client to start or shut down the timer. We also have two properties, `TimerID` and `Interval`. These properties tell the client if the timer is currently on (`TimerID` will be greater than 0 in this case) and what the current interval value is. However, these properties can only be changed by the object internally (i.e. read-only). We have two private methods, `SetCurrentTimer` and `KillCurrentTimer`, which will only be used by the object; the client will not be able to use these methods (and as you will see, we wouldn't want a client to mess with these methods). A third method, `APITimerIntervalReached`, is declared as a `Friend` method, but from the perspective of the client, it's private; only other objects within the component and procedures defined within a module can call this method. Finally, we have to let the client know when the timer fired, which is what the `IntervalReached` event is for.

It may not be perfect, but it's simple. The client doesn't have to worry about a lot of properties, methods, and events to confuse any implementation details. Even though this project is pretty simple in comparison to some enterprise-wide component models that I've seen, we could've made it much worse!

Before we start the implementation, I want to discuss one aspect of the design. You may have been confused when I mentioned using a collection to keep track of timer identifiers. The reason we'll do this stems from one of the rules of using the `AddressOf` operator; you can't pass the address of a function in a class module to an API call. Well, `TimerProc` is going to exist in a code module, not a class module. Once the interval is reached, the object has to raise an event to notify the client; `TimerProc` can't raise an event for an object.

To get around this problem, I use a global collection, `gcolTimers`, which will hold a set of `APITimer` object references. Whenever `SetTimer` is called successfully, I add the object reference to the collection along with the `Key` value equal to "T" concatenated with the identifying value. Therefore, when `TimerProc` is called, it will obtain the correct object reference by using the `Item` property of the collection, and setting the `Index` argument equal to "T" concatenated with the identifying value. When it gets a valid object reference, it calls a method on that object called `TimerIntervalReached`, which does the job of raising the appropriate event. To prevent the client from invoking this method, we will declare it with the `Friend` keyword.

Let's summarize the calling flow with a diagram:

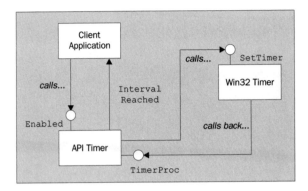

In the section that deals with subclassing, we'll use the ObjPtr *function to eliminate the need for a collection in this scenario.*

Coding the APITimer Object

Now we're ready to start coding. Open up the APITimerComponent project in VB and add the following API declarations to the TimerLibrary module file:

```
Declare Function SetTimer Lib "user32" (ByVal hWnd As Long, _
   ByVal nIDEvent As Long, ByVal uElapse As Long, _
   ByVal lpTimerFunc As Long) As Long
```

```
Declare Function KillTimer Lib "user32" (ByVal hWnd As Long, _
   ByVal nIDEvent As Long) As Long
```

We'll need to create the TimerProc function for the callback as well:

```
Function TimerProc(ByVal hWnd As Long, ByVal uMsg As Long, _
   ByVal idEvent As Long, ByVal dwTime As Long) As Long
```

We also need the collection gcolTimers defined in the module, so add it using this code:

```
Public gcolTimers As New Collection
```

We use the New keyword to ensure that we have a valid object reference. Also, add the following enumeration in the module file - we'll use these values for our own error handling:

```
Public Enum ErrorCodes
   UnanticipatedProgramError = 26000
   InvalidInterval
   SetTimerError
   NoCurrentTimer
   KillTimerError
End Enum
```

The 26000 value is purely arbitrary - these error codes are designed to be specific for our own timer component.

Starting the Timer

Let's start implementing the creation of the timer. We'll start with the `Enabled` method:

```
Public Sub Enabled(Val As Boolean, TimeInterval As Long)

    Dim lngTemp As Long

    If Val = False Then

        KillCurrentTimer

    Else

        If TimeInterval > 0 Then

            If TimerID <> 0 Then

                KillCurrentTimer

            End If

            SetCurrentTimer TimeInterval

        Else

            Err.Raise ErrorCodes.InvalidInterval, _
                "APITimer.Enabled", "Interval value must be positive."

        End If

    End If

End Sub
```

Let's walk through what this code does from a data validation standpoint.

First, we check the value of `Val`. If it's `False`, we'll try to turn off the timer using the `KillCurrentTimer` method (we'll define this later in the chapter). However, right now we're concerned with creating the timer:

```
If Val = False Then

    KillCurrentTimer

Else
```

If `Val` is `True`, then we check to make sure that `TimeInterval` is greater than zero:

```
If TimeInterval > 0 Then

Else
```

```
        Err.Raise ErrorCodes.InvalidInterval, _
            "APITimer.Enabled", "Interval value must be positive."

    End If
```

If we do get a value for `TimeInterval` that is less than or equal to zero, we raise an error to the client using the `Raise` method on the `Err` object.

The `Raise` method has one required argument - *number* - and up to four optional arguments, we'll deal with just two of them here, *source* and *description*.

Here we set the number argument to our code for an invalid interval - `ErrorCodes.InvalidInternal`; the source argument is set to the name of the function - `"APITimer.Enabled"`; and the description argument to a string value that briefly states why an error was raised - `"Interval value must be positive."`.

If `TimeInterval` is positive, we have to check to see if the timer has already been created.

```
        If TimeInterval > 0 Then

            If TimerID <> 0 Then

                KillCurrentTimer

            End If

            SetCurrentTimer TimeInterval
```

A read-only property called `TimerID` is used to expose this value - we'll define this property in a moment. If the value of `TimerID` is not equal to 0, i.e. if the timer already exists, we need to destroy it with the `KillCurrentTimer` method so that we can reset it.

If we get through all this data validation, we can call `SetCurrentTimer` in the class module with the appropriate interval value. Here's how this method is defined:

```
    Private Sub SetCurrentTimer(TimeInt As Long)

      Dim lngTemp As Long

      lngTemp = SetTimer(0&, 0&, TimeInt, AddressOf TimerProc)

      If lngTemp <> 0 Then

        ' Success!
        gcolTimers.Add Me, "T" & CStr(lngTemp)
        TimerID = lngTemp
        Interval = TimeInt

      Else

        ' Error!
        Err.Raise ErrorCodes.SetTimerError, "APITimer.SetCurrentTimer", _
          "Unable to set the timer."
```

```
            End If

      End Sub
```

This method is `Private`, so we don't have to worry that a client would inadvertently invoke this method.

The first thing we do is call `SetTimer`.

```
    lngTemp = SetTimer(0&, 0&, TimeInt, AddressOf TimerProc)
```

We don't care about the window handle property, so we'll set it to 0. We'll also let the call return an identifier for us. We pass in the address of `TimerProc` as the last argument using the `AddressOf` keyword.

If `lngTemp` is equal to 0 we raise an error.

```
        '   Error!
        Err.Raise ErrorCodes.SetTimerError, "APITimer.SetCurrentTimer", _
          "Unable to set the timer."
```

This is similar in structure to that in the `Enabled` method that we have just seen. However, this time the number argument is set to `ErrorCodes.SetTimerError`, the source argument is set to `"APITimer.SetCurrentTimer"` and the description argument to `"Unable to set the timer."`.

If `lngTemp` is non-zero, we know that the timer was created:

```
    If lngTemp <> 0 Then

      '   Success!
      gcolTimers.Add Me, "T" & CStr(lngTemp)
      TimerID = lngTemp
      Interval = TimeInt
```

We add a reference to this class to the `gcolTimers` collection along with a unique key. We also set the two properties in the class module, `TimerID` and `Interval`, with the appropriate values.

Here's the code to define the `Interval` property:

```
Public Property Get Interval() As Long

  Interval = m_lngInterval

End Property
```

```
Private Property Let Interval(Val As Long)

  m_lngInterval = Val

End Property
```

Here's the code that defines the `TimerID` property:

```
Public Property Get TimerID() As Long

  TimerID = m_lngTimerID

End Property
```

```
Private Property Let TimerID(Val As Long)

  m_lngTimerID = Val

End Property
```

Notice that these properties have `Private` scope for their `Property Lets`, making them read-only - the client cannot change these values. Also notice that these properties use two internal variables: `m_lngTimerID` and `m_lngInterval`.

Enter these variable declarations into the General Declarations section of the class module:

```
Private m_blnEnabled As Boolean
Private m_lngInterval As Long
Private m_lngTimerID As Long
```

Handling Timer Intervals

Now that the timer is started, we need to have a mechanism of notifying the client when the timer fires. We know that there's a callback involved and we know that the collection will help us out in some way. Let's go through the details of this notification.

At some point in time, `TimerProc` will be called by the timer. I'll show you the code for `TimerProc` first, and then we'll review it in detail. Enter this code into the `TimerLibrary` code module:

```
Public Function TimerProc(ByVal hWnd As Long, ByVal uMsg As Long, _
    ByVal idEvent As Long, ByVal dwTime As Long) As Long

  On Error GoTo error_TimerProc

  Dim m_objTimer As APITimer

  Set m_objTimer = gcolTimers.Item("T" & CStr(idEvent))

  If Not m_objTimer Is Nothing Then
      m_objTimer.APITimerIntervalReached
  End If

  Exit Function

error_TimerProc:

  If Not m_objTimer Is Nothing Then
      Set m_objTimer = Nothing
  End If

End Function
```

As we saw before, idEvent contains the timer identifier. We'll use that to try and obtain a reference to an APITimer object. We do this by invoking the Item method in our gcolTimers collection, and pass in a key containing the identifier.

```
Set m_objTimer = gcolTimers.Item("T" & CStr(idEvent))
```

If we get a valid reference, then we call a method on the object called APITimerIntervalReached.

```
If Not m_objTimer Is Nothing Then
    m_objTimer.APITimerIntervalReached
End If
```

But what's APITimerIntervalReached? It's a method on our APITimer object. This is the callback procedure to find out when the timer's interval has been reached. Here's its implementation - it's pretty straightforward:

```
Friend Sub APITimerIntervalReached()

    RaiseEvent IntervalReached

End Sub
```

Notice that it's declared as a Friend method. This means that only class module and code module functions within the component can call this procedure; clients using the APITimer object won't be able to use this procedure. There's only one line of code in this method, which raises an event by using the keyword RaiseEvent. To add this new event to our object, simply add this line to the Declarations section of the APITimer class:

```
Public Event IntervalReached()
```

Now if the client can support COM events, they'll get notified every time the timer fires (we'll see how to do this in VB shortly).

Ending the Timer

We already have the method declared to do this in our APITimer - it's contained in the Enabled event:

```
If Val = False Then
    KillCurrentTimer
Else
```

Notice that if Val is False, we call an internal method called KillCurrentTimer. Let's take a look at the code (you should enter this into your APITimer class):

```
Private Sub KillCurrentTimer()

  Dim lngTemp As Long

  If TimerID <> 0 Then
    lngTemp = KillTimer(0&, TimerID)
```

```
        If lngTemp <> 0 Then
        '   Success!
            gcolTimers.Remove "T" & CStr(TimerID)
            TimerID = 0
        Else
        '   Error!
            Err.Raise ErrorCodes.KillTimerError, _
                "APITimer.KillCurrentTimer", "Unable to kill the timer"
        End If

    End If

End Sub
```

Killing the timer is similar to starting it up. We begin by checking that `TimerID` is not equal to 0.

```
    If TimerID <> 0 Then
```

We use the Win32 API call `KillTimer` and pass in the current value of the timer's identifier.

```
    lngTemp = KillTimer(0&, TimerID)
```

If the call is successful, we remove this object's reference within the collection since it's no longer in an active state. We also reset the object's timer identifier to 0.

```
    '   Success!
        gcolTimers.Remove "T" & CStr(TimerID)
        TimerID = 0
```

However, if for some reason `KillTimer` failed, we raise an error to the client specifying the type of error.

```
    '   Error!
        Err.Raise ErrorCodes.KillTimerError, _
            "APITimer.KillCurrentTimer", "Unable to kill the timer"
```

That's it! If you go back and look at what we've done, there isn't a lot going on. In theory, you could create timers within any VB project simply by using the Win32 calls directly. However, by making a COM component, we've hidden the details away from another programmer. Also, we've now removed the requirement that any project that needs a timer must have a form to contain VB's Timer control.

Before we add it into the encryption program, we need to compile the component. To do this, select File | Make APITimerComponent.dll. If you didn't get any errors, then we can move to the final step in this chapter.

One technical comment on our DLL. You may wonder if a calling program can invoke `TimerProc`, *since it's a public procedure. The reason we're safe here is due to the fact that VB does not allow you to export functions in a DLL. If you're from the C or Pascal world, you know that you can do this, and may be wondering, "Why can't I?" Well, many other VB programmers have been begging for this for a while, but I wouldn't hold my breath for this feature in 7.0. In reading a chat transcript posted on Microsoft MSDN site on the new features of VB 6.0, one programmer asked if 6.0 would finally allow a developer to export functions. The response was no - COM is becoming a more widely used interface than the "old" way of entry-point functions in DLLs. I had to laugh! When you get down to it, COM is doing the same thing as an exported function (try calling* `CoCreateInstance` *in VB and you'll see what I mean). I was somewhat disappointed in this logic, but there are other third-party tools that let you create DLLs with exported functions in VB.*

Using the APITimer Object in the Encryption Project

Remember when we went a little overboard with the visual aspects of the About form in the encryption program? We had a timer that would randomly change the text within the picture box. Well, now that we have our own timer object, we're going to get rid of VB's Timer control, and use ours instead!

Referencing the Component

First, open up the encryption program. Once that's done, we need to let VB know that we want to use our component within the project. To do that, select Project | References... You'll get a screen that looks similar to this one:

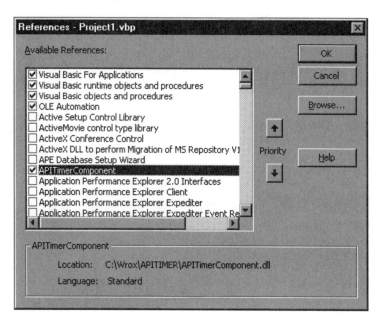

Your screen may look different from mine, but look through the list and try to find the APITimerComponent. Once you do, check the box next to the name. You'll notice that when you do this, the Location: label at the bottom of the screen tells you where the actual component file resides on your hard drive. If you can't find it, you'll have to press the Browse... button and find the component yourself. Once you're sure you've made the reference correctly, select OK.

Now what's going on here with referencing components? Whenever you make a component, be it an EXE or DLL, you have to let the computer know where it is, what kind of interfaces it supports, and a slew of other details that may or may not apply to your design. This information is stored within the computer's registry (under the HKEY_CLASSES_ROOT key, if you're interested in looking) using a **Globally Unique Identifier**, or GUIDs. This identifier uniquely defines your class interface, which is where the contract idea we saw before comes into play. The moral of the story is that VB reads all of this information to determine what components have been registered on your PC, and adds them to the list.

> *Since you probably compiled the timer component's code on the same computer that the encryption program resides, we won't need to register the component's information. However, if you have to install a COM component on a user's PC, or if you have problems getting components to work on a PC, you may have to register them yourself. Fortunately, using the commands* regsvr32 *and* regserver *(for DLLs and EXEs, respectively) will do all of the registration for you. For example, to register our DLL compoment, you can type* regsvr32 "C:\APITimerComponent.dll" *when you select* Run *from the* Start *menu in Windows.*

Changing the Code

Now, all we have to do is change frmAbout's code around a bit to use the APITimer object. First, add this line of code to the Declarations section of the form:

```
Private WithEvents m_objAPITimer As APITimer
```

The WithEvents keyword notifies VB to add all of the events for this object to the code editor. Let's go over a couple of restrictions that WithEvents has before we continue. The WithEvents keyword only works with objects declared at the module level of a form or class module; you can't use WithEvents in code modules or within a procedure. In addition, you can't use the New keyword with the WithEvents keyword. Therefore, the following line of code won't work:

```
Private WithEvents m_objAPITimer As New APITimer
```

Now, if we go to the Object drop-down box in the code editor, we'll see m_objAPITimer listed there. If you select it, we'll see our IntervalReached event! Here's a screen shot to illustrate this:

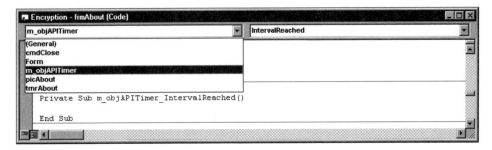

Before we move our code from the old timer to the new one, let's make sure we create and destroy m_objAPITimer correctly:

```
Private Sub Form_Initialize()

    Set m_objAPITimer = New APITimer
    m_objAPITimer.Enabled True, 5000

End Sub
```

```
Private Sub Form_Terminate()

    If m_objAPITimer.TimerID > 0 Then
        m_objAPITimer.Enabled False, 0
    End If

    Set m_objAPITimer = Nothing

End Sub
```

VB's Timer control does have the advantage of allowing you to change the properties using the Properties window, so that's why we have to explicitly start the timer in the form's Initialize event. Now, all we have to do is delete our code from tmrAbout's Timer event procedure:

```
Private Sub tmrAbout_Timer()

  AlterLabels

End Sub
```

and enter the following code into m_objAPITimer's IntervalReached event.

```
Private Sub m_objAPITimer_IntervalReached()

  AlterLabels

End Sub
```

Now we must alter the code that changes the interval from 5 seconds to 1 in AlterLabels procedure. Replace these lines of code:

```
If tmrAbout.Interval = 5000 Then
  tmrAbout.Interval = 1000
End If
```

with this new code, which calls the component:

```
If m_objAPITimer.Interval = 5000 Then
  m_objAPITimer.Enabled True, 1000
End If
```

This may seem a bit weird, since we already have the timer enabled. However, our implementation is different from that of VB's Timer. To change the timer's `Interval` value, we need to invoke `Enabled` with the new value. If you go back to the code for this method, you'll see that we actually destroy, then start up a new timer.

```
If TimeInterval > 0 Then

    If TimerID <> 0 Then

        KillCurrentTimer

    End If

    SetCurrentTimer TimeInterval

Else
```

Now that all of the changes are there, delete `tmrAbout` from the form. Now save your project. Start up the project and we'll find we have the same behavior as before. We've successfully created a COM component that uses the Win32 API and integrated it into an existing project. That's not a small feat!

Improvements to the Design

As with any design, hindsight is 20/20. I've tried to make the component easy and straightforward to implement, but I can already hear the derision from the audience: "Hey, you should've done it this way!" I've already seen some places where the design can be improved upon, but I'll leave them as exercises for the interested reader. Most of them start getting in the details of COM and object design, which is somewhat out of our scope, but if you're curious, take a look at these possible changes:

❑ **Keep the Same Identifier.** In the example above, we changed the interval value from 5 seconds to 1. If you noticed, the `TimerID` may have changed because we internally destroyed and created a timer to do this. You could add code to preserve the identifier once the first timer is created (remember, you can identify the timer yourself, so once you get use, you should be able to reuse it).

❑ **Expand the Interval Property's Implementation.** You could change the behavior of the `APITimer` class to change the timer's interval simply by changing this property. This starts to get into the issues of component versioning and interface contracts, but you'll learn more about the benefits and frustrations of component design - specifically, trying to get it right the first time!

❑ **Waitable Timers.** You'll only be able to use this kind of timer if you're using NT, but I'd take a look at this one if you can. There are more options with this timer in terms of how and when it will fire, but the most interesting aspect that I've seen is that you can share it across processes. If done properly, you can set up your own scheduled processes with this timer.

Creating a Subclassing Component

In my opinion, this section is by far the hardest one in the entire book. That's not to say that it's the hardest implementation you'll ever do in VB or COM, but subclassing is a topic that starts to push the limits of VB. However, it's not impossible, and if done correctly, it opens up the floodgates to Windows (just make sure you don't drown). First, we'll go over subclassing in detail so we understand the concept in depth. Then, we'll start designing the component to see what problems we'll run into. Finally, we'll implement the component and test it out on a simple form.

The Details of Subclassing

As I've mentioned before, each window is based on a class (remember the discussion over `GetClassName?`). Therefore, whenever you create a window in Windows, your window has all of these attributes predefined. One of these attributes is the window's message handler, which is just a function that handles any message that is sent to a window (usually through a call like `SendMessage`). This is analogous to a user clicking on a command button and having VB raise the `Click` event for that button. As simple as this concept sounds, the message handler cannot break for your application to work correctly. If it does, your window will not function properly. When you stop and think about all of the events that occur during a window's lifetime (mouse movements and clicks, keyboard events, minimize/maximize/resize, etc.), you realize just how important this message handler is. Here's a diagram to illustrate how this works:

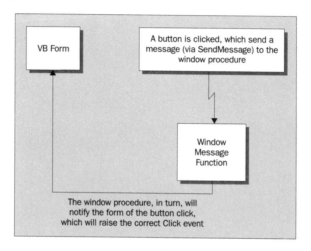

Fortunately, we don't have to worry about this in VB. VB handles all of the low-level window messages and translates them into events. This definitely makes our programming lives easier! However, there is a trade-off to this world of comfort. VB has about 30 form events, but if you ever do a search to see how many window messages there are, the message count far outweighs the event count. This is by design, since VB is meant to be an easy tool to use, and some messages are tricky to handle.

In essence, VB has subclassed, or redirected, the original message procedure. It intercepts all of the messages that are received by the window, and raises events for only a handful of them. Of course, all of the messages are directed to the original message procedure; otherwise, your form would never look like a window. In fact, it would never function at all. Here's a diagram to show what is going on underneath the scenes:

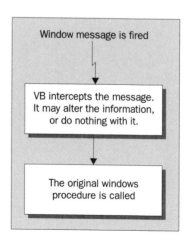

When a message procedure is subclassed, another function receives the message (which we'll call `MyMessageProc`). When `MyMessageProc` is invoked by the OS, it has a couple of choices. It can:

❑ Simply pass the information back to the original message procedure
❑ Do something with the message, and then invoke the original procedure
❑ Invoke the original procedure, and then do something with the information
❑ Do something with the message and never call the original procedure

The last option is the most dangerous by far. It can allow you to prevent certain actions from occurring, but care must be taken to ensure that this will not incur erratic results. For example, if you prevented any menu messages from occurring, your form would never have any menus, which may be catastrophic for your application.

The first one is the easiest, since you're simply an "observer" of the message – no interaction takes place. The other two options are in the murky area of implementation, since errors may occur depending upon what you do before and/or after the original procedure is invoked. However, in all of the options except the last one, you're following a standard rule of subclassing:

> **Always pass the message to the original procedure.**

Subclassing a VB Form

With the `AddressOf` operator, you have the ability to subclass VB's form to look at all of the messages that Windows is sending VB. Let's take a look at how we will do this in more detail.

First, we have to define a function in a module that will be used to handle window messages. Its signature looks like this:

```
Public Function WindowProc(ByVal hWnd As Long, _
    ByVal Msg As Long, ByVal wParam As Long, ByVal lParam As Long) _
    As Long
```

These arguments have exactly the same meaning as the ones in `CallWindowProc`. Now, whenever we want to start subclassing the form, we make a call to `SetWindowLong` like this:

```
lngOldProcAddr = SetWindowLong(hWnd, GWL_WNDPROC, AddressOf WindowProc)
```

Where `SetWindowLong` is declared as follows:

```
Public Declare Function SetWindowLong Lib "user32" _
    Alias "SetWindowLongA" (ByVal hWnd As Long, _
    ByVal nIndex As Long, ByVal dwNewLong As Long) As Long
```

The constant `GWL_WNDPROC` notifies Windows that you want to start receiving window messages through your own window procedure, which is specified by using the `AddressOf` operator on `WindowProc`. The `hWnd` argument tells Windows which window we want to subclass. If this function is successful, the non-zero value on return is the address to the old window procedure. Keep it handy – we'll use it in a moment.

From this point on, any time the form is notified of anything, even if it's a message that VB doesn't expose to us through an event, we get it though `WindowProc`. Of course, if we still want our form to work, we need to call the old window procedure, which we do by making a call to `CallWindowProc`, setting the third argument equal to the address of the old window procedure (I told you to keep it handy!).

If we want to stop the subclassing, we make a call to `SetWindowLong`, and set the second argument equal to the address of the old window procedure (you still have it around, right?).

Subclassing Problems in VB

With subclassing, we can see everything that is going on within a window. If you don't see how powerful this is, step back a moment and hit your head with this book for a while to clear out those cobwebs. (Just kidding – I don't want to get sued). Before someone sat down with me and explained what this technique was doing, I had no clue what the fuss was with all of the values being sent to my own window procedure. Once you understand that **EVERY** window message is sent to your subclassed form, you'll realize that a lot of things that you knew Windows was processing are not hidden from you anymore (like when you move a form). Moreover, you can send your own application-specific window messages via `SendMessage` to your form, which can be processed by your own window procedure.

With power comes an equal amount of responsibility and care. Subclassing can be done in VB, but apart from its own perils, VB is not a fun language to subclass in. Here are just some of the issues involved:

❑ **Module Functions.** Oh, sure, we can get the messages, but how do we call the correct form, especially if we're in a MDI program? We saw this problem with the timer component, and we used a collection to get around this limitation, but a collection just won't cut it in this case. Window messages will be coming down on us like an avalanche, and trying to search for the correct form in a collection will be too time consuming.

❑ **Debugging.** We can solve this within our own application using code modules and class modules, but what happens when we hit a breakpoint in our application? Guess what, the whole environment freezes. To illustrate this point, add some code to the `Resize` method on any form that changes the form's caption, and put a breakpoint on that line. When you hit the breakpoint and hit F8, you'll notice that VB handles that operation without a glitch. Do this when you're subclassing the form and you have all the code included in your project, and the next line of code you'll step into will be your own window procedure, again, and again, and again, and…you get the point.

However, even with these and other problems, the temptation to open a proverbial Pandora's box is just too great. In the next section, we'll take a look at how we can create a subclassing component that will expose other events that VB's form doesn't give.

Extending the Form With IFormEx

The `FormEx` project is an ActiveX DLL project that we will use to create the `IFormEx.DLL` component. Create a new DLL project called `FormEx` and add one class module called `IFormEx`, and one code module called `IFormExLib`. Check that the `Instancing` property of `IFormEx` is set to `5 - MultiUse`. Add the following API calls to `IFormExLib`:

```
Public Declare Function CallWindowProc Lib "user32" Alias _
   "CallWindowProcA" (ByVal lpPrevWndFunc As Long, _
   ByVal hWnd As Long, ByVal Msg As Long, ByVal wParam As Long, _
   ByVal lParam As Long) As Long
```

```
Public Declare Sub CopyMemory Lib "KERNEL32" Alias _
   "RtlMoveMemory" _
   (lpvDest As Any, lpvSource As Any, ByVal cbCopy As Long)
```

```
Public Declare Function SetWindowLong Lib "user32" Alias _
   "SetWindowLongA" (ByVal hWnd As Long, ByVal nIndex As Long, _
   ByVal dwNewLong As Long) As Long
```

Also, add the `WindowProc` function to the library as well – we'll expand on it later.

```
Public Function WindowProc(ByVal hWnd As Long, _
   ByVal Msg As Long, ByVal wParam As Long, ByVal lParam As Long) _
   As Long
```

Now add the following events and variables to `IFormEx` class:

```
Private m_strLastError As String
Private m_objFormRef As Form

Public Event AppActivate()
Public Event AppDeactivate()
Public Event SystemTimeChange()
Public Event PowerChange(wParam As Long)
Public Event PowerResumeFromCritical()
Public Event PowerResumeFromStandby()
Public Event PowerResumeFromSuspend()
Public Event PowerStandBy()
Public Event PowerSuspend()
```

Now add the following constant to the `IFormExLib` code module:

```
Public Const GWL_WNDPROC = (-4)
```

We'll go over how each of these will be used in a moment. Now let's go over just what this component will do for us.

The New Form Events

The `IFormEx` class exposes nine events that the VB form doesn't expose. They are:

❑ **Power Save.** If you computer has power save abilities, then these messages (`PowerChange`, `PowerResumeFromCritical`, `PowerResumeFromStandby`, `PowerResumeFromSuspend`, `PowerStandBy`, `PowerSuspend`) may come in handy. They will let you know when your computer is going in a power save mode, and when it's coming back online.

- ❑ **Application Activation/Deactivation.** VB forms have `Activate` and `Deactivate` events, but `AppActivate` and `AppDeactivate` are form-specific, which means they don't tell you when the user leaves the entire application or comes back to it. These do, although the event only fires on the top-level form of the application.
- ❑ **System Time Change.** Depending upon your application, it may be crucial to know that the user changes the system clock. The `SystemTimeChange` event will let you know when it occurs.

Of course, there are many more events that Windows has, but that's one of the beauties of component development. You can extend `IFormEx` at will by adding events when you feel comfortable with other window messages. If you do it right, you won't break the client that are using an older version of your DLL with, and newer clients get the new events.

Technically, power and time changing events can also be received using the `SysInfo` control that comes with VB, which leads to an interesting question: what are legitimate form events and what are application events? For example, `AppActivate` effects every form in the application, so there are some communication issues that have to take place between all forms if this event gets fired. I don't want to tackle that design issue here, but keep it in mind when you add new events to `IFormEx` in the future.

For now, let's take a look at how this component handles the subclassing from start to finish.

Implementing IFormEx

The first thing we need to do is add a read-only property called `HookFormHWnd` to our `IFormEx` class:

```
Public Property Get HookFormHWnd() As Long

If Not m_objFormRef Is Nothing Then
    HookFormHWnd = m_objFormRef.hWnd
End If

End Property
```

This property's sole function is to return the window handle of the form that is currently being subclassed. We'll see how this is used later.

Next, add a method called `HookForm`:

```
Public Function HookForm(FormRef As Object) As Boolean

On Error GoTo error_HookForm

    Dim blnContinue As Boolean
    Dim blnRet As Boolean

    If Not FormRef Is Nothing Then

        If TypeOf FormRef Is Form Then

            blnContinue = True
            If Not m_objFormRef Is Nothing Then
```

```
                    If ObjPtr(FormRef) = ObjPtr(m_objFormRef) Then
                        HookForm = True
                    Else
                        blnRet = UnhookForm
                        If blnRet = False Then
                            HookForm = False
                            blnContinue = False
                        End If
                    End If
                End If
                If blnContinue = True Then
                    Set m_objFormRef = FormRef
                    HookForm = Hook(Me)
                End If
            End If
        End If

    Exit Function

error_HookForm:

    HookForm = False
    LastError = CStr(Err.Number) & "  " & Err.Description

End Function
```

This function sets the subclassing for `FormRef`, the form to hook. It returns `True` on success and `False` on failure (`LastError` holds the details).

Most of the code at the beginning of the method is there as a "safety net".

We begin by checking that `FormRef` is not `Nothing`:

```
If Not FormRef Is Nothing Then
```

We're using `Object` as our argument data type, so we must make sure that `FormRef` is a form:

```
If TypeOf FormRef Is Form Then
```

Now we check to see if we already have a form reference, which would mean that we're already subclassing a form:

```
If Not m_objFormRef Is Nothing Then
```

We then check to see if `FormRef` is the same as `m_objFormRef`. If it is then everything is OK - we're already subclassing this form - so set `HookForm` equal to `True`:

```
If ObjPtr(FormRef) = ObjPtr(m_objFormRef) Then
        HookForm = True
```

If `FormRef` is not equal to `m_objFormRef`, we're hooking a different form so we must unhook and rehook. After setting `blnRet` equal to `UnhookForm` we check that `blnRet` isn't `False`. If it is then `LastError` already contains the error so we must set `HookForm` and `blnContinue` equal to `False`:

```
Else
  blnRet = UnhookForm
  If blnRet = False Then
     HookForm = False
     blnContinue = False
  End If
End If
```

If we want our form to be hooked, `blnContinue` will have been set to `True`, therefore we run this final check:

```
If blnContinue = True Then
    Set m_objFormRef = FormRef
    HookForm = Hook(Me)
End If
```

Now we need to add a `Property Get` and a `Property Let` for `LastError`. The `LastError` property holds details of the last error - the `Err.Number` and the `Err.Description`.

```
Friend Property Let LastError(Val As String)

   m_strLastError = Val

End Property
```

```
Public Property Get LastError () As String

   LastError = m_strLastError

End Property
```

Notice that the `Property Let` is declared as a `Friend` method. This means that only functions within the `IFormEx` class module can call this `Property Let`; clients using the `IFormEx` object within another project won't be able to use this. This effectively makes the `LastError` property read-only as far as any client is concerned.

Finally, here's the `Hook` function that does the dirty work (note that this function should reside in the `IFormExLib` module):

```
Public Function Hook(FormEx As IFormEx) As Boolean

   On Error GoTo error_Hook

   Dim lngLocalPtr As Long
   Dim lngOldProcAddr As Long
   Dim lngPtr As Long
   Dim lngRet As Long
```

```
        If Not FormEx Is Nothing Then

            lngLocalPtr = ObjPtr(FormEx)

            lngOldProcAddr = SetWindowLong(FormEx.HookFormHWnd, _
                GWL_WNDPROC, AddressOf WindowProc)
            If lngOldProcAddr <> 0 Then
                lngRet = AddIFormExValues(FormEx.HookFormHWnd, _
                    lngLocalPtr, lngOldProcAddr)
                If lngRet > 0 Then
                    ' We're done.
                    Hook = True
                End If
            End If
        End If

        Exit Function

    error_Hook:

        Hook = False

    End Function
```

The Hook function actually does the subclassing of the form. The reason it exists in a code module and not a class is because we need to store the object reference as well as the hWnd value at the module level. The windows callback function exists here, and we'll need a way to callback to the correct object later.

First of all, note that we're passing in a reference to the IFormEx object instance, and **not** the form itself:

```
    Public Function Hook(FormEx As IFormEx) As Boolean
```

As I mentioned before, we have to be able to call back to the class to raise events, so this object reference will be used to get an object pointer to call the correct object instance. We get this object pointer using the undocumented function ObjPtr:

```
    lngLocalPtr = ObjPtr(FormEx)
```

Once we have the object pointer, we call SetWindowLong to start the form subclassing:

```
    lngOldProcAddr = SetWindowLong(FormEx.HookFormHWnd, _
            GWL_WNDPROC, AddressOf WindowProc)
```

If we get a nonzero return value from SetWindowLong, the subclassing was successful:

```
        If lngOldProcAddr <> 0 Then
            lngRet = AddIFormExValues(FormEx.HookFormHWnd, _
                lngLocalPtr, lngOldProcAddr)
            If lngRet > 0 Then
                ' We're done.
                Hook = True
```

```
        End If
    End If
```

As I stated before, unless we like living on the edge, we should call the old window procedure whenever we subclass, so we should store this window procedure along with the object pointer and the form's window handle. Therefore, we need a UDT called `IFormExValues` to store this information. Add this to the Declarations section of `IFormExLib`:

```
Private Type IFormExValues
    IFormExPtr As Long
    hWnd As Long
    OldWindowProcAddr As Long
End Type
```

Since this component can subclass more than one form at a time (the object only handles one form at a time, but there can be multiple `IFormEx` objects instantiated) there's a private array of this UDT type called `m_udtFormValues`. Type this into the Declarations section of `IFormExLib`:

```
Private m_udtFormValues() As IFormExValues
Private m_lngFormValuesL As Long
Private m_lngFormValuesU As Long
```

This array is used to store information about each form that's subclassed. The other two values, `m_lngFormValuesU` and `m_lngFormValuesL`, are used to store the upper and lower bounds of the array. I realize that we can use `UBound` and `LBound` to figure this out, but I wanted to cache these values for performance reasons. Since we're adding a new subclassed form, we need to add the values to `m_udtFormValues`. The `AddIFormExValues` function does just that. Type this into `IFormExLib`:

```
Private Function AddIFormExValues(hWnd As Long, _
    IFormExPtr As Long, OldProcAddr As Long) As Long

    On Error GoTo error_AddIFormExValues

    If m_lngFormValuesL = 0 Then
        m_lngFormValuesL = 1
        m_lngFormValuesU = 1
        ReDim m_udtFormValues(1 To 1) As IFormExValues
    Else
        m_lngFormValuesU = m_lngFormValuesU + 1
        ReDim Preserve m_udtFormValues(1 To m_lngFormValuesU) As _
            IFormExValues
    End If

    With m_udtFormValues(m_lngFormValuesU)
        .hWnd = hWnd
        .IFormExPtr = IFormExPtr
        .OldWindowProcAddr = OldProcAddr
    End With

    AddIFormExValues = m_lngFormValuesU

    Exit Function

error_AddIFormExValues:
```

```
AddIFormExValues = -1

End Function
```

By having the "add" capability stored away in a function, we can call it anywhere we want in the code. Furthermore, if we find a way to improve it (and it can be improved, that's for sure), you don't have to change the "add" capability everywhere in the code.

The `AddIFormExValues` function adds the values to the array in a first in-first out manner. It returns the array index on success and -1 on failure.

If `m_lngFormValues` = 0 then this is the first call. We set `m_lngFormValuesL` and `m_lngFormValuesU` equal to 1 and resize the `m_udtFormValues` array using `ReDim`:

```
If m_lngFormValuesL = 0 Then
    m_lngFormValuesL = 1
    m_lngFormValuesU = 1
    ReDim m_udtFormValues(1 To 1) As IFormExValues
```

However, if `m_lngFormValues` is non-zero we need to add 1 to the value of `m_lngFormValuesU` and use the new value to resize the array. We use `Preserve` here so that any data present in the array is not lost when we resize it:

```
Else
    m_lngFormValuesU = m_lngFormValuesU + 1
    ReDim Preserve m_udtFormValues(1 To m_lngFormValuesU) As _
        IFormExValues
End If
```

Now we add the data into the top level of the `m_udtFormValues` array:

```
With m_udtFormValues(m_lngFormValuesU)
    .hWnd = hWnd
    .IFormExPtr = IFormExPtr
    .OldWindowProcAddr = OldProcAddr
End With
```

Finally, we return the array index:

```
AddIFormExValues = m_lngFormValuesU
```

As you can probably guess, we're going to need some "remove" and "get" functions to complement the "add" function.

Add the following to `IFormExLib` as well:

```
Private Function RemoveIFormExValues(IFormExPtr As Long) As Boolean

    On Error GoTo error_RemoveIFormExValues

    Dim lngC As Long
```

```
If m_lngFormValuesL > 0 Then

    lngC = m_lngFormValuesL
    Do Until lngC > m_lngFormValuesU Or _
        m_udtFormValues(lngC).IFormExPtr = IFormExPtr
        lngC = lngC + 1
    Loop

    If lngC <= m_lngFormValuesU Then

        Do Until lngC = m_lngFormValuesU
            m_udtFormValues(lngC).hWnd = _
                m_udtFormValues(lngC + 1).hWnd
            m_udtFormValues(lngC).IFormExPtr = _
                m_udtFormValues(lngC + 1).IFormExPtr
            m_udtFormValues(lngC).OldWindowProcAddr = _
                m_udtFormValues(lngC + 1).OldWindowProcAddr
            lngC = lngC + 1
        Loop
        m_lngFormValuesU = m_lngFormValuesU - 1
        If m_lngFormValuesU = 0 Then
            Erase m_udtFormValues
            m_lngFormValuesL = 0
        Else
            ReDim Preserve _
                m_udtFormValues(1 To m_lngFormValuesU) As IFormExValues
        End If
        RemoveIFormExValues = True
    End If
End If

Exit Function

error_RemoveIFormExValues:

  RemoveIFormExValues = False

End Function
```

This function removes the values from the local array, given the `IFormExPtr` value. It returns a
`True` on success and `False` on failure.

We begin by checking that the array actually contains values:

```
If m_lngFormValuesL > 0 Then
```

We start at the value of `m_lngFormValuesL` (the lower bound of the array) and proceed through a
`Do Loop` until we have exceeded the upper bound of the array (`m_lngFormValuesU`) or reached
the array value for the given object pointer.

```
lngC = m_lngFormValuesL
Do Until lngC > m_lngFormValuesU Or _
    m_udtFormValues(lngC).IFormExPtr = IFormExPtr
    lngC = lngC + 1
Loop
```

If the value of `lngC` is less than or equal to the value of `m_lngFormValuesU` then we've found the pointer. Now we must shift all the values back in the array:

```
Do Until lngC = m_lngFormValuesU
    m_udtFormValues(lngC).hWnd = _
        m_udtFormValues(lngC + 1).hWnd
    m_udtFormValues(lngC).IFormExPtr = _
        m_udtFormValues(lngC + 1).IFormExPtr
    m_udtFormValues(lngC).OldWindowProcAddr = _
        m_udtFormValues(lngC + 1).OldWindowProcAddr
    lngC = lngC + 1
Loop
```

Now we remove the last element:

```
m_lngFormValuesU = m_lngFormValuesU - 1
```

If the value held in `m_lngFormValuesU` is now equal to zero we start a new array from scratch. Otherwise, we `ReDim Preserve` the array to resize it:

```
If m_lngFormValuesU = 0 Then
    Erase m_udtFormValues
    m_lngFormValuesL = 0
Else
    ReDim Preserve _
        m_udtFormValues(1 To m_lngFormValuesU) As IFormExValues
End If
```

Here's the "get" function, `GetIFormExData`. Type this into the `IFormExLib` code module:

```
Private Function GetIFormExData(hWnd As Long, _
    DataType As IFormExValueTypes) As Long

  On Error GoTo error_GetIFormExData

  Dim lngC As Long

  GetIFormExData = 0

  If m_lngFormValuesL > 0 Then
    lngC = m_lngFormValuesL
    Do Until lngC > m_lngFormValuesU Or _
        m_udtFormValues(lngC).hWnd = hWnd
        lngC = lngC + 1
    Loop
    If lngC <= m_lngFormValuesU Then
        If DataType = ObjectPointer Then
            GetIFormExData = m_udtFormValues(lngC).IFormExPtr
        ElseIf DataType = OldWindowProcAddress Then
            GetIFormExData = m_udtFormValues(lngC).OldWindowProcAddr
        Else
            GetIFormExData = 0
        End If
    End If
  End If
End If
```

```
Exit Function

error_GetIFormExData:

  GetIFormExData = 0

End Function
```

If a procedure needs to get information out of the m_udtFormValues array, the GetIFormExData function can return specific information (specified by DataType) on a subclassed form given its window handle (hWnd). It returns 0 if no pointer could be found and the pointer on success.

The implementation in the GetIFormExData function right now is a brute-force search (ugh!). This should be changed in the future, but for demonstration purposes, it'll suffice.

We begin by initializing the return value:

```
GetIFormExData = 0
```

If the value held in m_lngFormValuesL is greater than 0, there is data to search for:

```
lngC = m_lngFormValuesL
Do Until lngC > m_lngFormValuesU Or _
   m_udtFormValues(lngC).hWnd = hWnd
   lngC = lngC + 1
Loop
```

If the value of lngC after exiting the Do Loop is less than or equal to m_lngFormValuesU we've found the pointer. We can now get the data specified by DataType:

```
If lngC <= m_lngFormValuesU Then
    If DataType = ObjectPointer Then
        GetIFormExData = m_udtFormValues(lngC).IFormExPtr
    ElseIf DataType = OldWindowProcAddress Then
        GetIFormExData = m_udtFormValues(lngC).OldWindowProcAddr
    Else
        GetIFormExData = 0
    End If
End If
```

You'll notice that with GetIFormExData, the second argument uses an enumerated type called IFormExValueTypes to let GetIFormExData know if we want to look for an object pointer or the address to the old window procedure. Add the following enumeration to the code module:

```
Private Enum IFormExValueTypes
    ObjectPointer
    OldWindowProcAddress
End Enum
```

With all that said, we have subclassed the form and saved any information we need to raise events that extend the form. But how do we do that? Read on...

How Our Window Procedure Raises Events

This is the core of subclassing. We've hooked our form, and our `WindowProc` is being called at a furious pace. Every so often, however, a window message will come along that we need to catch and raise an extended event. Therefore, we need a way to callback on the correct object to raise the event. Let's take a look at `WindowProc` and see how this is done:

```
Public Function WindowProc(ByVal hWnd As Long, ByVal Msg As Long, _
    ByVal wParam As Long, ByVal lParam As Long) As Long

    On Error Resume Next

    Dim blnCallProc As Boolean
    Dim lngData As Long
    Dim lngObjPtr As Long
    Dim lngRet As Long
    Dim lngWindowRet As Long
    Dim objFormEx As IFormEx

    blnCallProc = True

    lngData = GetIFormExData(hWnd, OldWindowProcAddress)

    If lngData > 0 Then
        lngObjPtr = GetIFormExData(hWnd, ObjectPointer)
        If lngObjPtr <> 0 Then
            CopyMemory objFormEx, lngObjPtr, 4
        End If
        If Not objFormEx Is Nothing Then
            If objFormEx.HookFormHWnd = hWnd Then
                lngRet = objFormEx.BeforeWindowProc(Msg, wParam, lParam)
                If lngRet = 0 Then
                    blnCallProc = False
                End If
            End If
        End If
        If blnCallProc = True Then
            WindowProc = CallWindowProc(lngData, hWnd, Msg, wParam, _
                            lParam)
        End If
        If Not objFormEx Is Nothing Then
            If objFormEx.HookFormHWnd = hWnd Then
                lngRet = objFormEx.AfterWindowProc(Msg, _
                    wParam, lParam)
            End If
        End If
        CopyMemory objFormEx, 0&, 4
    'Else
    '   WARNING!  WARNING!
    '   This is a big problem!
    End If

End Function
```

For now, all we'll do is call the old window proc for the given hWnd. Note that this function **should not be called** by anything other than a callback by SetWindowLong.

We always call the original windows procedure unless IFormEx tells us not to:

```
blnCallProc = True
```

The first thing we do is get a valid function pointer to the old window procedure along with the object pointer that is associated with hWnd.

```
lngData = GetIFormExData(hWnd, OldWindowProcAddress)

If lngData > 0 Then
    lngObjPtr = GetIFormExData(hWnd, ObjectPointer)
```

If we get valid values (which we should), we create an instance of the object using CopyMemory like this:

```
If lngObjPtr <> 0 Then
    CopyMemory objFormEx, lngObjPtr, 4
End If
```

After some validation of objFormEx, we call BeforeWindowProc to perform pre-processing:

```
If Not objFormEx Is Nothing Then
    If objFormEx.HookFormHWnd = hWnd Then
        lngRet = objFormEx.BeforeWindowProc(Msg, wParam, lParam)
```

If the value of lngRet is now equal to zero then BeforeWindowProc has worked but we shouldn't call the windows procedure:

```
If lngRet = 0 Then
    blnCallProc = False
End If
```

Now if the value of blnCallProc is still True we call the old window procedure:

```
If blnCallProc = True Then
    WindowProc = CallWindowProc(lngData, hWnd, Msg, wParam, _
                    lParam)
End If
```

Again, after validating objFormEx we call AfterWindowProc, which performs the post-processing:

```
If Not objFormEx Is Nothing Then
    If objFormEx.HookFormHWnd = hWnd Then
        lngRet = objFormEx.AfterWindowProc(Msg, _
            wParam, lParam)
    End If
End If
```

`CopyMemory` comes to our aid again to get around a very tricky scenario. We could've used the same technique of storing an object reference in a collection like we did in the timer component, but in this case, this doesn't work. If we hold a reference to the object, we've increased the object reference count by 1. Every COM object implements something called the `IUnknown` interface (see Appendix C for more information). This interface has only three methods: `QueryInterface`, `AddRef`, and `Release`. The last two are the ones we're concerned about.

When we reference a COM object in VB, an implicit call to `AddRef` is made, so the reference count is incremented. When we set our object reference to `Nothing`, the `Release` method is called, so the reference count is decremented. COM will only destroy the object when the reference count goes to zero. This is meant to prevent objects from being orphaned or destroyed prematurely, and that's a good thing. However, in our subclassing scenario, it's not. If we hold a reference to an `IFormEx` object in our `IFormExValues` UDT array, that reference count will always be at least 1. If the user tries to close the form if the form is still subclassed, the form should set its own object reference to `Nothing`. All fine and good, but that extra object reference is getting in the way! If the programmer doesn't make a call to `Unhook` on the object, the `Terminate` event will always check to make sure it's done if it needs to be. But with an extra reference to the object, the object's `Terminate` event will not fire, the original window procedure will not be reset, and we're in for a lot of support calls.

However, if you "reference" the object via the call to `CopyMemory` using its object pointer, the call to `AddRef` is never made. Only `Set` calls in VB increment the object reference count (and `Nothing` assignments decrement it). This is exactly what we want, since the extra reference is not there, and the `Terminate` event will fire as it should. (Note that the byte size in the `CopyMemory` call is 4, since the size of the pointer is 4 bytes.)

Of course, there's one little catch. If you get a reference to an object using this technique, you have to de-reference the object like this:

```
CopyMemory objFormEx, 0&, 4
```

Although the reference count wasn't set, the object `objFormEx` contains some information. When `WindowProc` is done, VB will see that the variable goes out of scope, and try to set it equal to `Nothing`. This, however, would decrement the object reference count by 1. If in doing this the object reference count goes to zero, the object will automatically be destroyed. Not a good situation to be in. By setting `objFormEx` to a null value, we are essentially de-referencing `objFormEx` without decrementing the object reference count.

Before we continue with the discussion on the window procedure, please re-read the last two or three paragraphs on object references. It's something that we don't usually deal with to any great extent in VB, but in this case, it's very important to understand why we did what we did. You may have to break open a book on COM to get more information (if you haven't already), but object reference counts are a critical piece of COM.

Now that we have a way to reference the correct object, let's look at what we do with the window messages. The first thing we do is call `BeforeWindowProc` (you should enter this into the `IFormEx` class module:

```
Friend Function BeforeWindowProc(ByVal Msg As Long, _
    ByVal wParam As Long, ByVal lParam As Long) As Long
```

```
On Error GoTo error_BeforeWindowProc

    BeforeWindowProc = 1

Exit Function

error_BeforeWindowProc:

    BeforeWindowProc = -1
    LastError = CStr(Err.Number) & "  " & Err.Description

End Function
```

As you can see, we don't do any pre-processing with the message information - we just return a value of 1. We created this function in case we ever need to do something before the old window procedure gets a hold of it. Note that the return value determines not only if everything went OK, but if we should also prevent the old window procedure from doing anything with the information. A return value of 1 means success and continue, whereas 0 means success but don't call `CallWindowProc`.

Once `BeforeWindowProc` is done and we have returned a value to `WindowProc`, we call the old window procedure using `CallWindowProc` if `BeforeWindowProc` says it's OK to do so. Note that we set the return value of `WindowProc` equal to the return value of `CallWindowProc`.

```
WindowProc = CallWindowProc(lngData, hWnd, Msg, wParam, lParam)
```

If we ever did any special processing of our own, we may need to change the return value as well, but for now, whatever the window procedure returns, we return.

Finally, `WindowProc` calls the `AfterWindowProc` method on the object, which is where the extended events finally get raised. Here's what `AfterWindowProc` looks like (you should also enter this into the `IFormEx` class module):

```
Friend Function AfterWindowProc(ByVal Msg As Long, _
ByVal wParam As Long, ByVal lParam As Long) As Boolean

    On Error GoTo error_AfterWindowProc

    Dim blnMessages As Boolean

    Select Case Msg
        Case WM_POWERBROADCAST
            blnMessages = RaisePowerMessage(wParam)
        Case WM_TIMECHANGE
            RaiseEvent SystemTimeChange
            blnMessages = True
        Case WM_ACTIVATEAPP
            If wParam <> 0 Then
                RaiseEvent AppActivate
            Else
                RaiseEvent AppDeactivate
            End If
            blnMessages = True
        Case Else
        ' Other window message could go here.
            blnMessages = True
```

```
        End Select

    AfterWindowProc = blnMessages

    Exit Function

  error_AfterWindowProc:

    AfterWindowProc = False
    LastError = CStr(Err.Number) & "  " & Err.Description

  End Function
```

The `AfterWindowProc` function is used to handle any post-processing once the real windows procedure is called. It returns `True` on success and `False` on failure. The arguments of `AfterWindowProc` are standard windows message arguments.

The function looks at the value of `Msg` and determines what event to raise.

If the `Msg` is of type `WM_POWERBROADCAST` then the message is a power broadcast - we'll handle this in another function - so we set the `blnMessages` variable equal to `RaisePowerMessage(wParam)`:

```
        Case WM_POWERBROADCAST
                blnMessages = RaisePowerMessage(wParam)
```

If `Msg` is of type `WM_TIMECHANGE` then we raise the `SystemTimeChange` event and set `blnMessages` equal to `True`:

```
        Case WM_TIMECHANGE
                RaiseEvent SystemTimeChange
                blnMessages = True
```

If `Msg` is of type `WM_ACTIVEAPP` we first have to determine if this is an activation or deactivation. If `wParam` is non-zero then the application just got the focus, so this is an activation message and we raise the `AppActivate` event. Otherwise, this is a deactivation so we must raise the `AppDeactivate` event. Note that only the form that is getting or has lost the focus will receive this event. Regardless of whether this was a activation or deactivation however, we set `blnMessages` to `True`:

```
        Case WM_ACTIVATEAPP
                If wParam <> 0 Then
                        RaiseEvent AppActivate
                Else
                        RaiseEvent AppDeactivate
                End If
                blnMessages = True
```

Finally, we have a `Case Else` to handle any other types of messages:

```
        Case Else
            '  Other window message could go here.
                blnMessages = True
```

Before exiting the function we set `blnMessages` as its return value:

```
AfterWindowProc = blnMessages
```

Right now, these three window message constants are used (please add them to `IFormExLib`):

```
Public Const WM_POWERBROADCAST = &H218
Public Const WM_ACTIVATEAPP = &H1C
Public Const WM_TIMECHANGE = &H1E
```

However, note that we can easily extend this by adding more `Case` statements for other window messages.

Power Messages

If we get the `WM_POWERBROADCAST` message, we call the `RaisePowerMessage` function (please enter this into the `IFormEx` class module):

```
Private Function RaisePowerMessage(ByVal wParam As Long) As Boolean

    On Error GoTo error_RaisePowerMessage

    Select Case wParam
        Case PB_APMRESUMECRITICAL
            RaiseEvent PowerResumeFromCritical
        Case PB_APMRESUMESTANDBY
            RaiseEvent PowerResumeFromStandby
        Case PB_APMRESUMESUSPEND
            RaiseEvent PowerResumeFromSuspend
        Case PB_APMSTANDBY
            RaiseEvent PowerStandBy
        Case PB_APMSUSPEND
            RaiseEvent PowerSuspend
        Case Else
            RaiseEvent PowerChange(wParam)
    End Select

    RaisePowerMessage = True

    Exit Function

error_RaisePowerMessage:

    RaisePowerMessage = False
    LastError = CStr(Err.Number) & "  " & Err.Description

End Function
```

The `wParam` value tells us which power message has been sent to our application. Depending upon the value of `wParam`, we raise the corresponding object event. The `Case Else` raises a general `PowerChange` event in case we don't know what the `wParam` value means, but we still want the form to know that something with the power is happening. To be complete, here's a list of the power constants, which you should type into the `Declarations` section of the code module:

```
Public Const PB_APMRESUMECRITICAL = &H6
Public Const PB_APMRESUMESUSPEND = &H7
Public Const PB_APMRESUMESTANDBY = &H8
Public Const PB_APMSTANDBY = &H5
Public Const PB_APMSUSPEND = &H4
```

Unhooking a Form

When the client application goes out of scope, we need to clean up our subclassing. Therefore, we need an `UnhookForm` method in our `IFormEx` class module:

```
Public Function UnhookForm() As Boolean

    On Error GoTo error_UnhookForm

    Dim blnRet As Boolean

    LastError = ""

    If Not m_objFormRef Is Nothing Then
        blnRet = Unhook(Me)
        If blnRet = False Then
            UnhookForm = False
            LastError = "Could not unhook the form."
        Else
            Set m_objFormRef = Nothing
            UnhookForm = True
        End If
    Else
        UnhookForm = True
    End If

    Exit Function

error_UnhookForm:

    UnhookForm = False
    LastError = CStr(Err.Number) & "  " & Err.Description

End Function
```

This function unhooks the form specified by `m_objFormRef`. It returns `True` on success and `False` on error (check `LastError` for details).

First, we check to make sure we already have a form referenced:

```
If Not m_objFormRef Is Nothing Then
```

If the value of `blnRet` (returned from `Unhook`) is `False`, we set `UnhookForm` to `False` and report the error:

```
If blnRet = False Then
    UnhookForm = False
    LastError = "Could not unhook the form."
```

Otherwise, if `blnRet` was set to `True`, we set the form reference, `m_objFormRef`, to nothing and `UnhookForm` to `True`:

```
Else
    Set m_objFormRef = Nothing
    UnhookForm = True
End If
```

Finally, if `m_objFormRef` is `Nothing` there is no reason to unhook, but no error occurred so we set `UnhookForm` to `True`:

```
UnhookForm = True
```

Realistically, the `UnhookForm` method should be called when a form unloads, but it's called during the class's `Terminate` event just to be safe:

```
Private Sub Class_Terminate()

    UnhookForm

End Sub
```

Again, most of the code in `UnhookForm` is safety net code to make sure that the form really needs to be unhooked. If it does, we call the `Unhook` method located within `IFormExLib`:

```
Public Function Unhook(FormEx As IFormEx) As Boolean

    On Error GoTo error_Unhook

    Dim lngOldAddr As Long
    Dim lngRet As Long

    If Not FormEx Is Nothing Then
        lngOldAddr = GetIFormExData(FormEx.HookFormHWnd, _
                OldWindowProcAddress)
        If lngOldAddr <> 0 Then
            lngRet = SetWindowLong(FormEx.HookFormHWnd, GWL_WNDPROC, _
                lngOldAddr)
            If lngRet <> 0 Then
                RemoveIFormExValues ObjPtr(FormEx)
                Unhook = True
            End If
        End If
    End If

    Exit Function

error_Unhook:

    Unhook = False

End Function
```

It is this function that actually does the unhooking of the form.

After validating that the `FormEx` object exists, we get the old window proc for it:

```
If Not FormEx Is Nothing Then
        lngOldAddr = GetIFormExData(FormEx.HookFormHWnd, _
            OldWindowProcAddress)
```

If the value of `lngOldAddr` is non-zero we can unhook the form. The main part of this function is to reset the original window procedure, which is done by calling `SetWindowLong`. We place its return value into `lngRet`. If `lngRet` is also non-zero we remove the entries from the `IFormExValues` array using the `RemoveIFormExValues` function. Finally, we set `Unhook` equal to `True`:

```
If lngOldAddr <> 0 Then
    lngRet = SetWindowLong(FormEx.HookFormHWnd, GWL_WNDPROC, _
        lngOldAddr)
    If lngRet <> 0 Then
        RemoveIFormExValues ObjPtr(FormEx)
        Unhook = True
    End If
End If
```

Creating Our FormEx Component

Finally, we need to create our component just as we did with `APITimerComponent`. Select Ma<u>k</u>e FormEx.dll from the <u>F</u>ile menu.

Testing IFormEx

We've now compiled our component. However, we're far from done. Even with this short test section, this component needs a lot more work to make sure it's bulletproof. But for the moment, let's create a Standard EXE project called `FormExClient` to see if our component works as expected. Here's a picture of the one and only form of the application:

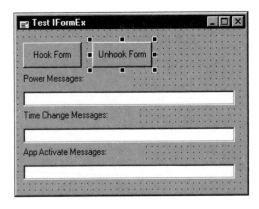

Here's a list of the form and control properties:

Object	Property	Value
Form	Name	frmMain
	Caption	Test IFormEx
Command Button	Name	cmdHook
	Caption	Hook Form
Command Button	Name	cmdUnHook
	Caption	Unhook Form
Label	Name	lblMain(0)
	Caption	Power Messages:
Text Box	Name	txtPowerMsg
	Locked	True
Label	Name	lblMain(1)
	Caption	Time Change Messages:
Text Box	Name	txtTimeChangeMsg
	Locked	True
Label	Name	lblMain(2)
	Caption	App Activate Messages:
Text Box	Name	txtAppActivateMsg
	Locked	True

Make sure that you reference the new FormEx component in this project as we did with timer project:

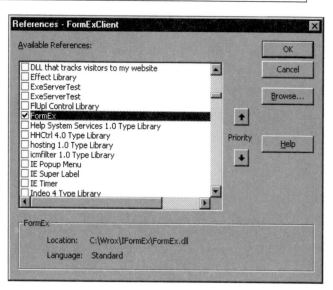

As we did with the timer component, we create a form-level object of an `IFormEx` type declared `WithEvents`:

```
Private WithEvents m_objIFormEx As IFormEx
```

The `WithEvents` keyword is crucial to extending the form; if we don't include this keyword, we might as well pack up our bags and go home. By including this keyword, we'll get all of the events defined by `IFormEx`, just like the `IntervalReached` event for the timer object.

Hooking the Form

Now that we have the class defined correctly on our form, we can use it to subclass the form at will. To do this, we have to call the `Hook` method on the object and pass a reference to the form as its only argument. We do that from the client-side using the `HookMyself` method, which is called from the `Click` event of `cmdHook`:

```
Private Sub cmdHook_Click()

    HookMyself

End Sub
```

Here's the `HookMyself` method which tries to subclass the form:

```
Private Sub HookMyself()

    On Error GoTo error_HookMyself

    Dim blnRet As Boolean

    If Not m_objIFormEx Is Nothing Then
    '   We have to unhook it first.
        blnRet = m_objIFormEx.UnhookForm
    Else
        Set m_objIFormEx = CreateObject("FormEx.IFormEx")
    End If

    blnRet = m_objIFormEx.HookForm(Me)

    If blnRet = False Then
        MsgBox "Could not subclass the form."
    End If

    Exit Sub

error_HookMyself:

    MsgBox CStr(Err.Number) & "  " & Err.Description

End Sub
```

We first check to see if the `m_objIFormEx` object is valid; if it isn't, we create a new object using the `CreateObject` call:

```
If Not m_objIFormEx Is Nothing Then
    ' We have to unhook it first.
    blnRet = m_objIFormEx.UnhookForm
Else
    Set m_objIFormEx = CreateObject("FormEx.IFormEx")
End If
```

Alternatively, if m_objIFormEx is valid we have to unhook it first by calling UnhookForm.

Then, we simply pass in a reference to the form to HookForm:

```
blnRet = m_objIFormEx.HookForm(Me)
```

If we get a True value back, the form is subclasssed, and the events will fire when appropriate. If we get a False value back we send a message box to the user:

```
If blnRet = False Then
    MsgBox "Could not subclass the form."
End If
```

Receiving IFormEx Events

When we receive an extended form event, we simply update the appropriate text box with a new message:

```
Private Sub m_objIFormEx_AppActivate()

  txtAppActivateMsg.Text = "App is activated."

End Sub
```

```
Private Sub m_objIFormEx_AppDeactivate()

  txtAppActivateMsg.Text = "App is deactivated."

End Sub
```

```
Private Sub m_objIFormEx_PowerChange(wParam As Long)

  txtPowerMsg.Text = "Unrecognized power message:  " & CStr(wParam)

End Sub
```

```
Private Sub m_objIFormEx_PowerResumeFromCritical()

  txtPowerMsg.Text = "Resume operation from critical suspension."

End Sub
```

```
Private Sub m_objIFormEx_PowerResumeFromStandby()

  txtPowerMsg.Text = "Resume operation from standby suspension."

End Sub
```

```
Private Sub m_objIFormEx_PowerResumeFromSuspend()

  txtPowerMsg.Text = "Resume operation from suspend suspension."

End Sub
```

```
Private Sub m_objIFormEx_PowerStandBy()

  txtPowerMsg.Text = "Going on standby."

End Sub
```

```
Private Sub m_objIFormEx_PowerSuspend()

  txtPowerMsg.Text = "Going on suspend."

End Sub
```

```
Private Sub m_objIFormEx_SystemTimeChange()

  txtTimeChangeMsg.Text = "Time has changed"

End Sub
```

Unhooking the Form

Once the form is closed, we should reset the old window procedure to prevent any nasty error from occurring. The test form does this by calling `UnhookThyself`:

```
Private Sub UnhookThyself()

  On Error Resume Next

  Dim blnRet As Boolean

  If Not m_objIFormEx Is Nothing Then
      blnRet = m_objIFormEx.UnhookForm
      If blnRet = False Then
          MsgBox "Could not stop the subclassing."
      End If
  End If

End Sub
```

This is called in the `Click` event of `cmdUnhook` as well as the `Unload` event of the form, just to be safe:

```
Private Sub cmdUnhook_Click()

  UnhookThyself

End Sub
```

```
Private Sub Form_Unload(Cancel As Integer)

  UnhookThyself

End Sub
```

As a final clean-up, we set our extended form object to `Nothing` when the form terminates:

```
Private Sub Form_Terminate()

  If Not m_objIFormEx Is Nothing Then
      Set m_objIFormEx = Nothing
  End If

End Sub
```

Running the Client Project

So what happens when you subclass the form? Well, two scenarios that we can test out are activating and deactivating the form, and changing the system time.

Run the `FormExClient` application and click on the **Hook Form** button. Now click somewhere in Windows such that the application loses the focus, the form should report the event like this:

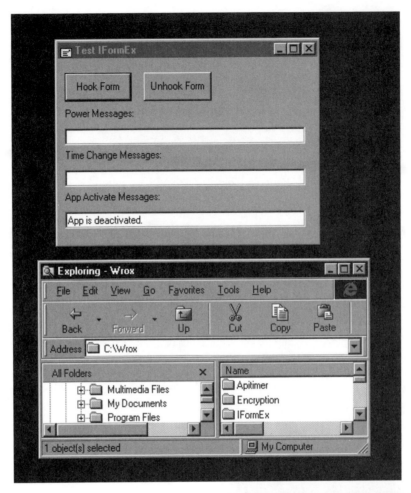

Now find your <u>C</u>ontrol Panel from the Start menu and select Date/Time. The Date/Time Properties dialog will appear:

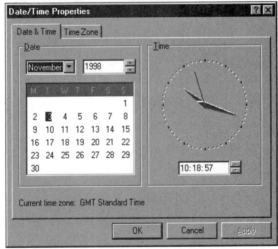

If we change the system clock, the form informs us of this in another text box:

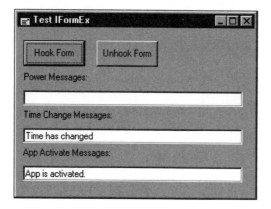

The power events depend upon your PC and its ability to shutdown and startup after a specified passage of time. Most modern laptops have this feature, but I can't assume that your PC has this feature, so don't worry if you can't get this event to raise.

Subclassing and Component Summary

There's a lot more I can say on subclassing, but we don't have the space to go over every Window message available. I'd suggest that you break open the Windows SDK and start playing with other window messages. There's really nothing to hold you back from obtaining more control over your VB applications with this subclassing component. Plus, having it in a component hides all the nasty details away from the client. However, I want to warn you of an issue that came up when I was designing this component, and I don't want you to have the same inspirational moment.

The IFormEx class used to have another event called WindowMessage, which contained all of the values that we receive in WindowProc. I did this to make sure that my subclassing code worked, and having an event raise every time the form received a message seemed to make sense. Well, it worked, but look what I did with the event:

```
Private Sub WindowMessage(Msg as Long, wParam as Long, lParam as Long)

    txtWindowsMessage.Text = "Msg = " & CStr(Msg) & _
        ", wParam = " & CStr(wParam) & ", lParam = " & CStr(lParam)

End Sub
```

(Note: txtWindowsMessage was another text box that was on the form to show this event's information). So every time I got a window message, I reasoned, I would see it in a text box. At least that's what my logical brain decided without coffee at 2:00 in the morning. The result left me desperately screaming at my computer for control. By updating the text box **every** time I got a message...well, I end up sending another message to the window. That message gets reported by the event, which sends another message to the window...and I never saw my app again during that Windows session (in fact, the program locked up so bad that *Ctrl+Alt+Del* wouldn't work; I had to power the machine down and restart it).

The moral of the story is don't code like I did; late at night without coffee. Seriously, I really should have thought about what I was doing, but I didn't. The event isn't the problem, but exposing that information leaves a hole open that decaffeinated programmers will go wild with. The result is catastrophic. Therefore, if you add another event to `IFormEx`, think about the ramifications of doing so. What would another programmer do with that event? Could it cause some serious damage to the application? If you spend some time analyzing the effects of exposing a particular window message, you'll save yourself a lot of pain in the future.

> *Actually, there's a simple way to get around what I did. You can check to see if* `Msg` *is equal to* `WM_PAINT`. *If it is,* **don't** *update the text box or do anything else that will cause another repaint of the window. By adding this filter, you should be able to do what I did with no problems.*

Lastly, there are a couple of items that I want to point out about the component, and they really have nothing to do with the design of `IFormEx`.

The first thing to look at is the Compile tab of the Properties window:

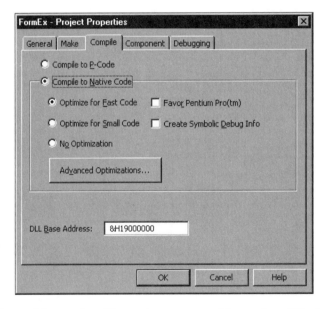

Look at the DLL base address value. This is the memory address where Windows will try to load you DLL. By default, this is set to `&H11000000`, but in this project, it's set to `&H19000000`. Why? Well, for the most part, you can leave this value alone, since Windows will resolve any base address conflicts that occur when it loads the DLL into memory. However, if you're working in an organization where component creation thrives, you may want to override this value to prevent a lot of conflicts from occurring. Remember, there are other VB component developers out there who probably aren't changing the default base address. If you make the effort to do so, you'll make you DLL loads a bit faster.

The other item resides a tab away:

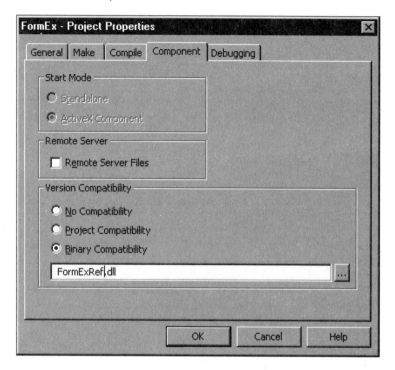

Here, <u>B</u>inary Compatibility is chosen as the Version Compatibility mode. Once you have compiled your project and clients start using it, you can't change your interface without breaking everything else. This is the contract that I talked about at the beginning of this chapter. Since VB generates all the GUIDs for your interfaces, it has to have a way to maintain them. The way you do it is by renaming a copy of your compiled component and using that as the referenced component. VB will use that component to maintain the interface IDs. If you change an interface that's already been published, VB will notify you of the error the next time you try to compile the component, and for good reason. If you don't heed its message, the users of your component might send you some really nasty messages when their application doesn't work with your component anymore. (I'd also suggest that you do this with the timer component as well to preserve the identifiers.)

Revisiting the APITimerComponent Project

Well, we've just implemented a component that does a lot of complex operations underneath the scenes. The nice thing is that if we use it to subclass a form, we only have two methods to worry about, Hook and Unhook. However, in this project, we used CopyMemory to grab an object reference in a code module via an object pointer; in the timer component, we used a collection to store an object reference. This has the same problem we were trying to avoid in the subclassing project, which is that a collection has a reference to a timer object. Therefore, the Terminate event may not fire in the timer object, and we're stuck. Let's go back in the APITimerComponent project, and clean this up.

Fortunately, we don't have a lot to change. First, change the SetCurrentTimer method in the APITimer class like this:

```
Private Sub SetCurrentTimer(TimeInt As Long)

  Dim lngTemp As Long

  lngTemp = SetTimer(0&, 0&, TimeInt, AddressOf TimerProc)

  If lngTemp <> 0 Then
      '  Success!
      gcolTimers.Add CStr(ObjPtr(Me)), "T" & CStr(lngTemp)
      TimerID = lngTemp
      Interval = TimeInt
  Else
      '  Error!
      Err.Raise ErrorCodes.SetTimerError, "APITimer.SetCurrentTimer", _
            "Unable to set the timer."
  End If

End Sub
```

The only thing we've changed here is that now we're storing an object pointer into our collection instead of a direct object reference.

> *For simplicity's sake, I decided not to create a UDT array to relate an object pointer to a unique identifier like we did in the subclassing component.*

The other function we have to change is `TimerProc` in the `TimerLibrary` module:

```
Public Function TimerProc(ByVal hWnd As Long, ByVal uMsg As Long, _
ByVal idEvent As Long, ByVal dwTime As Long) As Long

On Error GoTo error_TimerProc

Dim lngObjPtr As Long
Dim objTimer As APITimer

lngObjPtr = CLng(gcolTimers.Item("T" & CStr(idEvent)))

If lngObjPtr <> 0 Then
    '  Get a reference to the object.
    CopyMemory objTimer, lngObjPtr, 4
    '  Call the method.
    objTimer.APITimerIntervalReached
    '  Set the reference to null.
    CopyMemory objTimer, 0&, 4
End If

Exit Function

error_TimerProc:

If lngObjPtr <> 0 Then
    '  Set the reference to null.
    CopyMemory objTimer, 0&, 4
End If

End Function
```

As we did in the subclassing component, we use `CopyMemory` to grab an object reference without incrementing the reference count, add it to your TimerLibrary code module now:

```
Public Declare Sub CopyMemory Lib "KERNEL32" Alias "RtlMoveMemory" _
    (lpvDest As Any, lpvSource As Any, ByVal cbCopy As Long)
```

Once we've called `APITimerIntervalReached`, we set `objTimer` equal to a null pointer via `CopyMemory`.

That's it! The great thing about this is that we didn't change the interface. Once you recompile the project, the encryption project **About** window will still run fine. As far as it's concerned, no change occurred in the component.

Summary

In this chapter, we saw how callbacks can be implemented into a COM component. We saw some of the limitations of the `AddressOf` operator, and how you can get around these issues. We created two components in VB that used the `AddressOf` operator. One was a timer component, which we included it into the encryption program as a replacement to VB's Timer control. The other was a subclassing component that could be used to extend a VB form with new events.

To achieve all this we learnt:

- ❑ The basics of COM
- ❑ The advantages and disadvantages of EXE and DLL components
- ❑ How to redirect Windows messages
- ❑ How to expose other events that VB's form doesn't provide

Conclusion

Well, we've finally made it to the end of the book. I would hope that however you have chosen to use my book that you now feel confident of programming in the Win32 environment.

In essence, there is no "right" way to learn anything. Each person has their own style of learning and responds to particular techniques better than others. However, in the VB community, most of the developers seems to jump on its ease of use to quickly bring an in-house application to production in a short amount of time and forget to learn the operating system they were working on. Let me illustrate this point.

Many moons ago, one of the only ways you could develop an application in Windows was to use a lower-level language like C or C++. Personally, I know enough C to make myself extremely dangerous in the bad sense of the phrase, but I've done enough with it to see what it takes to create, manage, and destroy windows without much of a safety net, and it's painful. Granted, anyone can become dull to continuous pain after a while, but most people don't like to suffer needlessly.

Here's the point. Try doing what VB does for you by yourself. It's not a ploy to learn C++ nor am I trying to dish VB, but it's an illuminating exercise to see just how much VB is saving you from. I've tried to do it (and I failed horribly), but I gained a lot of appreciation for those who can actually use C++ in a robust manner for Windows development. I've also gained a lot of insight into the rather complex world of Windows.

Unfortunately VB's salvation in its ease of use has a bad side. More and more VB developers are running amok with bloated recordsets, overloaded forms with too many controls, and just bad Windows designs. Again, I don't claim to be the Windows guru, and there are a lot of decent projects written in VB, but I've seen enough VB programs in my life to cringe at what our community is producing.

As an aside I'm still amazed at the amount of VB code that I see in magazines and books that put a lot of code in the events. Technically, it's not wrong, but if the user can open an account by clicking the Open Account button, should the mnuOpenAccount menu item call cmdOpenAccount_Click to open the account? I don't think so; the better approach is to create a form-level method called OpenAccount that any control can call when appropriate.

Therefore, if anyone out there is learning VB as their first Windows language, I hope that you back up a second and pick up some books on Windows, not only from the UI perspective but also from the down-and-dirty perspective. Jeffrey Richter's "Advanced Windows" by Microsoft Press is one of the best books I've seen on the more technical aspects of Windows, and I recommend it for anyone who is working in Windows. His is not the only source out there, but spend some time getting acquainted with the Windows world so you have some insight as to what VB is doing. This may save you some really bad headaches in the long run.

The Final Conclusion

There's a lot that I covered in this book, but there's a lot more that I didn't. Keep exploring and playing with whatever you find out about Windows. Sometimes you'll run into a wall where you just can't get past, but that's OK. One of the best phrases I ever heard about development was that the fun part was discovering where the tool finally broke down, because you pushed it to an extreme where few ever dare go. In doing so, you'll have more experience and knowledge than your peers, and that gives you the development advantage. Have fun expanding the VB environment ... just remember to save your work often!!

Data Type Summary

This appendix provides a quick summary of the data types in VB and how they map to the ones found in Win32 API calls. Note that there are always strange twists in the calls where you need more information than just the procedure declaration. As we saw with `GetEnvironmentStrings` in Chapter 2, we're getting a `String` back, but we receive a pointer to a string as the return value. Therefore, we have to use a `Long`. So please don't take this list as gospel; rather, use it as a general guide.

VB Type	Can be used when you see…
Byte	Unsigned Char, Byte
Integer	Short, WORD
Long	Int, BOOL, Long, UINT, pointers (they usually have the * character next to the variable), hwnd (or any handle)
String	LPSTR
UDT	Structure
Arrays	Match the data type, and pass in the first element `ByRef`.
Single	Float
Double	Double
Any	Not a real data type; can be used to allow different data types to be passed through the argument.

Hungarian Notation

Hungarian notation was introduced by Charles Simonyi to minimize the possibility of misusing a variable due to interpreting it differently from that intended.

Prefix	Meaning
b	a logical variable of type BOOL, which is equivalent to int
c	type char
dw	type DWORD, which is unsigned long
fn	a function
h	a handle, which is used to identify something (usually an int value)
l	type long
lp	long pointer
n	type int
p	a pointer
s	a string
sz	a zero terminated string
w	type WORD, which is unsigned short

C

That Thing Called COM

Components and COM

The basic principle behind COM is the concept of **components**. In many ways, it is easy to think of a component as an object, except that crucially a component is pre-compiled binary code. The idea is to try and create a plug-and-play application built up of various components each of which only interacts with the others dynamically at run time. Thus should you need to change or upgrade one particular component then the change can be easily made without having to recompile and re-publish the entire app. Because all the components are binary then this allows the components to be language independent. For example, you could quite easily use a component written in C++ in your VB app. This is all possible due to COM.

Interfaces and COM

COM is a specification for building components which can be dynamically interchanged. (Before I go any further I should say that COM is not the only way to do this but it is Microsoft's way and since we're using VB we don't have much say in the matter.) Central to COM is the concept of the **interface**. Although you may have a C++ component seemingly conversing with VB, in fact, neither can see the other at all. All each component communicates with, is the other's COM interface. This interface is a memory structure containing an array of function pointers or a **vtable** as it is called. In the same way that we used the `AddressOf` operator to find the memory address of a function, the interface holds a list of these addresses that can be called by other components.

As components can only communicate via an interface, this allows for language independence (providing a few rules such as using general data types are followed) and it also allows each component to hide its implementation. Exactly what goes on inside each component is private and consequently can be changed at any time.

So far you may think this all sounds great and you can see the future is here. However, before you get too excited there's one small thing you have to remember. You can modify, upgrade, and even completely rewrite a component, but once you've published it you can never, ever change the interface. If you change the interface then it all falls apart. Think for a moment what happens if forget to add a parameter to a function call. What happens? VB gets in a stress and tells you so. Now imagine if this were to happen in a compiled distributed app. It wouldn't do your reputation much good now would it? It's not all doom and gloom though - there are ways around this.

However, before we get into that, you may be wondering more about these interfaces and how you define them in VB. Interfaces are abstract things. Both it and the functions it supports have to be implemented in the programming language, but the interface needs to language-independent and this is where the **interface definition language** (IDL) comes in (or MIDL in Microsoft's case). However, although MIDL may be integrated into the VC++ development environment in VB, you never really have to worry about any of this. Basically, you can think of the interface as any `Public` methods (or properties).

Into the Unknown

Before we get into some object-oriented theory, I just want to 'dip below the hood', so to speak, and discuss object lifetimes. All COM objects have the **IUnknown** interface. (In fact all interfaces inherit the `IUnknown` - again this is something that VB handles for you and you will rarely see `IUnknown`.) `IUnknown` contains just three functions: `QueryInterface`, `AddRef` and `Release`. We won't bother discussing `QueryInterface` - it's used to get a pointer to an interface. I want to briefly discuss `AddRef` and `Release`, both of which are used to determine an object's lifetime. Object lifetimes (or how long an object is loaded in memory) are managed by reference counting. Each client of an object using an interface pointer calls the `AddRef` function, which increases the object's reference count. Conversely, when a client has finished it calls the `Release` function, which decreases the object's reference count. When an object's reference count reaches zero the object unloads itself. Again, VB handles these calls for us. When we use the `New` keyword or `CreateObject`, VB increases the reference count for us, and when we set an object to `Nothing`, the count is decreased for us.

Visual Basic and COM

Finally, I just want to talk about how VB object capabilities are so well matched with COM. To do this let's discuss a `House` class which defines the basic characteristics of a house, such as the height of the walls, the angle of the boards for the roof, and the number of windows. If we were to build this class and compile it, we would then be able to instantiate COM objects from it. The interface that we would see of this object could be `Height`, `AngleToRoof` and `NoWindows` properties (if they were declared as `Public`). We might also have a `HighestPoint` property, which returns the height of the highest part of the house. However, this might not be as simple as adding a few numbers together, but instead requires a complex algorithm. Now you don't want to have to document this algorithm so that someone else can use it, so you implement it as a private routine of the object. This demonstrates how the implementation of COM objects is hidden from the interface, and hence any other objects. Now let's say one day you get out of your car, and you're hit with a moment of programming inspiration. You run to your computer, and confirm that, yes, you've just improved your `HighestPoint` algorithm tenfold. Because you've implemented the algorithm as a private routine, you can quite easily update your class (providing of course that you don't change the interface of `HighestPoint`) and no one would be any the wiser.

COM objects typically have multiple interfaces and so too can VB objects. Let's say that we also want to create a `Mansion` class. Now a `Mansion` is clearly a type of house and as such, will have a `Height`, `AngleToRoof` etc. properties. Now, it would be much easier if we could simply use the interface we have already defined for `House`, rather than have to implement a new one. Thus by a process called **interface inheritance** (by using the `Implements` keyword), the `Mansion` class can have its own interface, as well as the `House` interface. We also have a rather natty algorithm for calculating the `HighestPoint`. Wouldn't it be great if we could also inherit this entire algorithm. Unfortunately, COM (like VB) has no support for true **inheritance**, where one object can share the behavior of another. We can get around inheritance by using **containment** and **delegation**, such that our `Mansion` object would contain an instance of the `House` object and any work, such as calculating the `HighestPoint`, would be delegated down to the `House` object.

Therefore, I hope you can begin to see that although VB hides much of the COM implementation, it is in fact ideally suited to the task of developing in the COM environment.

Summary of API Declarations

Following is a list of every API call that we have covered in this book, along with a very brief description of their purposes. I've tried to group them into categories to make lookup time a bit faster. The purpose of this appendix is to give you the location in the book where you can find the definition of any API call that I've used. So, use this appendix as a lookup table for API calls; please don't use the descriptions as full-blown documentation. I have also included a few additional calls which although weren't covered in the main text I still feel could be used to complement some of the calls I have discussed.

Device Contexts

A device context is a Windows object which is set up to manage input and output to screens, printers etc. The device context allows you to define attributes (e.g. text color in a picture) independently from the hardware used. The following API calls are used to manipulate device contexts.

Create a memory device context compatible with the one given:

(Chapter 5)

```
Declare Function CreateCompatibleDC Lib "gdi32" _
    (ByVal hDC As Long) As Long
```

Delete a created DC:

(Chapter 5)

```
Declare Function DeleteDC Lib "gdi32" (ByVal hDC As Long) As Long
```

Delete a created object from memory:

(Chapter 5)

```
Declare Function DeleteObject Lib "gdi32" (ByVal hObject As Long) As Long
```

Enumerate all of the objects currently defined in the DC:

(Chapter 7)

```
Declare Function EnumObjects Lib "gdi32" (ByVal hdc As Long, _
    ByVal n As Long, ByVal lpGOBJEnumProc As Long, _
    ByVal lpVoid As Long) As Long
```

Get the DC value for the specified window:

(Not used in book)

```
Declare Function GetDC Lib "user32" (ByVal hwnd As Long) As Long
```

Obtain specific information about a device context:

(Chapter 5)

```
Declare Function GetDeviceCaps Lib "gdi32" (ByVal hDC As Long, _
    ByVal nIndex As Long) As Long
```

Replace an object in a device context with one specified by hObject:

(Chapter 5)

```
Declare Function SelectObject Lib "gdi32" (ByVal hDC As Long, _
    ByVal hObject As Long) As Long
```

Release a DC obtained by GetDC:

(Not used in book)

```
Declare Function ReleaseDC Lib "user32" (ByVal hwnd As Long, _
    ByVal hdc As Long) As Long
```

Dialog Boxes

*The **Windows Common Dialog Boxes** (e.g. the Open File box, the Save File box) are common to all Microsoft Windows applications. You can use these API calls to call Common Dialog Boxes from your applications.*

Display the Color dialog box:

(Chapter 6)

```
Declare Function ChooseColor Lib "comdlg32.dll" _
    Alias "ChooseColorA" (pChoosecolor As ChooseColor) As Long
```

Display the Open File dialog box:

(Chapter 6)

```
Declare Function GetOpenFileName Lib "comdlg32.dll" Alias _
    GetOpenFileNameA"(pOpenfilename As OPENFILENAME) As Long
```

Display the Save File dialog box:

(Chapter 6)

```
Declare Function GetSaveFileName Lib "comdlg32.dll" _
    Alias "GetSaveFileNameA"(pOpenfilename As OPENFILENAME) _
    As Long
```

DLLs

Dynamic Link Libraries (DLLs) are collections of external functions that can be connected to programs during runtime (i.e. dynamically). The following API calls are used to perform various operations on both DLLs and on specific functions from DLLs.

Call a `WindowProc` function:

(Chapters 7,8)

```
Declare Function CallWindowProc Lib "user32" _
    Alias "CallWindowProcA" (ByVal lpPrevWndFunc As Long, _
    ByVal hWnd As Long, ByVal Msg As Long, _
    ByVal wParam As Long, ByVal lParam As Long) As Long
```

Free a specified DLL from memory:

(Chapter 1)

```
Declare Function FreeLibrary Lib "kernel32" _
    (ByVal hLibModule As Long) As Long
```

Retrieve the address of an exported function in a DLL:

(Chapter 1)

```
Declare Function GetProcAddress Lib "kernel32" _
    (ByVal hModule As Long, ByVal lpProcName As String) _
    As Long
```

Load a specified DLL into memory:

(Chapter 1)

```
Declare Function LoadLibrary Lib "kernel32" _
    Alias "LoadLibraryA" (ByVal lpLibFileName As String) As Long
```

Errors

Errors in Win32 OS can be accessed with API calls.

Retrieve an error message based off of a Win32 API error code:

(Chapter 2)

```
Declare Function FormatMessage Lib "kernel32" _
    Alias "FormatMessageA" (ByVal dwFlags As Long, _
    lpSource As Any, ByVal dwMessageId As Long, _
    ByVal dwLanguageId As Long, ByVal lpBuffer As String, _
    ByVal nSize As Long, Arguments As Long) As Long
```

Get the error number of the last Win32 error:

(Chapter 2)

```
Declare Function GetLastError Lib "kernel32" () As Long
```

Files

Manipulating files and file content using API calls is an alternative to using VB file operations:

Copy a file:

(Chapter 3)

```
Declare Function CopyFile Lib "kernel32" Alias "CopyFileA" _
    (ByVal lpExistingFileName As String, _
    ByVal lpNewFileName As String, ByVal bFailIfExists _
    As Long) As Long
```

Create and/or open a file (also works with pipes, mailslots, etc.):

(Chapter 3)

```
Declare Function CreateFile Lib "kernel32" Alias "CreateFileA" _
    (ByVal lpFileName As String, ByVal dwDesiredAccess _
    As DesiredAccess, ByVal dwShareMode As Long, _
    ByVal lpSecurityAttributes As Long, _
    ByVal dwCreationDisposition As Long, _
    ByVal dwFlagsAndAttributes As Long, _
    ByVal hTemplateFile As Long) As Long
```

Delete the specified file:

(Chapter 3)

```
Declare Function DeleteFile Lib "kernel32" Alias "DeleteFileA" _
    (ByVal lpFileName As String) As Long
```

Take data from a FILETIME UDT and translates it into a system time format:

(Chapter 4)

```
Declare Function FileTimeToSystemTime Lib "kernel32" _
    (lpFileTime As FILETIME, lpSystemTime As SYSTEMTIME) As Long
```

Close a file opened by FindFirstFile:

(Chapter 3)

```
Declare Function FindClose Lib "kernel32" _
    (ByVal hFindFile As Long) As Long
```

Find the first occurrence of a file:

(Chapter 3)

```
Declare Function FindFirstFile Lib "kernel32" _
    Alias "FindFirstFileA" (ByVal lpFileName As String, _
    lpFindFileData As WIN32_FIND_DATA) As Long
```

Retrieve file attributes (normal, hidden, etc.) of a specified file:

(Chapter 4)

```
Declare Function GetFileAttributes Lib "kernel32" _
    Alias "GetFileAttributesA" (ByVal lpFileName As String) As Long
```

Receive extended information on a given file:

(Chapter 4)

```
Declare Function GetFileInformationByHandle Lib "kernel32" _
    (ByVal hFile As Long, lpFileInformation As _
    BY_HANDLE_FILE_INFORMATION) As Long
```

Retrieve the file size of a specified file in a 64-bit format:

(Chapter 3)

```
Declare Function GetFileSize Lib "kernel32" _
    (ByVal hFile As Long, lpFileSizeHigh As Long) As Long
```

Retrieve file time information of a specified file:

(Chapter 4)

```
Declare Function GetFileTime Lib "kernel32" _
    (ByVal hFile As Long, lpCreationTime As FILETIME, _
```

Read information in an INI file:

(Chapter 2)

```
Declare Function GetPrivateProfileString Lib "kernel32" _
    Alias "GetPrivateProfileStringA" (ByVal lpApplicationName _
    As String, ByVal lpKeyName As String, ByVal lpDefault As String, _
    ByVal lpReturnedString As String, ByVal nSize As Long, _
    ByVal lpFileName As String) As Long, lpLastAccessTime As
    FILETIME, lpLastWriteTime As FILETIME) As Long
```

Obtain a temporary file name:

(Chapter 3)

```
Declare Function GetTempFileName Lib "kernel32" _
    Alias "GetTempFileNameA" (ByVal lpszPath As String, _
    ByVal lpPrefixString As String, ByVal wUnique As Long, _
    ByVal lpTempFileName As String) As Long
```

Read a specified number of bytes from a file:

(Chapters 2,3)

```
Declare Function ReadFile Lib "kernel32" (ByVal hFile As Long, _
    lpBuffer As Any, ByVal nNumberOfBytesToRead As Long, _
    lpNumberOfBytesRead As Long, ByVal lpOverlapped As Long) As Long
```

Move the file pointer in a file:

(Chapter 3)

```
Declare Function SetFilePointer Lib "kernel32" _
    (ByVal hFile As Long, ByVal lDistanceToMove As Long, _
    ByVal lpDistanceToMoveHigh As Long, _
    ByVal dwMoveMethod As Long) As Long
```

Write a specified number of bytes to a file:

(Chapter 3)

```
Declare Function WriteFile Lib "kernel32" (ByVal hFile As Long, _
    lpBuffer As Any, ByVal nNumberOfBytesToWrite As Long, _
    lpNumberOfBytesWritten As Long, ByVal lpOverlapped As Long) As Long
```

Fonts

You can create a custom font using an API call.

Create a font based on information in the LOGFONT UDT:

(Chapter 5)

```
Declare Function CreateFontIndirect Lib "gdi32" Alias _
    "CreateFontIndirectA" (lpLogFont As LOGFONT) As Long
```

Imaging

These are just a few of the many API calls that can be used to alter images and graphics in Visual Basic.

Copy a bitmap from one DC to another:

(Chapter 5)

```
Declare Function BitBlt Lib "gdi32" (ByVal hDestDC As Long, _
    ByVal x As Long, ByVal y As Long, ByVal nWidth As Long, _
    ByVal nHeight As Long, ByVal hSrcDC As Long, _
    ByVal xSrc As Long, ByVal ySrc As Long, ByVal dwRop As Long) As Long
```

Create a brush object with a specific RGB color value:

(Chapter 5)

```
Declare Function CreateSolidBrush Lib "gdi32" _
    (ByVal crColor As Long) As Long
```

Color a rectangular region:

(Chapter 5)

```
Declare Function FillRect Lib "user32" (ByVal hDC As Long, _
    lpRect As RECT, ByVal hBrush As Long) As Long
```

Menus

The standard Visual Basic menus can be customized using API calls.

Get the first menu item in the specified window:

(Chapter 4)

```
Declare Function GetMenu Lib "user32" (ByVal hWnd As Long) As Long
```

Get a menu ID from a window from a particular location in the menu tree:

(Chapter 4)

```
Declare Function GetMenuItemID Lib "user32" (ByVal hMenu As Long, _
    ByVal nPos As Long) As Long
```

Get a menu item that has submenus:

(Chapter 4)

```
Declare Function GetSubMenu Lib "user32" (ByVal hMenu As Long, _
    ByVal nPos As Long) As Long
```

Set a bitmap image next to the specified menu item:

(Chapter 4)

```
Declare Function SetMenuItemBitmaps Lib "user32" _
    (ByVal hMenu As Long, ByVal nPosition As Long, _
    ByVal wFlags As Long, ByVal hBitmapUnchecked As Long, _
    ByVal hBitmapChecked As Long) As Long
```

Miscellaneous

There are numerous things you can do with API calls. The following calls are just a sample of what is possible.

Close the specified handle:

(Chapter 2,3)

```
Declare Function CloseHandle Lib "kernel32" _
    (ByVal hObject As Long) As Long
```

Copy a block of memory from one location to another:

(Chapter 8)

```
Declare Sub CopyMemory Lib "KERNEL32" Alias "RtlMoveMemory" _
    (lpvDest As Any, lpvSource As Any, ByVal cbCopy As Long)
```

Create a mutex:

(Chapter 2)

```
Declare Function CreateMutex Lib "kernel32" _
    Alias "CreateMutexA" (ByVal lpMutexAttributes As Long, _
    ByVal bInitialOwner As Long, ByVal lpName As String) As Long
```

Enumerate all of the time formats for the specified locale:

(Chapter 7)

```
Declare Function EnumTimeFormats Lib "KERNEL32" Alias _
    "EnumTimeFormatsA" (ByVal lpTimeFmtEnumProc As Long, _
    ByVal Locale As Long, ByVal dwFlags As Long) As Long
```

Retrieve environment information from the OS:

(Chapter 2)

```
Declare Function GetEnvironmentStrings Lib "kernel32" _
    Alias "GetEnvironmentStringsA" () As Long
```

Get the current system color:

(Chapter 4)

```
Declare Function GetSysColor Lib "user32" (ByVal nIndex As Long) _
    As Long
```

Display a message box to the user:

(Chapter 4)

```
Declare Function MessageBox Lib "user32" Alias "MessageBoxA" _
    (ByVal hWnd As Long, ByVal lpText As String, _
    ByVal lpCaption As String, ByVal wType As Long) As Long
```

Show a file operation window (when copying, moving or deleting files):

(Chapter 6)

```
Declare Function SHFileOperation Lib "shell32.dll" _
    Alias "SHFileOperationA" (lpFileOp As SHFILEOPSTRUCT) As Long
```

Sound

Sound is just one of the multimedia that you can manipulate using the Win32 API

Retrieve extended error information from an error returned by mciSendString:

(Chapter 6)

```
Declare Function mciGetErrorString Lib "winmm.dll" _
    Alias "mciGetErrorStringA" (ByVal dwError As Long, _
    ByVal lpstrBuffer As String, ByVal uLength As Long) As Long
```

Execute a multimedia function depending upon the command given:

(Chapter 6)

```
Declare Function mciSendString Lib "winmm.dll" _
    Alias "mciSendStringA" (ByVal lpstrCommand As String, _
    ByVal lpstrReturnString As String, ByVal uReturnLength As Long, _
    ByVal hwndCallback As Long) As Long
```

Control the execution of **WAV** files:

(Chapter 6)

```
Declare Function PlaySound Lib "winmm.dll" Alias "PlaySoundA" _
    (ByVal lpszName As String, ByVal hModule As Long, _
    ByVal dwFlags As Long) As Long
```

Timers/Time

*It can often be useful to use the APIs to handle **time** and **timers** in your VB apps.*

Get the current tick count in Windows in milliseconds:

(Chapter 1,8)

```
Declare Function GetTickCount Lib "kernel32" () As Long
```

Kill a timer specified by the timer ID:

(Chapter 8)

```
Declare Function KillTimer Lib "user32" (ByVal hWnd As Long, _
    ByVal nIDEvent As Long) As Long
```

Determine the tick count of the high-resolution timer:

(Chapter 1)

```
Declare Function QueryPerformanceCounter Lib "kernel32" _
    (lpPerformanceCount As LARGE_INTEGER) As Long
```

Determine the frequency of the high-resolution timer:

(Chapter 1)

```
Declare Function QueryPerformanceFrequency Lib "kernel32" _
    (lpFrequency As LARGE_INTEGER) As Long
```

Create a timer with a specific interval:

(Chapter 8)

```
Declare Function SetTimer Lib "user32" (ByVal hWnd As Long, _
    ByVal nIDEvent As Long, ByVal uElapse As Long, _
    ByVal lpTimerFunc As Long) As Long
```

Windows

*Managing **windows** is a crucial part of API programming. The term 'window' encompasses everything from a command button on a form to a full screen display. Anything with a visible user interface is classed as a window and can be accessed via API calls.*

Create an elliptic region for a window:

(Chapter 5)

```
Declare Function CreateEllipticRgn Lib "gdi32" _
    (ByVal X1 As Long, ByVal Y1 As Long, ByVal X2 As Long, _
    ByVal Y2 As Long) As Long
```

Enumerate all of the windows created by the specified thread:

(Chapter 7)

```
Declare Function EnumThreadWindows Lib "user32" _
    (ByVal dwThreadId As Long, ByVal lpfn As Long, _
    ByVal lParam As Long) As Long
```

Retrieve a handle to a window:

(Chapter 2)

```
Declare Function FindWindow Lib "user32" Alias "FindWindowA" _
    (ByVal lpClassName As String, ByVal lpWindowName As String) _
    As Long
```

Get the class name for the given window:

(Chapter 7)

```
Declare Function GetClassName Lib "user32" _
    Alias "GetClassNameA" (ByVal hwnd As Long, _
    ByVal lpClassName As String, ByVal nMaxCount As Long) As Long
```

Obtain information about a specified window:

(Chapter 4)

```
Declare Function GetWindowLong Lib "user32" _
    Alias "GetWindowLongA" (ByVal hWnd As Long, _
    ByVal nIndex As Long) As Long
```

Get the title (or caption) of a window:

(Chapter 7)

```
Declare Function GetWindowText Lib "user32" _
    Alias "GetWindowTextA" (ByVal hwnd As Long, _
    ByVal lpString As String, ByVal cch As Long) As Long
```

Get the full path of the Windows Directory:

(Chapter 2)

```
Declare Function GetWindowsDirectory Lib "kernel32" _
    Alias "GetWindowsDirectoryA" (ByVal lpBuffer As String, _
    ByVal nSize As Long) As Long
```

Set window information:

(Chapters 4,8)

```
Declare Function SetWindowLong Lib "user32" _
    Alias "SetWindowLongA" (ByVal hWnd As Long, _
    ByVal nIndex As Long, ByVal dwNewLong As Long) As Long
```

Set the window region to another region:

(Chapter 5)

```
Declare Function SetWindowRgn Lib "user32" (ByVal hWnd As Long, _
    ByVal hRgn As Long, ByVal bRedraw As Boolean) As Long
```

Send a window message to a specific window:

(Chapter 4)

```
Declare Function SendMessage Lib "user32" Alias "SendMessageA" _
    (ByVal hWnd As Long, ByVal wMsg As Long, ByVal wParam As Long, _
    lParam As Any) As Long
```

Index

wrox

Register Visual Basic 6 WIN32 API Tutorial
and sign up for a free subscription
to The Developer's Journal.

A bi-monthly magazine for software developers, The Wrox Press Developer's Journal features in-depth articles, news and help for everyone in the software development industry. Each issue includes extracts from our latest titles and is crammed full of practical insights into coding techniques, tricks, and research.

Fill in and return the card below to receive a free subscription to the Wrox Press Developer's Journal.

Visual Basic 6 WIN32 API Tutorial Registration Card

Name _____

Address _____

_____

_____

City_____ State/Region_____

Country_____ Postcode/Zip_____

E-mail _____

Occupation _____

How did you hear about this book? _____

☐ Book review (name) _____

☐ Advertisement (name) _____

☐ Recommendation _____

☐ Catalog _____

☐ Other _____

Where did you buy this book? _____

☐ Bookstore (name)_____ City_____

☐ Computer Store (name)_____

☐ Mail Order_____

☐ Other_____

What influenced you in the purchase of this book?

☐ Cover Design

☐ Contents

☐ Other (please specify) _____

How did you rate the overall contents of this book?

☐ Excellent ☐ Good

☐ Average ☐ Poor

What did you find most useful about this book? _____

What did you find least useful about this book? _____

Please add any additional comments. _____

What other subjects will you buy a computer book on soon? _____

What is the best computer book you have used this year? _____

Note: This information will only be used to keep you updated about new Wrox Press titles and will not be used for any other purpose or passed to any other third party.

WROX PRESS INC.

Wrox writes books for you. Any suggestions, or
ideas about how you want information given in
your ideal book will be studied by our team.
Your comments are always valued at Wrox.

Free phone in USA 800-USE-WROX
Fax (312) 397 8990

UK Tel. (0121) 706 6826   Fax   (0121) 706 2967

———— *Computer Book Publishers* ————

NB. If you post the bounce back card below in the UK, please send it to:
Wrox Press Ltd. 30 Lincoln Road, Birmingham, B27 6PA

NO POSTAGE
NECESSARY
IF MAILED
IN THE
UNITED STATES

BUSINESS REPLY MAIL
FIRST CLASS MAIL   PERMIT#64   CHICAGO, IL

POSTAGE WILL BE PAID BY ADDRESSEE

WROX PRESS
1512 NORTH FREMONT
SUITE 103
CHICAGO IL 60622-2567